21 March 1992

To Sophie—
Go for it!
Sandra Kurtz

CEO:
BUILDING A
$400 MILLION
COMPANY
FROM THE
GROUND UP

CEO:
BUILDING A $400 MILLION COMPANY FROM THE GROUND UP

by

Sandra L. Kurtzig

with

Tom Parker

W · W · NORTON & COMPANY
New York   London

Printed in the United States of America.

The text of this book is composed in Goudy Old Style,
with the display set in Eurostile and Goudy Old Style.
Composition and manufacturing by
Haddon Craftsmen, Inc.
Book design by Jacques Chazaud.

First Edition.

Library of Congress Cataloging-in-Publication Data

Kurtzig, Sandra L.
CEO: Building a $400 Million Company from the Ground up /
by Sandra L. Kurtzig and Tom Parker.
p. cm.
Includes index.
1. Kurtzig, Sandra L.   2. Women executives—United States—Biography.
3. Computer industry—United States—History.
I. Parker, Tom, 1943–   . II. Title.
HD9696.C62K8755   1991
338.7′61004′092—dc20
[B]   90-45743

ISBN 0-393-02963-8

W.W. Norton & Company, Inc., 500 Fifth Avenue, New York, N.Y. 10110
W.W. Norton & Company, Ltd., 10 Coptic Street, London WC1A 1PU

1 2 3 4 5 6 7 8 9 0

To the memory of my father, Barney Brody, whose ingenuity, perserverence, and organization were an inspiration to me.

To my mother, Marian, whose love and helpful advice have been important to my success.

To my children, Andy and Kenny, who are the loves of my life.

To my wonderful brother, Greg, who always makes me laugh.

Contents

Part V: Working for Shareholders 239

Part VI: Working Again 281

PART I

WORKING
FOR OTHERS

1

A Modest Proposal

If you had told me in 1971 that *Business Week* would one day name me one of America's most influential business leaders and that I'd be chairman, president, CEO, and a major shareholder of a company with nearly four hundred million dollars in revenues, I'd have said you were crazy. After all, in 1971 I was a twenty-four-year-old working wife thinking about starting a family, not a business. But things didn't turn out quite the way I'd planned.

In 1971 I was selling computer time for a division of General Electric called GE Computer Time-sharing Service. Back then time-sharing, as it was called, was becoming increasingly popular. For a relatively low monthly fee plus a per minute usage charge, businesses could buy time on a mainframe computer to perform a host of financial or engineering functions. For the first time managers and researchers had direct access to computing power, rather than have to turn their problems over to professional programmers. All you needed was a terminal in your office and a phone line to a time-shared computer running the software program that fitted your needs. The programs most commonly available at the time were financial analysis and engineering applications.

In early December I made a sales call on a company called Halcyon Communications, run by a guy named Larry Whitaker. Halcyon was a brand-new enterprise—a start-up—located in Palo Alto, California, the northern end of what was just becoming known as the Silicon Valley. Back then most companies in the Valley made silicon chips—also called semiconductors—or manufactured electronic instruments for laboratories. The U.S. military was the single largest customer. Halcyon wanted to build telecommunications equipment, a relative novelty for the area in 1971. Their product would improve the accuracy and speed at which data could travel along phone lines.

In the late 1930s the first pioneers had settled the Valley. They were engineers like William Hewlett and David Packard who turned to business in order to invent and build the research instruments they couldn't find on the shelves of existing manufacturers. Now they were being joined by a new breed of young men—and they all were men—engineer-entrepreneurs as intent on profit as on product. All over the Valley high-tech towns were sprouting new start-ups.

I knocked on Halcyon's door. When there was no answer, I let myself in.

No one was in the reception area so I walked into a back room, where a shirt-sleeved man in his early thirties sat at a single desk, a lone outpost perched at the edge of thousands of square feet of darkened floor space. Two other men in their twenties wearing T-shirts chatted nearby. The floor was littered with piles of paper, and cartons were stacked everywhere. It didn't look promising.

"Larry Whitaker?" I asked. The man at the desk stood, shook my hand, then pulled a stack of papers from a chair and motioned for me to sit. Following my standard ice-breaking chitchat and direct sales pitch, I handed him GE's list of ready-made, "canned" applications programs. Certainly one of these programs would provide what he needed. After all, Whitaker had contacted us rather than the other way around, so he was obviously eager to buy.

He glanced at the list and handed it back. "Nope," he said.

"What I'm looking for isn't there. I need something special."

"What do you mean by special?"

"Listen, I'm interested in your service. But we're going to be a fifty-million-dollar manufacturing company in a few years, and we're going to need some way of keeping track of things around here." He swept his arm through the enormous empty space behind him.

"What sorts of things?" I asked. (Fifty million dollars, incidentally, while considered a good-size company today, was even more impressive by early seventies standards.)

"You know. Inventory. Orders. Bills of materials . . ." He went on confidently, a man on a mission, an entrepreneur. True, he'd never run a manufacturing company before, but he knew that inventory was like cash sitting on a shelf. So before he assembled his first product, he wanted a system in place to keep track of it all. Also, he was convinced that the trick to making money in manufacturing was in being able to make fast, smart decisions about what could and couldn't be delivered. Finally, he wanted Halcyon to *look* organized when customers like RCA and AT&T came around for a site inspection. A handwritten list of parts wouldn't fit the bill. "So you can see, I *do* need your service. But I also need a special program written just for Halcyon."

He was right on both counts. He needed a computer, or at least regular access to one, to accomplish his goals. He was not alone. In the early seventies more and more savvy manufacturers were shopping around for the same thing.

He also needed a custom program. While we had dozens of canned engineering and accounting programs in our 1971 catalog, GE and its competitors offered little for monitoring a company's inventory and manufacturing operations.

I was still gazing into the huge expanse of warehouse behind Larry when he suggested we talk more about Halcyon's needs over lunch. When he said he wanted to see how I might be able to fit into his plans, I assumed he meant GE, not me personally, so I accepted.

Over lunch he was all business. "I want to know what I have in stock, on order, and in process. I want a list of every part that goes into every assembly. And if we substitute a part, I want it reflected immediately on my bill of materials." He checked to see if he was losing me.

I was right with him. I'd sold time-sharing to other manufacturers. I'd even written a few simple programs for prior customers, nothing too elaborate, just a few lines of what was called program code to get them up and running on the GE service.

"Well, then" he tossed his napkin on the table—"it seems we've solved the problem. Will you do it?"

The question caught me off guard. "I don't mean to be dense, but do *what?*"

"You know, write the program. But not just a few lines," he cautioned. "I'll need you to write the whole thing."

I was genuinely surprised. "You're asking me to write a program to control the inventory for your entire operation after talking to me for only a couple of hours? What makes you even think I could do it?"

He fended off my objection with a raised hand. "Well, you seem like a smart woman. Besides, I'm not asking for the theory of relativity here. Just something that tells me what I have in stock, what I need to order."

Larry's style was entrepreneurial: driving hell-bent toward a goal, minimizing obstacles, accomplishing more than anybody thought you could. It was a style I soon developed myself.

Sitting across from him at lunch that day, I was already thinking that I probably *could* write the program he was looking for. After all, I'd always loved solving problems, and that's what programming was. Larry wanted to keep track of his inventory and his bills of materials. It would require a number of programs to do what he wanted. I knew a simple programming language that would work on GE's computer. Sure, writing these programs would take concentration and common sense, but finally it would be like writing a recipe, with one instruction logically following the next. It certainly wouldn't take an Einstein.

"Well?" Larry insisted. "Can you do it?"

"Sure, I *can,*" I said, "but I've already got a full-time job, a husband, I want to start a family . . . I just don't have a third life to moonlight writing programs."

"Quit then. Quit and write my program."

"Come on . . ." I said.

He stood. "Don't answer yet. Think about it." He insisted I follow him back to Halcyon.

Back at his desk he started in on me again. "Seriously you should go into business for yourself. It's easy." He swept his arm through his empty building.

I looked beyond him into all that square footage. "Gee," I thought, "if this guy can do it, why can't I?"

The hardest part of going into business for myself was simply the idea of it: leaving the security of a large corporation like GE to become a contract programmer, a gypsy, wandering from company to company, living off my wits. No regular paycheck, no benefits, no set hours. After a while the idea seemed less outrageous. I'd been extremely successful selling for GE. I'd even been asked to give a speech about my sales techniques at GE Time-Share's National Sales Conference. For nearly three years I'd been making all kinds of money for GE. Maybe I could do the same for myself.

That night I discussed with Arie, my husband of three years, the possibility of quitting my job to go out on my own. Arie and I had met at Stanford when we both were graduate students. "Sure," he said. "Go ahead if you want." I wasn't surprised by his advice, although he was much more conservative with his own career. At the time he was heading a research project for a company manufacturing disk drives. "You could work part-time out of the apartment. After all," he added, "it *is* about time we started a family."

I was up most of the night, thinking. I was making an okay living at GE, but my manager was a jerk. He was more concerned with paper work than performance. Only the day before, he'd had me redo my entire expense report because some figures were in the wrong column. Also, selling for GE in California was an uphill battle against a much more aggressive time-sharing service called Tymshare. So while I was doing well, I wasn't having much fun.

I figured I had three choices: I could stay at GE for business as usual, I could find another job, or I could wait three weeks until the end of the year, collect the two thousand dollars in commissions I had coming from GE, and set myself up in business. The worst case would be I'd lose the two thousand dollars and have to get another job. The best case would be I'd wind up my own boss, make some money, and start the family Arie and I were planning. At 2:00 A.M. I switched on the lamp next to the bed and wrote out my list of pros and cons. "Maybe," I thought. "Maybe."

A major con was that in 1971 the man leaving a corporation to start his own company was often the black sheep, the guy who didn't fit in anywhere else. And the woman starting her own company was considered a pariah, a piranha, or both.

Fortunately my parents both had been in business for themselves most of their lives, so going out on my own was in my blood. My father, Barney Brody, was the son of Russian immigrants. His father had walked out on the family when Dad was very young, leaving his mother with three small children to raise on her own. During the depression Dad quit high school and built a small candy store next to his home in Omaha to help out his mother. He didn't like selling, but he loved building, so he went into construction. He built his first dream house in Chicago in 1951, when I was four years old. It was a rambling California-style ranch with floor-to-ceiling windows, and it created quite a stir in our neighborhood of two-story Georgians.

My mother's family were relatively well-to-do Chicago merchants. My mom, Marian Brody, née Boruck, was graduated from the University of Illinois during the depression, then worked for a newspaper. Eventually she became a police reporter in one of the toughest precincts in Chicago. The men she worked with weren't ready to accept a woman as their equal, so they nicknamed her Steve. After I was born, she took a stay-at-home job training interviewers for the University of Michigan Social Research Center, working, as she tells it, while I napped.

In the early fifties, after my brother, Greg, was born, Mom and Dad built a few "spec" houses in a nearby suburb and promptly sold them. Flush with their success, they decided they could repeat it in the promised land—California. With Greg and me in tow they headed west to Los Angeles to start a joint venture: Dad would design and build homes and apartment houses, and Mom would decorate them, do the advertising and promotions, and handle the sales and rentals. I was eleven when we moved, so except when I was very young, I never saw either of them work regular nine to five hours. Instead, I saw two people with their own schedules, working as a team, usually working very long hours, but also taking time off when they wanted.

Still, when I called my parents in L.A. to tell them my plans, they weren't very enthusiastic. Sure, *they* could beat the depression, rise from the ashes, make it on their own. But their daughter? Over the next few days they each called me with their reservations. Mostly they were concerned about their grandchildren. When *would* there be grandchildren? And how would these innocent babes fit into my scheme? "Soon," I said in response to the first question. To the second I said, "When the baby sleeps, Mom. That's when I'll work. Just like you did."

I didn't win them over. But a few days after Larry Whitaker's offer I decided to go for it. Like my father, I'd always been a bit of a risk taker. Not that I wasn't thoughtful or analytic, but only up to a point. Then I'd make a decision and leave regret behind. I'd discovered that no matter how much upside or downside planning you do, there'll always be something to come along and blindside you. It was about the only thing I knew I could count on. So I called Larry and told him I'd write his programs. We agreed on a fee of twelve hundred dollars with a three-hundred-dollar down payment. I stayed at GE through the end of the year, collected my commissions, then quit. I was in business.

2

Why Computers?

My curiosity about computers began during my sophomore year at UCLA, where I was a math major with a chemistry minor. Every day on the way to class I walked past the computer center, where "nerds," guys with mechanical pencils in their shirt pockets and slide rules dangling from their belts, hung out. They were a pale, sickly-looking crowd by L.A. standards, but unlike the surfers and the Hollywood dreamers, they asked smart questions in class and had something to talk about besides themselves. I figured they knew something I didn't. I was also frustrated with the theoretical math courses I had to take. I thought computers might give me a chance to work with some real-world applications.

Never shy about going after what I wanted, I asked the head of the center, Dr. Charles B. Tompkins, for a summer job. Tompkins was a well-known mathematician who probably wasn't accustomed to talking to brash undergraduates, particularly not brash undergraduate women. A bit flustered, he said he'd see what he could do. A couple of days later I had a job as a summer research assistant in the computer center.

Right away I ran into some snags. First, I hadn't the faintest notion how to tackle the problem I was assigned: how to determine where radio waves beamed behind the iron curtain would land after they had bounced off the ionosphere.

The second snag was that most of the programmers in the center programmed in a special code called assembly language, which *may* have been easy to learn, but not from the manuals I was given. They were undecipherable.

The third snag was that I was simply in over my head. Everyone else at the center was talking assembly language as if they'd been born with 0 and 1 chromosomes, instead of Xs and Ys. I remember one guy in particular, one of the first hackers. He sat at his desk surrounded by two-foot-high piles of green-lined eleven-by-seventeen inch fanfold computer paper printed mostly with combinations of 0s and 1s, which he pored over like some weird alchemist. He was the great god Assembler, and I had a crush on him all summer.

The fourth snag was that Tompkins left town for the summer the day I began work. By the end of the summer I hadn't caught a single radio wave bounding behind the iron curtain. I was prepared to believe that computers *could* be used to solve problems, just not *my* problems.

The following summer I took a job as a math aide at a division of TRW that designed aircraft systems. As a math aide I was actually a high-level flunky for a group of aeronautical engineering Ph.D's. Mostly I plotted elaborate graphs and did complex calculations using a large four-function adding machine. Each calculation took days to work. The alternative was to submit the problem to a TRW programmer to feed to TRW's in-house mainframe computer. But that took weeks. There was a continuous backup because more important calculations from higher-ranking researchers were always being slipped into the queue ahead of you. Also, most of the programmers lived in a rarefied world of their own and worked according to their own strange internal clocks. Hence, the need for math aides. Ultimately all final calculations had to be fed into the computer to be checked and processed, but that was the programmer's job, not mine.

One of the first assignments I was given at TRW was the blunt body problem. It involved using a special mapping technique to illustrate how a blunt body like an aircraft would react under specific inflight conditions. Well, tackling blunt bodies was just about as easy for me to get a handle on as bouncing radio waves into the Kremlin. Fortunately one of the brighter engineers in the group, Frank Fendell, took a liking to me and helped me get started. It was all I needed. After that the summer was a real kick. I loved plotting the graphs, chugging away at the calculations. Most of all, it was fun to apply the math I knew to a bona fide practical problem.

After a few months of work—my summer job had turned into a part-time winter job—I gave my formulas, graphs, and calculations to a programmer to code and feed into TRW's mainframe for a final computation. Three key numbers would verify the accuracy of my work. When the computer printout arrived two weeks later, it was twice as thick as the Los Angeles phone directory. Frank and a few others were at my desk for the unveiling. It was an exciting gutwrenching moment—the solution to my first real engineering problem. I flipped open the print out and with a nervous laugh said, "Well, here it is, guys." Everyone applauded.

Later, alone at my desk, deciphering the printout, I was mortified to find that all the Mach numbers—the numbers representing the speed of the blunt body relative to the speed of sound—were negative. Meaning my blunt body was flying backward. At thousands of miles per hour. I'd obviously made an enormous error in my calculations. But where? How? Would I have to redo months of work? It never occurred to me that the programmer might have made a mistake or that the computer might have let me down.

At about that time a few time-sharing terminals were cropping up at TRW, so instead of working through all my calculations by hand or going back to the programmer, I gave one of the terminals a try. The programming language used by the system was called BASIC. Unlike assembly language, it was easy to learn because it used simple English instead of obscure abbreviations. Embarrassed by my negative Mach numbers, I burned the midnight oil to find my error. After only a few nights I discovered the mistake wasn't mine at all. On the contrary, using the on-line terminal, I was able to prove that the entire premise of the blunt body problem as it had been presented to me was incorrect. But with a few minor changes in the original equations I was given, we could get a working solution.

What a relief! Maybe computers could help me solve problems after all. The key, I realized, was direct access, being able to check results instantly. Sitting before my terminal, the mystery of the negative Mach numbers solved, I now knew that computers would be a part of my future.

3

Job Hunt

When I was graduated from UCLA at twenty, I was accepted to Stanford's aeronautical and astronautical engineering Ph.D. program—1 of only 2 women in a class of 250. I arranged my schedule to receive an M.S. degree at the end of my first year, in case I decided not to continue. It turned out to be a smart move. The more I saw what the life of an aeronautical engineer would be like—confined to desk number 603 in a room of 1,000 other engineers—the more I realized it wasn't what I wanted. Uncertain what I *did* want, I interviewed on campus for six jobs: with AT&T's Bell Laboratories in New Jersey, MIT's Lincoln Laboratories in Boston, General Electric in Syracuse, New York, and three different West Coast divisions of IBM. Four were research jobs; two were in sales. I was eventually offered all six.

I'd been interested in selling since I was a kid watching my mom show apartments to prospective tenants. I loved the strategy, the interaction, the give-and-take. Mom's specialty was making people feel they already lived in the apartment she was showing. "Imagine," she'd say, "it's seven in the evening and you're sitting on your couch, watching the sunset from this window." Her method stuck with me. When I had a part-time job in high school selling linens at Bullock's, a fancy department store, I'd ask customers, "Won't these towels look great hanging from the racks in your bathroom?" It was hokey, but it worked. At sixteen—I'd lied about my age to get the job—I was one of the top-selling part-timers in the store.

After visiting the East Coast companies during spring break—in the middle of a blizzard—I accepted a sales job with IBM in sunny Palo Alto, only a few miles from Stanford. IBM promised me three things: that my eight-week sales training would take place over the summer so I could continue my Ph.D. work part-time in the fall; that I could do the training in L.A., so I could live at home; and that I'd be assigned to an IBM sales group concentrating on aerospace companies, so I could put my aero background to use. When I showed up for my first day of work all excited about my career with Big Blue, I was told my training wouldn't start until August, that there wasn't any space in the L.A. program, and that when I finished the program, I'd be working with commercial rather than aerospace clients. I let this sink in, finished out the day at IBM, and quit. Instead of working, and still uncertain what I would do that fall, I spent the summer on a low-budget tour of Europe.

When I returned from Europe, I had to change planes in New York on my way back to California. Arie greeted me at JFK Airport with a large bouquet of roses and on bended knee asked me to marry him. Of all the offers I received that year, Arie Kurtzig's proposal was the least expected. We'd met at Stanford the prior fall, and though we'd dated much of the year, in the late spring, when Arie finished his Ph.D., he announced he was going back east to seek his fortune. I figured that was the end of "us." Now, after only six months of being on his own on the East Coast, he'd reappeared.

As for many women of the time, marriage for me was part of a natural progression of events that included children, grandchildren, and growing older. Getting married was something you'd eventually do when someone marriageable came along. Arie was certainly that:

He was a great companion, a good listener, and generous with his time and attention. He was also Jewish and a doctor—of sorts—which I knew would make my parents happy.

When Arie proposed, I was still heady from my European jaunt. I was unsure of what I'd do with my life and intrigued by the possibilities. I was also a bit scared and lonely, not ready, I realized, to face the uncertainty alone. Without dwelling on it for too long, I accepted Arie's proposal. We were married on December 1, 1968.

Following a brief honeymoon in Acapulco, we moved to Short Hills, New Jersey, where Arie was working at Bell Labs' nearby Murray Hill facility. Less than five months after I "retired" from IBM, I was one of the overeducated and unemployed. But not for long.

After settling in, I interviewed for a research position at Bell Labs' Murray Hill facility and for a sales and customer service job at Rapidata, a time-sharing company. Bell Labs offered me a position, but I delayed giving them my answer until I heard from Rapidata. By then I was certain I wanted to sell, not work in a lab. When the Rapidata job finally came through, I accepted it on the spot.

"I should tell you, though," the guy hiring me leaned over his desk to whisper, "next week I'm starting my own time-sharing company called Virtual Computing, and I can offer you the same deal as Rapidata, with a lot more potential for growth."

The offer came from left field. Accepting it meant turning down not only one of the most prestigious research institutes in the country, but also spurning Rapidata, a thriving concern. Yet it was this off-the-wall offer I went for, mostly because I'd always liked new things and because the idea of a brand new company with growth potential was appealing. It was a reckless decision. But I was young, a bit of a maverick, and a little cocky.

I lasted longer at Virtual than at IBM. Though they hired me in sales and customer service, they put me to work writing programs for Virtual's partially-installed mainframe computer. There were only about 6 employees in this new company. After about 3 months, the guy from Rapidata who had started the company with some investors' money brought in an executive manager. The new manager's first act was to have everyone sign a nondisclosure and noncompete agreement. The agreement forbade me to disclose anything that was happening at the company or to take a job with any competitive company for two years if I left. I wondered, "What's 'competitive'?" A computer company? A time-sharing company? Was engineering competitive? I had no idea whether or not the agreement was enforceable. In any event I refused to sign it.

"Sign it or you're fired," I was told. I didn't, so I was.

4

Learning
from Mistakes

By the time I left Virtual I was itching for excitement. I didn't want to
write programs; I wanted to sell. And because I believed in the product, computer time-sharing was what I wanted to sell. GE Computer
Time-Sharing was the service I had used at TRW and was the leading
service in the East. I decided that was where I'd work. I tried to
contact a manager there but was told, "Send your résumé." I'd heard
that jobs were tight that winter and that it was tough even to get an
interview, but I wasn't about to sit around until the job market improved.

Instead, one cold, miserable, slushy morning I drove to the GE
Computer Time-sharing Service district offices in Teaneck, New Jersey, to ask the district manager for a job. I had no idea if there even
was a job, and I didn't have an appointment, but I was determined to
meet the boss and make my case. Shivering from the cold, wet
weather, I sat in the lobby for hours until the head honcho finally
consented to give me a few minutes. Once in his office I got right to

the point. I told him my credentials. I told him how my experience at TRW had convinced me that time-sharing was invaluable. I told him I could sell others on that conviction. He offered me a job on the spot. My first account: Bell Labs in Murray Hill.

While the Murray Hill facility setting was pastoral, the Bell Labs compound, set back from the road on a wooded hill, was stark and foreboding. If you didn't know it was a hotshot research lab, you might think it was a penitentiary. No jailhouse ever had inmates like this, though. The research fellows at Murray Hill were divided into two groups, theoretical and applied, with the theoretical guys looking down their noses at the applied guys though virtually everyone had a Ph.D. Of the five Bell Labs sites, Murray Hill was where the most advanced research was taking place. The atmosphere was more like that of a university physics department than the research arm of a large corporation. Anytime, day or night, there'd be scientists working in their labs or walking down the halls, spaced out on pure math and theoretical physics, bumping into drinking fountains, saying, "Excuse me," and continuing on. Not to knock the system; it clearly worked. Bell Labs had produced thousands of patents for such things as the transistor, one of the most important scientific and business achievements of the twentieth century.

With GE in Teaneck, a deadly hour commute on the Garden State Turnpike, and Murray Hill only a few minutes away from Arie's and my Short Hills apartment, I figured the smartest thing to do was to set up shop right at Bell Labs. At first Bell would issue me only a visitor's day pass, which got me into the compound but required I be escorted from lab to lab and office to office. This really put a crimp in my style. After seeing my face every day for a few weeks, security gave up and let me have a permanent visitor's pass. I now had unescorted access, snooping privileges. On one foray I spotted an unused cubicle with a desk. I asked to move in, someone said, "I don't see why not," and I was home free.

What made Bell Labs a potentially lucrative account for GE was that virtually everyone there could benefit from direct access to a computer. Murray Hill's in-house mainframe was guarded by full-time programmers. Researchers who wanted computer results had to take their data downstairs into the guts of the building to the windowless cells where the programmers lived. Although the programmers were whizzes at talking to the mainframe, they were often less fluent with the high-level formulas and equations being worked on at Murray Hill. As a result, a research and development (R&D) guy might wait a day, a week, or more for an answer only to find out the programmer had goofed. Using the in-house mainframe compromised both response time and accuracy. Time-sharing, on the other hand, offered a way around the mainframe and its middlemen, providing independent access to computing power.

Bell Labs had seen early the potential of the service and had already installed quite a few time-sharing terminals. But GE had apparently dropped the ball. Prior to my arrival, there were no GE sales reps talking up usage, no mailings announcing new programs—or old ones, for that matter. So it was only a matter of time before the terminals started gathering dust in the corner.

My sales strategy at Murray Hill was first to get every researcher with a terminal up and running. Next, with researchers in one lab boasting of their progress to guys in another, I'd broaden GE's installed base by selling more terminals. Finally, I would concentrate on increasing usage. In this scenario, the in-house mainframes and their gatekeepers, the programmers, were the enemy.

I started my campaign by calling on the researchers with terminals and going through the GE programs they might be able to use. This required some scientific knowledge on my part, but mostly common sense. For example, if a guy was running a lot of tests, I talked up how our statistical programs could help organize, correlate, and evaluate masses of lab data. Often I saw the gears meshing behind his eyeballs before I could even finish my spiel. Here was the key to research heaven. "Statistical programs?" He'd blow the dust off his terminal and crank it up.

GE's programs addressed a lot of problems. Once they were humming on their terminals, many researchers even started writing programs of their own. While I rarely understood the specific problems they were working on, my math and engineering background gave me enough insight into researchers' needs to suggest a viable path for using the tool I was selling.

Soon dozens of Murray Hill R&Ders were burning time on their terminals, while I fed the flames. "... *and* you can work all night," I always suggested, knowing that was when a lot of guys at Murray Hill really cooked. I was taking them one by one off the mainframe and putting them onto the terminals. The money was good, but it was particularly satisfying to have an impact on the quality and quantity of other people's work. I'd come a long way from Bullock's.

Four months into my fabulous success, my manager asked me to come to Teaneck for a chat. "Why?" I wondered. It was too soon for a raise. An "attagirl" from higher up? Hard to say. To break the tedium of the Garden State Parkway drive, I tossed enough quarters into the toll machines to stake myself and the car behind me. I was feeling flush.

"We're taking you off the Bell Laboratories account," my boss said the second I sat down. "They want you outta there."

"What? Who's 'they'?"

"*They.* The company. GE. They don't want you in there."

I listened to his explanation, but I was so upset I hardly heard what he said. Here I was doing such a great job, doing just what they wanted, and now they were giving me the ax. Tears welled, but I refused to cry in front of my manager. The second he was through, though, I ran to the ladies' room and bawled for about ten minutes.

It turned out that the cards were stacked against me from the beginning. In addition to selling time-sharing, GE had sold Bell Labs its mainframes, the very mainframes from which which I was systematically weaning everyone. To keep those super-big-buck mainframe orders coming, GE needed Bell to use up the resources on the ones they had. Then GE could say, "Hey, you're running out of gas. It's time to buy some more." Aside from interfering with GE's mainframe sales, my success was also making the Bell programmers nervous. In fact, the entire data processing department was getting jittery. So they closed my office, took away my pass.

Back in Teaneck, banned from Bell Labs, I considered the lesson I'd just learned. It was not about computing—I already knew the value of hands-on computing power—but about business politics. My mistake at Bell Labs—largely the fault of GE's management—was in not looking at the big picture before developing a sales strategy. I should have asked more questions, found out whom or what I was competing against: not only the programmers whose jobs my success threatened but, as it turned out, a division of my own company more powerful than the one I was working for. At Murray Hill I was trying to be a good team player. Only no one told me that would require throwing the game. I was in a lose-lose situation. It was inevitable that my success would be my downfall.

Who knows, it could even have been that GE sent me to Murray Hill thinking I was so green they wouldn't have to worry about my doing as well as I did. But the demand for access to computing power was about to become a juggernaut, much larger than GE or any one company. In the years to come, some would try to control the wave. Others, like myself, in the right place at the right time would end up riding it.

5

"Let's Start with This"

After a brief stint in Teaneck I was assigned to a newly created GE sales office in West Orange, New Jersey. The office was a converted, folksy old house, complete with kitchen, fireplace, and pleasant rooms. There was even an attic I could escape to if I needed a quiet place to work. It was a lot nicer than the apartment in Short Hills and made me homesick for my parents' house in California. My new sales territory was in north-central New Jersey, as smokestack industrial as Murray Hill was high-tech.

One of my first sales calls was to Pulverizing Machinery, an eight-million-dollar manufacturing company with two hundred employees. Pulverizing made large custom-designed industrial filters and pollution control equipment. It was the summer of 1969, and new federal air pollution standards were helping Pulverizing to prosper.

On a typical hot, muggy, killer New Jersey June day, the air in Pulverizing's parking lot, thick with smog and grit, was enough to show how big its market could be.

Pulverizing's R&D manager, Evan Bakke, a young Ph.D. from Sweden, wearing a white lab coat, showed me around. Multimillion-dollar Pulverizing was dark, noisy, and dirty, a glorified machine shop. Also, the only filters I was familiar with were for making coffee, so seeing a completed pollution filter measuring twelve by twelve by one hundred feet was a real eye-opener.

As we clambered over catwalks and traipsed through the production floor, Bakke gave me a task-by-task rundown of the manufacturing process. Together we stood ankle-deep in filings and watched sheets of steel being cut, bent, molded, and drilled, then married to other materials and components, such as motors that had been bought from other manufacturers. Sparks flew as Bakke rattled on in his Swedish accent. Reticent at first, he grew more and more animated. Two things about him were clear: He knew his job, and he loved it.

My initial thoughts as Bakke took me from workstation to workstation were of the canned time-sharing programs I could sell. Certainly Pulverizing would benefit from a program that measured how much stress their custom-made filters could withstand or from a program that calculated the efficiency of a given filter for a prospective client or the Environmental Protection Agency (EPA). In any event, my goal was to make a quick sale, then hurry off to another prospect. But as I walked alongside Bakke, I was caught up in his interest and excitement and challenged by the prospect of helping his business in a more basic way. Through the din I fired dozens of questions at Bakke to get a sense of how Pulverizing's manufacturing process worked and what the thinking was behind their operations.

One thing that caught my eye in particular was a partially fabricated component at a workstation. It sat for twenty minutes as a worker reset his machine to drill a single hole. The drilling of the hole took only a minute or two. The part then traveled to another machine for another operation and back again to the first for a second hole of a different size, with each operation requiring a lengthy resetting of a machine before the task was performed. During my tour I saw similar time-wasting, labor-intensive operations.

Back in Bakke's office, when I should have been hauling out GE's catalog of programs, I told him I was struck by what seemed to be a lot of wasted production time. "You take twenty minutes or more, depending on the task, to set up a machine for a single operation."

Bakke looked at me from behind the steeple he'd formed with his fingers. "And. . . . ?"

"There must be a way of scheduling a machine to run the same operation on many components in a row."

Actually he'd given this some thought, he said, but his first priority had always been to keep inventory at a minimum. Drilling holes into a part, then letting it sit for days was a no-no.

"What's more expensive, the labor time to repeat the setup or the increased inventory?"

Bakke smiled ruefully. He'd given this some thought, too, but to schedule a custom shop like Pulverizing—one where a different product or part of a product was manufactured every day—around labor time, well, that would take a huge amount of calculation.

He was right, of course. That kind of scheduling couldn't be done efficiently by hand. There were far too many variables, each custom job would require a completely new calculation. If a machine broke down, or a part from another manufacturer didn't arrive on time, the whole shop would have to be rescheduled around that down machine or that missing part. Then any labor time saved would most likely be offset by the time it took to recalculate the schedule.

Unless the scheduling could be done by computer. If Pulverizing had a program that took into account how many machines they had, what each machine could do, how much setup time it took to perform various operations, etc., their manufacturing process could then be scheduled to optimize the load for each machine and minimize the labor time to perform each operation. Then, if a part didn't arrive, it would be easy enough to go back to the computer to find something else for that machine to do, or if a machine went down, to find a way to work around it.

So I said to Bakke, "It seems to me we could write a program that could schedule your operations and keep your machines and your people working at top efficiency." The program could, for example, tell Pulverizing that if drilling four holes in a single part requires twenty minutes of setup time, ten minutes of drill time per hole, and one minute of move time each, what the advantage or disadvantage would then be of keeping more inventory in stock and drilling forty holes in ten parts with only a single setup time. Or if one drill went on the fritz, how efficiently the operation could be performed on another.

Bakke heard me out. Whereas all day I'd been the listener, now my own enthusiasm carried me, and he leaned back in his chair. "Listen," I said, "I think we can figure out a program. I don't even think it'll be that hard. In fact," I went on, "I'll start on it tonight. Just a sample, of course, to get you started."

That was fine with Bakke. He was savvy enough to know that computers could help his operation. Now I was there, leading him to it. Good timing, good luck for us both.

It wasn't until I hit the parking lot that I realized again how hot and muggy it was. But the weather no longer bothered me. I was already too involved in solving Bakke's problem, too wrapped up in the program I was going to write. As I drove through Short Hills, my first impulse was to head home and wait for Arie to tell him about my day. But Arie wouldn't be home for hours. So I took the back road to the office in West Orange. There was a terminal there, and I had work to do.

I got so involved in writing the program that I forgot what time it was. It was midnight before I looked at my watch. By then I had realized that writing even a simple program was going to be a lot harder than I thought. What if a machine is down and the alternate machine is already on overtime? What if you drill three of four holes and your bit breaks? What if too many parts are on back order? What if, what if?

A bit sheepish but still enthusiastic, I arrived at Pulverizing the next day with dozens of lines of program code on a sheet of paper to show Bakke. "It's not perfect," I said, "but it's a beginning. Let's start with this."

Bakke looked over the program and handed it to Bruce Preston, another young engineer and Bakke's sidekick. It was clear from the time they spent with it that they thought I was on to something. "Okay," Bakke said, a faint smile crossing his face, "let's start with this." They signed up for the time-sharing service that day, with Preston given the job of developing the program.

I'd check in with them from time to time to see how they were doing, but my job at Pulverizing was over. I'd already gone farther with them than most sales reps would have, but if I hadn't taken the extra time to get them started, I would have never made the sale. It was a lesson I applied again and again.

Following my success at Pulverizing I called on dozens of manufacturing companies. Some were glorified machine shops like Pulverizing. Others had immaculate manufacturing processes with "clean" rooms with employees wearing protective clothes that made them look like spacemen—Merck Pharmaceuticals, for example. Like Murray Hill, Merck had an in-house mainframe—*not* a GE, I was quick to check—and had also invested early in time-sharing terminals that were for the most part sitting unused. To clear Food and Drug Administration (FDA) approval for newly developed drugs, Merck researchers were required to catalog the results of thousands of lab tests, correlate drug characteristics, tabulate responses from clinical trials, and finally prepare a cohesive report. Working with Merck researchers, I demonstrated how GE's statistical analysis programs could speed this cumbersome process, saving enormous amounts of time and accelerating a drug's entry into the market. They were sold.

Another company I worked with was General Foam. They stamped out sponges in a variety of sizes from large foam sheets. I helped them develop a program to maximize the number of sponges that could be stamped out from each sheet. The parent company, Tenneco, was so impressed with the money the program saved, they flew me by helicopter to check out their other manufacturing operations and recommend areas where they could put time-sharing to work. I was twenty-four and on top of the world.

But I was also homesick for California. So in the summer of 1971, after nearly three years in New Jersey, Arie and I moved back to California, where I transferred to GE Computer Time-sharing Service's Palo Alto office. There, however, GE wasn't number one and I often called on one of our accounts only to be told, "We're unplugging GE and going with the competition." So the job was as much shoring up the dam as it was fresh selling. I was working with a partner, Del Ball. The two of us staved off the flood and virtually doubled our sales office's business in just a few months. I was going gangbusters, I finally had the sales career I wanted. Then I answered the Halcyon call.

PART II

WORKING
FOR MYSELF

6

Halcyon Days

At the time I took on the Halcyon job, Arie and I were living in a low-slung apartment complex in Mountain View, about thirty-five miles south of San Francisco, in the very heart of the Silicon Valley. Compared with our bare one-bedroom apartment in New Jersey—a place so small that two people couldn't fit into the kitchen, a place so close to the tracks that the Erie-Lackawanna Railroad seemed to high-ball through the bedroom every few minutes—our new apartment was heaven. We had draperies, carpets, even a self-cleaning oven. Outside, a small stream ran through lush gardens. There was a pool, a sauna, and a recreation room. Most important, we had a second bed-room, which is where I set up shop.

"I couldn't even afford a garage," I've joked since the success of my company, alluding to the Valley's famous garage start-ups of Hewl-ett-Packard's Bill Hewlett and David Packard and Apple's Steve Jobs and Steve Wozniak. Actually a second bedroom was just fine. It only had to hold a part-time business.

With my two-thousand-dollar GE commission check and my three-hundred-dollar Halcyon advance I bought a desk, filing cabinet, and chair. I ordered a second residence phone rather than a business line to qualify for unlimited calls. Thriftily I combed the local papers for sales on office supplies and once drove fifteen miles to save a few cents on yellow legal pads. Another time I read that the price of sending a first-class letter was going from eight cents to ten. A whiz at math but not always strictly logical, I bought five-hundred eight-cent stamps to realize the savings. "You know," the helpful postal clerk told me "the first-class rate is going up to a dime tomorrow." "I know," I said, giving him a conspiratorial wink.

To do my programming, I rented a time-sharing terminal for sixty-five dollars per month. The computer terminal of the early seventies was like a Western Union teletype—no video monitor, no disk drive. Crude and slow, it was the size of a large office typewriter and sat on a heavy-duty stand with casters. A roll of continuous paper ready to receive data was perched atop the machine. Programs were stored on spools of skinny paper tape, onto which every letter or number of program code had to be stamped with a mechanical paper-tape punch. With a tiny hundred-line program gobbling up forty feet of tape or more, my biggest problem as a programmer was my lack of manual dexterity. The tape was constantly unspooling, and there was always some on the floor for me to put a heel through, ruining an hour's worth of work.

Fully equipped, all I needed now was a business name. But I didn't want to use my own name the way other contract programmers did. I wanted a short, punchy name, like IBM. I also wanted a name at the beginning of the alphabet, for prime yellow pages positioning. Borrowing the A from Arie, the S from Sandy, and the K from Kurtzig, I came up with ASK. It was perfect—easy to find, easy to remember.

Also memorable were my lavender business cards and my olive green stationery. And no prospect could every forget my pink briefcase.

I worked like crazy on the Halcyon programs, day and night, often till three in the morning. Writing the program involved developing a series of instructions for the computer to control all the inventory, bills of materials, and purchasing functions of Halcyon's manufacturing process. It took concentration and common sense, but establishing the program's basics was a thicket from which I knew I could emerge.

Larry Whitaker hadn't mentioned it, but I knew that the success of the program depended on its being easy to use. Back then computers were science fiction for most people, and parts managers, no matter how high-tech the company, still lived in an old-fashioned, pencil-and-paper world. So the real callenge of the Halcyon job was to create a user-friendly program—a term that had not yet been coined. The user needed a simple, direct way to identify parts, enter withdrawals from stock, flag reorders, and verify incoming parts against open purchase orders. Often this would be handled automatically by the program, and in those cases the parts person had to have faith in the information that was being provided. After all, it would be his job on the line, computer or not. I was determined that my program would earn that faith.

Despite the long hours I put in writing Halcyon's program, it never felt like work. I broke the task down into component parts with defined goals, knowing that as each goal was attained, there'd be a verifiable answer, a reward. Throughout school I had always enjoyed solving math and chemistry problems and whenever possible, had steered clear of English and social studies, where clear-cut answers were hard to come by.

Actually my parents were told when I was in elementary school that I had an average IQ. I'm certain it was more upsetting to them than it was to me. Since there was nothing I could do about it, I just worked as hard as I could and concentrated on doing the things I liked. In junior high, when the teachers said I wasn't sharp enough for admission into an advanced math class, I was determined to prove them wrong. I studied the prior semester's text for the advanced class, did all the assignments, took the qualifying exam and ended up with the highest grade in the class. Then in high school I was mistakenly placed in an *all-*advanced program, and though English and history were difficult for me, I decided I'd stay where I was rather than ask to be switched to regular-level classes. It was hard work, but I was graduated with an A-minus average.

Larry Whitaker's job took five weeks to complete. By the middle of February my Halcyon days were over. The program wasn't a masterpiece, but it gave Larry what he was looking for, and more. When I received my nine-hundred-dollar check, I was tremendously pleased and proud. If I'd been paid in cash, I would have taken a dollar, framed it, and hung it on the wall, the way they do at family restaurants. Instead, I photocopied the check and started my ASK scrapbook.

7

Woman
on the Loose

I'd sold towels for Bullock's and time-shares for GE. Now it was time
to sell myself. GE had generated business cost-effectively with direct
mail, so with my mom's help, I worked up a flyer to send to potential
customers. Borrowing from Mom's experience as a police reporter, we
created a wanted poster, complete with a mug shot and the headline
WARNING: DANGEROUS WOMAN ON THE LOOSE! After some offbeat copy
about my experience and skills, the flyer closed with the warning "DO
NOT ATTEMPT TO RESIST THIS WOMAN! SHE IS ARMED with facts and
figures on how she can save you money and improve your company's
efficiency, and SHE IS DANGEROUS to any less-than-perfect computer
plan you are using."

Mom did the writing. All through high school and college she'd
helped me with my papers, and there was no one I trusted more with
the printed word. I focused on my own strengths and performed the
less literary chores, including typing and rubbing down each letter of
the headline with transfer type. I even had envelopes printed with the

word *WARNING* . . . in red ink across the front. Finally I hand addressed each envelope. The flyer certainly didn't look anything like the mail crossing most executives' desks in 1972.

After scouring a local industrial directory for prospects, I mailed my flyers to the presidents of thirty-five small to medium-size businesses in the area and waited for my phone to start ringing. A week went by without a single call. Frustrated, I started phoning the thirty-five presidents on the list. But I couldn't even get through to their secretaries. I'd sometimes be referred to data processing, who said, "We have our own staff," or pawned off on a middle manager, who said, "We're not interested." Most often I was just cut off. I finally figured out that the best time to call the president of a company was after 6:00 P.M., when the switchboard was manned by a security guard who'd put me through to whomever I wanted. Bingo! I'd get right to the top. And when these guys answered, they were usually more relaxed than during the working day and more likely to spend a few minutes talking before they said no, they weren't interested. That was more often than not the case, though I was never certain whether it was the flyer that put them off or the fact that they just didn't think they needed computer programs.

The president who expressed the most interest was Suburban Newspapers' Dave MacKenzie. Suburban published three local papers that were delivered door to door in the Silicon Valley towns of Cupertino, Los Altos, and Sunnyvale. "We don't need any computers here," MacKenzie said. Recalling my flyer, he added, "But we *do* need a clever writer. How'd you like to come write for us?"

I told him I didn't know how to write and changed the subject back to computer applications. He changed it back to my poster. I changed it back to software. Finally he passed me on to his circulation manager. Maybe he could figure out something for me to do.

"Well," said John Scroggs, Suburban's circulation manager, "I *do* have this problem. . . . I really don't think you can help, but I do have this problem."

John's problem was that each of Suburban's twelve hundred deliverers—mostly school kids—was an independent contractor. Each had to buy rubber bands, plastic bags to put the papers in when it rained, and accident insurance from Suburban. Commissions were based on collections minus the cost of the newspapers, insurance, and supplies. Not only did Scroggs have to keep track of these twelve hundred independent contractors and their little businesses, but he also had to divide and label twelve hundred packets of papers, develop twelve hundred routes, and make certain the kids were delivering only to current or new subscribers, not to those who let their subscriptions lapse. In addition, at the end of every month Scroggs had to generate twelve hundred commission checks and a variety of reports. I told him I could write a program to simplify the entire process. He was dubious but agreed to let me try.

Later Scroggs introduced me around. "This is the woman who'll be computerizing our circulation department," he said to a guy running a press. I might as well have been from Mars, because no one, Scroggs included, knew what that meant. Still, they seemed impressed that a professional had been called in.

Suburban's program would have to be created from scratch. None of GE's nifty programs would help. So I plugged out GE and switched over to one of the less expensive local time-share services that were cropping up. Most used downsized computers and offered a further reduced rate for nighttime use.

But Suburban needed more than a program. Without a computer of their own, or anyone in-house to run a time-share program, they needed what was called a service bureau. So I wrote the program for Scroggs and also offered to run it and keep it up-to-date: to provide him with weekly labels and routing reports and monthly commission statements as well as printed checks. Hustling for the additional work was the logical move since at the time Suburban was my only client. Still, without giving it much thought, I had changed the nature of my business. Contract programmers write a program and move on. A service bureau stays on the job forever.

The good news of taking on the extra tasks was I'd responded to the needs of my customer. The bad news was I'd created a monster. Every week I was running twelve hundred labels on my teletype-terminal, clunk-clunk, clunk-clunk, at ten characters per second. They clunked out for hours. Since the teletype wasn't really meant to run production jobs, the gummed labels often jumped the sprockets and jammed the machine. Wanting the job perfect, I'd start over again, all the while on-line at about ten dollars per hour, five dollars at night. Every week, too, there'd be changes to the carrier lists that had to be hand punched onto paper tape and inserted into the program. I'd solved Suburban's circulation problem and converted their ungainly operation into a well-oiled machine. But I'd overloaded my own machine.

The problem was exacerbated when MacKenzie—now that his circulation department ran so smoothly—bought three more newspapers. This more than doubled my work load. Where before routes already existed, now a whole bunch of start-up information had to be keypunched into the program. There were twice the number of labels and twice the number of reports. My teletype groaned.

In short order the Suburban job evolved from a programming challenge to a repetitive number-crunching and printing service. This was not at all what I'd set out to do at ASK—or what my second bedroom was equipped to handle. I soon realized the obvious: With the basic program written, it was no longer necessary to be on-line and pay the premium for direct computer access week after week. On the contrary, the Suburban job had become a perfect candidate for batch processing. This was an old-fashioned mainframe technology that involved feeding data in batches to a computer on keypunch cards.

So I canceled my time-share terminal and took my program to a data processing service in Palo Alto called OSI that had IBM mainframes. For the next three weeks, working only nights to take advantage of OSI's cut rates, I rewrote the Suburban program from BASIC to FORTRAN, a language mainframes understood. Next, I transferred all the data from paper tape to keypunch cards. Now it was simply a matter of running the cards through the mainframe once a week to provide Scroggs with his statements and reports. OSI's relatively speedy printers would handle the printing chores.

Still, with six newspapers, ever-changing subscriber lists, and thousands of paperboys and girls, I couldn't do all the keypunching myself and keep my business going. Initially I turned the chore over to a keypunch service—one of the mini-industries that sprang up around computers in the early seventies. I soon learned that a truly great keypuncher was like a truly great typist—rare and valuable. Jan

Korpella, the woman at the service who keypunched the Suburban job for me, was just that. She was so impressive, in fact, I asked her to work for me part-time. About a year after opening its doors, ASK had its first employee.

Just about the time ASK was taking shape as something more than a contract programming business, I started assuming a new shape myself. In early summer 1972 I was pregnant.

8

California
Microwavin'

I get a kick out of entrepreneurs who boast about the strategic decisions that led them to their successes. Some probably do have a master plan, but the brilliant pattern usually emerges only as you look back. Charting the future in business can be like one of those game shows where you have to choose from door number one, door number two, or door number three. You can as easily walk away with the set of carving knives as the trip to Hawaii. However, my first year in business I did make two strategic decisions that were crucial to ASK's success.

The first was to build up ASK's service bureau, now that I had figured out how to make it efficient. Writing the initial program for a customer would give me a chunk of money up front; then running it on the service bureau would provide me with a steady stream of income. Once each program had been written, I'd have time to hustle more business.

My second decision was to concentrate on manufacturing companies. By then I'd spent a lot of time with Halcyon, Pulverizing Machinery, Merck, and other manufacturers, and it was becoming clear that as varied as their products were, their needs were more similar than dissimilar. Perhaps I could use the code I'd written for one manufacturer as a foundation to build upon for another. I thought, too, I'd be better off solving a universal problem like inventory control rather than something as complex as the shop floor scheduling program I'd started at Pulverizing. Focusing on the basics, I could get in, get out, get paid, and not be a slave to a single company.

So I targeted the second mailing of my wanted poster to small manufacturing companies. This time a few companies responded, but the only prospect that turned into a job was a no-response I'd followed up on by phone. A manufacturer of microwave communication equipment, California Microwave was run by a guy named Dave Leeson, who remembered the poster and was curious enough to meet me for lunch. We hit it off.

Dave had been working with a competing service and was dissatisfied. He wanted pretty much what Larry Whitaker had wanted at Halcyon. But because California Microwave was already a going concern, he needed a program that was more finely tuned. It took me a couple of months to write the program, then make California Microwave my second service bureau client.

Late that summer Arie and I went house hunting for a place large enough for a baby and a business. We found a rambling five-bedroom house in the nearby town of Los Altos Hills. It was on a hillside and built partially on stilts, with a continuous deck that thrust out into space, a good fifty feet above ground level. Just about every room had a terrific view. We bought it at a bankruptcy auction for the amount of the first mortgage—about one hundred thousand dollars, an excellent buy at the time. The only problem was there were tens of thousands of dollars of liens on it—far more than it was worth—including one by the IRS. Most of the liens were wiped out by the bankruptcy auction, but the IRS had 120 days after we had bought the place to decide whether they could get a better price for it than we paid. When they sent their man to look around, I was a very visible eight months pregnant, and I told him he couldn't come in the house without my husband at home. He asked if he could walk around the outside. I told him the deck needed repair and we weren't able to afford insurance. He could look at his own risk. He took a quick glance at the drop from the deck, gave me a sick little smile, and that was the last we heard from the IRS.

My pregnancy was even easier. I never had morning sickness, and though I ate the obligatory crackers to settle my stomach, I didn't really need them. Arie and I went to Lamaze classes, furnished the baby's room, and bought a lifetime supply of paper diapers at an after-Christmas sale.

My mom supplied the crib, along with lots of advice. When I was born, my father had turned part of the dining room into a nursery, complete with a window, like that in hospitals, where visitors could view the baby. Anyone actually allowed into the nursery was given a mask to wear until I was many months old. "You were never sick as a child," Mom said, waiting for similar construction to begin in Arie's and my new house. But it never did, and my children got the normal childhood diseases at the usual times. Having been shielded from illness as a child, I eventually got to share the mumps with my kids in my thirties.

I worked throughout my pregnancy and was at lunch with Mom and a friend when I went into labor. We were sitting in a lovely restaurant with pink tablecloths and little bud vases when I felt the first contractions. I didn't want to ruin the lunch, so I kept to myself the fact that the contractions were coming at ten-minute intervals. At home twelve hours later I wakened Arie to take me to the hospital. After nine months of possibly the easiest pregnancy in history, Andrew Paul Kurtzig was born.

After a few days in the hospital—Andy was in a breech position and had to be delivered by caesarean section—and two more days in bed at home, I was ready to go back to work. Mom was still with us, and she, Arie, and I split the baby care duties, making my transition from mother of a newborn son to mother of a newborn business an easy one.

Two weeks later Mom flew back to L.A., leaving a significant void in the infant care department. After interviewing a number of housekeepers, we hired a woman named Eldemira Mejie, who quickly became a part of the family. She loved kids and had a passel of nieces and nephews, whom she'd often bring by. She lived in Monday through Friday, took care of Andy, cooked, and cleaned. Eldemira, Andy, and Arie and I had the three upstairs bedrooms. The ASK offices were in the two bedrooms downstairs. It was a perfect arrangement.

The only problem was me. I was disappointed in myself. I'd expected Andy's birth to change me into a full-time homemaker. But I'd never been interested in cooking or cleaning. And while I loved taking care of Andy and playing with him, I was also lonely for my work. Sometimes I resented being kept from it.

I ended up feeling a double dose of guilt: first, that I wasn't spending all my time with Andy or on the house and second, that I didn't want to. My parents couldn't understand it. When I was born, Mom had quit her full-time job and for the first few years devoted virtually all her waking hours to me. Now she was upset that I didn't do the same.

There was no real resolution, and finally I decided I'd just have to live with the situation. I knew it wouldn't do Andy any good to have me around all the time if that only made me feel trapped. With Eldemira on the job, Andy was safe and well cared for. I'd give him all the love and attention I could, knowing that I always had the option of going downstairs to work.

Actually I couldn't understand my mother's reaction to my working. Her own mother had emigrated from Austria to New York in 1909, at the age of sixteen. She married after a year and moved to Chicago, where she and her husband rented a tiny store from one of her cousins, a wholesale butter-and-egg man. Her husband didn't like the business, but Grandma was such a great saleslady that the little store quickly grew to be the most successful of all the cousins' outlets. Denied a share of the profits, she bought the store outright. By that time she had a loyal clientele, some of whom had prospered and moved to ritzier neighborhoods. But they still sent their chauffeurs around for their butter and eggs. After a few years she moved to a larger location and sold groceries along with butter and eggs. When my mother and her brother were born, Grandma hired a woman to take care of both kids in the back of the store. Mom often spoke of the excitement of growing up in this environment. The way I saw it, it wasn't all that different from what I was doing with Andy, who spent many a day toddling around the ASK offices.

A month after Andy was born I rented a keypunch machine and made Jan Korpella a full-time keypuncher-secretary-typist. By then Suburban Newspapers and California Microwave were running smoothly and I was working with a company called Farinon Microwave that had responded to the third mailing of my wanted poster. They competed with California Microwave and had many of the same needs, but Floyd McGee, Farinon's vice-president and division general manager, wanted a unique feature built into his system, a way of keeping Farinon's inventory at an absolute minimum.

"I know what we need to build for the next few months. I know what parts and assemblies go into these orders. I only want to make and order parts and assemblies when we need them," he explained. Building assemblies and taking delivery of materials in this way, Floyd wouldn't tie up his cash for any longer than was absolutely necessary. Also, he would lessen the risk of his inventory's being obsoleted by engineering changes and would cut down on the amount of warehouse space needed to house parts and subassemblies. What Floyd wanted made sense, and I was eager for the new challenge, though it meant tinkering with the recipe that had already worked at Halcyon and California Microwave.

That spring I spent my days programming, doing my billing, putting out my modest payroll, and filing the thousands of forms required of small businesses by the government. My nights I spent running jobs. Andy fell asleep around seven, and I'd be at OSI by eight ready for action. There were always glitches, and often what should have taken an hour to run took three, four, or five hours. And when I got out the glitches, I'd want to improve the program, invariably creating a whole new set of problems. I often called Arie to say, "Honey, I'll be home in an hour," then called him two hours later with the same message, until finally it was too late to call. Then there were Sundays, when a Suburban commission statement was due the next morning and I'd take Andy in his stroller down to OSI to keep me company while I worked.

After I finished programming the Farinon job, ASK had a service bureau base of three companies—Suburban Newspapers, California Microwave, and Farinon—making the business large enough, I felt, to support a new employee. So I hired Jim Parker, OSI's night shift manager, to handle the service bureau.

Hiring Jim was a model for how I was to build ASK. At first, I wanted to do all of ASK's programming as well as run the service bureau. I needed to do it, to learn how to create a good product and keep my customers satisfied. But as soon as I understood how to make the service bureau a success, I was ready to turn it over to someone else. In much the same way I later turned over programming, new product development, sales, marketing, and ASK's financial functions to my successors in each area. Having a basic understanding of each function, I could oversee it without letting myself be snowed by someone who wasn't reliable.

Growing a business, I found myself constantly ceding territory and giving up running different areas of the company. It was the smart thing for me to do. As ASK grew, I found my strength lay less in details than in my ability to sell, communicate, hire good people, see the big picture, and strategically seize opportunities and guide ASK's overall operations.

Of course, with a business the size of ASK's—our 1973 gross receipts were less than fifty thousand dollars—the big picture was not so big. But it was a great time. I wouldn't have traded it for anything. It taught me the value of hands-on participation, of building a team and delegating responsibility. It also taught me the importance of a fledgling business's having a cash cow like ASK's service bureau.

Finally I learned an important personal lesson. I simply couldn't be the type of mother I had grown up expecting to be. I was who I was—a woman who wanted a child and was looking forward to having a second—but I also wanted something else. So I did what I could to have them both. In the end it made me happier, and it also made me a better mother than I would have been if I had just stayed home.

9

From MAMA to MANMAN

I'd survived my first year in business and was chugging along in my second when in mid-1973 a salesman named Gary Kettleson called from Tymshare, the small, aggressive time-sharing company that was outselling GE on the West Coast. Gary said, "I've got a customer who's seen the programs you've done for California Microwave and Halcyon and wants one of his own." When Kettleson wouldn't say who the customer was, I figured he was angling for a finder's fee. In fact, he wanted me to write a manufacturing program for the Tymshare network—a canned, one-size-fits-all program like the accounting and engineering programs I'd sold for GE.

The idea felt wrong. I liked being a heroine to individual customers. Writing a program for a time-sharing company instead of end users, I'd lose the satisfaction of customer contact. Besides, the current wisdom—what IBM was selling along with in-house mainframes—was that manufacturing companies needed custom programs tailored to specific operations. Mostly, though, I wanted my independence. So I said to Gary, "I don't do programs for time-sharing. I develop custom programs and run them as a service. So thanks, but no, thanks."

"Okay. But you're missing a terrific opportunity."

My first thought after hanging up was, Why didn't GE call? Hadn't I been one of their star employees? But Gary's call indicated precisely why Tymshare was trouncing GE in the California market. GE was simply not creative enough to see value in the software I'd been developing. My second thought was that maybe Gary was right. Maybe I *was* missing a terrific opportunity.

When he called back a couple of weeks later, I heard him out. What he said reinforced my own thinking that manufacturing companies were far more similar than dissimilar. From my point of view this meant each program I wrote could build on others I'd already written. From Gary's point of view it meant that a single, universal program could be developed for thousands of manufacturers.

The argument for a universal program made a great deal of sense. First, every manufacturer kept an inventory. One might inventory truck parts, another parts for assembling stereo loudspeakers, and another parts for building toys. Whatever the parts, they all could be assigned identifying names or numbers, making them perfect grist for the computer mill.

Second, most companies broke down their product assemblies into discrete subassemblies, with different assembly due dates for each—meaning not all parts for a finished product had to be on hand when the first assembly began but had to be scheduled to arrive when needed.

And third, most manufacturers purchase some of their parts and assemblies from outside vendors. These, too, had to be ordered, tracked, and scheduled.

I could see where Gary was heading. I just wasn't sure I wanted to go there. Finally, after a few days, the light went on. The reason this guy kept calling was that I really *did* have something that could make his company a lot of money and broaden the marketplace, a program that would work for all small and medium-size manufacturing companies that couldn't afford computers.

Maybe my program had the potential for reaching hundreds,

even thousands of customers. I called Gary back, we met a few times, and I agreed to write the universal program Tymshare wanted.

About the time I met Gary, I attended a talk given by a guy named George Plossl, who'd written a book called *Manufacturing Control: The Last Frontier for Profits.* An avuncular man in his late fifties, Plossl argued that manufacturing could be made into a science through computerized material requirements planning (MRP). Much of the manufacturing "science" he referred to in his talk I had already incorporated into the Farinon program. It was a pleasant surprise to learn that guided only by common sense and the needs of my customers, I'd unwittingly stumbled onto manufacturing's leading edge.

The program ASK developed for Tymshare was bare bones, allowing Tymshare's customers to enter their data quickly and be up and running within days. It had three segments, or modules, and a simple question-and-answer format. The inventory control module consisted of simple prompts, such as "ENTER PART NUMBER," "DESCRIPTION," "QUANTITY ON HAND," etc., and included a few interactive functions that would allow you to update the quantity of parts on hand as they were used and as replenishment parts arrived. The bill of materials module allowed you to list all the materials needed for a given assembly and then to break down each assembly into smaller and smaller subassemblies. The where used module showed all the assemblies with a given part. Say your company could no longer get No. 2 screws and engineering had to redesign every assembly that used them; the where used module would track them all.

Rudimentary as it was, ASK's program was a step into the next century, compared with the old-fashioned manual cardex system of inventory control—skinny little file drawers filled with tiny cards corresponding to each part number. Beyond eliminating the cardex hassle, the ASK program immediately helped companies cut inventory costs and operating expenses by enabling them to have in stock the correct parts in the optimum quantity needed. It also helped improve on-time deliveries to customers by allowing companies to tailor production to actual customer orders. So the faster my rudimentary product hit the market, the more money my potential users would save—and, of course, the faster I'd begin earning royalties.

Another reason for wanting the product out the door was that I didn't want to fall into the R&D trap of trying to create the perfect mousetrap. Some companies spend so long developing their mousetraps that by the time they hit the market, there are whole new kinds of mice to trap, mutant strains that have become dominant. Every product has its time. The trick is to be in the marketplace just as the demand for it is accelerating. Too early is sometimes as bad as too late.

In the early eighties the Xerox Star workstation was well ahead of its time. It was slick and—years before the Apple Macintosh—it featured icons rather than text commands. But the public was just getting used to the idea of computers and wasn't ready for anything quite so radical. The product was also overpriced.

Fax machines are another example of a technology ahead of its time. Fax machines have been around for more than a decade, but they were too expensive for a public that didn't consider the speed that they could provide that important. The mail was fast enough. Then along came Federal Express. Speed became critical. Now every business and lots of individuals have fax machines.

As for being too late, also in the early eighties VisiCorp, the company that developed the best-selling VisiCalc spreadsheet program for the Apple II, decided it needed a product for the growing IBM personal computer (PC) market. One of the company's programmers, Mitch Kapor, offered VisiCorp's president, Dan Fylstra, a package he'd developed on his own. Fylstra turned it down, thinking VisiCorp could develop a better package internally. Kapor quit to start his own company. By the time VisiCorp finally came out with their IBM product, VisiOn, Kapor's software, Lotus 1-2-3, owned the market.

Adam Osborne, on the other hand, was right on time with the first portable computer. Not only did he package the hardware into a machine that was highly compact for the times, but he also included software, all for less than two thousand dollars. Within two years his company had grown from nothing to nearly a hundred million dollars. But Osborne then took too long to respond to the trend to IBM compatibility, and within another year his company had gone bankrupt.

It took me about three months of day and night work to finish the universal manufacturing program for Tymshare. With only the user manual left to write, Arie and I and another couple went up to Lake Tahoe for a week to ski. It rained all week. Fortunately I had brought my briefcase along, and I wrote the entire manual at the ski lodge. Like the software, the manual had to be simple to use. After all, the person referring to it wouldn't be a computer expert or a Ph.D. in math. He'd be someone who knew what he wanted but would need his hand held through the process of finding it. So I built the same simplicity into the manual that I'd built into the software, making use of a similar question-and-answer format the user could easily walk through. All this is pretty obvious today, but it was ignored surprisingly often in those early days of computers.

My desire for simplicity extended to the name I gave the software: MAMA, short for MAnufacturing MAnagement—a nice, simple mnemonic. When I came back from the ski trip, I gave an advance copy of the manual to Fred Levien, one of the managers at Farinon, for his comments. The very first thing he did was draw a red circle around the "MAMA" on the cover and hand it back to me.

"Why the circle?" I asked.

"Can you imagine a hard-nosed executive getting up in front of his board of directors and asking for approval to run the company's manufacturing operations with the MAMA system? No way!"

At first I was ticked off. Not only was I the program's mama, but I was also a real-life mama. I felt insulted. Then I looked at it on the page and said, "You know, you might have something there. You often need two men to do the work of one mama." I scratched out MAMA and wrote MANMAN, same mnemonic, same idea. And to this day I've never heard of anyone having any trouble getting up before a board to ask for a hundred thousand, two hundred thousand, three hundred thousand dollars or more for MANMAN.

10

ASK, Inc.

By early 1974, with MANMAN on Tymshare, the atmosphere at ASK was changing. We were still operating out of the two extra bedrooms in my house, but ASK was growing. I had three full-time employees—Jan Korpella, Jim Parker, and another programmer—and if Tymshare panned out, I'd hire more. Also, by 1974 I'd completely given up on my original idea of working part-time. ASK was a full-time business, and my goal was to build it bigger and better.

One way to accomplish this was to make MANMAN on Tymshare a success. No matter how good it was, the program wasn't going to sell itself.

So I took another risk. Having already written the program on spec, I now decided to dedicate much of my time to helping Tymshare's sales reps sell it. After all, I knew the program, had a sense of the market, and was certainly no slouch in time-share sales. With ASK making around 20 percent of every dollar that Tymshare billed their customers for using my program, Tymshare would stand to benefit the most from my efforts, but I was happy to earn money for them in the process of earning money for ASK. By taking part in the sales process, I was able to exert more control over what happened to my baby.

I started by pitching MANMAN to Tymshare's field reps. I showed them how it worked and how they could sell it effectively. I was afraid they'd be put off by my butting in, but the reps loved the help. At their urging I even joined them on local sales calls and talked directly to their customers. It wasn't long before my involvement paid off. In just a few months we had dozens of customers on-line, including Coca-Cola, General Cable, Borden Chemical, and Varian.

Spending time again in a variety of manufacturing environments convinced me that not only was being on-line efficient, but the instant feedback it provided was imperative to running a successful operation. For example, when a good customer was on the phone asking how soon you'd be able to deliver a hundred more yellow widgets, you could tell immediately how many of the widgets you had in stock, how many were committed to other customers, and how long it would take to assemble and ship any widgets you had to manufacture. You also could tell your chief financial officer the exact value of your inventory when he went to the bank for a short-term loan.

Another advantage of being on-line was the speed at which you could correct errors. Working in batch on the OSI mainframe for my service bureau clients, I'd keypunch all their inventory and purchasing updates on cards and feed them into the computer. But if a stock clerk gave me the wrong number—a part number not matching those on file, for example—I'd get an error reading at the end of my computer run. The clerk would have to correct the error and resubmit the transaction, and it wouldn't show up on the printout until the next run, often as much as a week later. So even if the information was ultimately accurate, it was never up-to-date. Timely decisions just couldn't be made. With MANMAN, however, when the clerk entered an incorrect part number, the program responded immediately with "NOT A CURRENT PART NUMBER; RE-ENTER?" or "ADD AS NEW PART?"

The only disadvantage of being on-line with MANMAN in a time-sharing environment was cost. The more a company used MAN-MAN, the more they liked it and the longer they stayed on-line. This was fine with me because I received a royalty for every minute MAN-MAN was used. But it wasn't fine with the management of companies suddenly being socked with ten thousand, fifteen thousand, twenty thousand dollars or more in monthly bills. At some point the bean counters would start shouting that the system's costs outweighed its benefits.

But in 1974 far more companies were plugging in time-sharing than unplugging it. And MANMAN was seeing a great deal of play because it was one of the few programs of its type available and because the manufacturing industry as a whole was undercomputerized. However basic, MANMAN fitted the bill.

By spring 1974, as MANMAN on Tymshare caught on, ASK began to grow far faster than before. I'd bet on the "come," investing time and money up front before getting a penny from Tymshare, and now that bet was beginning to pay off. Not in hundred of thousands of dollars or anywhere near it, but after only a few months we'd made a few thousand dollars, and it seemed we'd soon be making even more—meaning we'd also be making more money than we were spending. This created a whole new set of concerns.

I'd initially established ASK as a proprietorship, which in 1974 was much the same as being self-employed from a tax standpoint. Like the self-employed person, a proprietor paid taxes quarterly on the estimated annual net of his or her business and at the same rate. There was no tax break for reinvesting profits in the business. A proprietor also assumed personal legal liability for his or her business. If one of my customers' manufacturing programs went haywire, he could have conceivably sued me personally for damages. And if he won, to satisfy the judgment, he could attach all the assets in my name as well as those in Arie's and my name together.

With MANMAN generating ASK's first real profits—above and beyond, that is, my meager 1973 salary of about twelve thousand dollars—on July 1, 1974, I took the next logical step—I filed for incorporation. As a corporation ASK would have its profits taxed at the 1974 corporate rate of 48 percent, considerably lower than the maximum personal rate of 70 percent I would pay on my salary from ASK. Thrifty as I was, this encouraged me to keep as much money in the company as possible.

A corporation is also considered a separate legal entity, so if ASK were sued, only its assets, not mine, were at risk. While the "veil of the corporation," as it's referred to, can be broken by the courts under some circumstances, our liability would nevertheless be limited by incorporating.

A third reason I incorporated was that a corporation issues shares of stock as evidence of ownership. I thought that as ASK grew, giving stock to my employees would be a way of rewarding them for work well done and providing them with a stake in the future of the company.

At twenty-seven I was president, chairman, and chief executive officer of a corporation.

11

The Big Connection

One evening around the time ASK incorporated I got a call from a fellow named Dick Breon. He was a technical support representative for Hewlett-Packard (HP), the largest corporation in the Silicon Valley. I was in the office winding down from the day's activities, answering mail, paying bills, occasionally checking in on Andy, and reading technical magazines—my way of keeping up-to-date with the computer industry and the industries ASK sold to. Someplace, somewhere, MANMAN was cooking on Tymshare, and ASK was earning royalties.

Dick had seen MANMAN in action and been impressed. HP wanted to sell its HP 2100 computer to a Los Angeles company called Powertec, which manufactured power supplies. The HP computer would run Powertec's factory, and Dick wondered if I'd consider rewriting MANMAN for HP's machine.

I was flattered—HP was not only big but highly respected—but there was just one problem. On a time-sharing network the user's terminal was linked by phone to a large mainframe. So although the user saw only his terminal, the MANMAN program was running on a machine with plenty of computing power and memory. The 2100, on the other hand, was one of the new *mini* computers just coming into wide use. These machines were supposed to be computing's next generation. One-tenth the cost of a mainframe, they were cheap enough to be dedicated to a single function like controlling an instrument in an automated process. The problem was they also had substantially less power and memory. In fact, the 2100 had only thirty-two thousand bytes of memory—only as much as some of today's hand-held calculators—and a five-megabyte disk storage system. No way was the HP machine large enough to run MANMAN, I told Dick.

"Well, we've solved that problem," he said. "We've got a new operating system that allows you to overlay programs to achieve more capacity. It's all in place and ready to go."

"Oh, yeah?" If Dick was right, there might be a whole new ball game for MANMAN. We met the following morning.

In 1974 there were only a few players in the minicomputer market. The two largest were Digital Equipment Corporation (DEC)—the company that developed the first minicomputer in the late fifties—and Data General. At that time both companies sold their machines primarily to original equipment manufacturers (OEMs), who repackaged them with other hardware, most often scientific instruments, and sold them under their own names.

In contrast, Hewlett-Packard was an instrument company that had developed minicomputers to run its own instruments. Widely regarded as one of the finest electronics companies in the world, HP was now trying to capitalize on that reputation to sell computers separately to the ultimate user.

Founded in 1939 in a Palo Alto garage by Stanford electrical engineers William Hewlett and David Packard, HP developed products using the "next bench syndrome." Hewlett was an inveterate putterer who was always searching for the gizmo that the engineer at the next bench would want or that he himself would want if he were at that bench. The most famous instance of this occurred in 1972, when Bill Hewlett tired of his slide rule and decided it would be easier and more accurate to work with a small calculator he could hold in his hand or slip into his shirt pocket. His market research department concluded that as long as there were forty-dollar slide rules, no one would pay four hundred dollars for a hand-held calculator, which, considering the technology of the times, was what the device would have to sell for. Hewlett came back with "I don't care if no one else wants one. *I* want one." HP built it, and the rest is history, along with the slide rule (my sons don't even know what one looks like).

If Hewlett was HP's spark plug who made sure that only the highest-quality products were developed, Packard was the exceptional manager who fostered the company's growth and sold its products in the marketplace. Even after both had become billionaires, they were often seen in shirt sleeves in the company cafeteria. Success never turned their heads nor dampened their curiosity.

But in 1974, when HP contacted me, I hadn't yet had access to the inner sanctum. I'd seen only the outsides of the HP buildings that dotted the Silicon Valley countryside. Their corporate headquarters in Palo Alto was as verdant and sprawling as a college campus, with low-slung buildings, covered pathways, and glass, glass, glass. HP was growing so fast that every few months or so a new building appeared on the landscape. Look close and you'd see HP engineers scurrying from building to building. Virtually all men, they were trim, crew-cut, and irrepressibly healthy, fresh out of the top universities, hired before they could be sullied by the outside world. Go for an interview at HP only a year after you'd graduated and, rumor had it, you'd have little chance of signing on. The uniform was a white shirt, slacks, a tie, a plastic breast pocket holder of pens, and a little blue HP badge. No need for a sport coat, certainly not for a suit. In the eyes of many it was *the* place to work in the Valley.

So when Dick Breon called, I was flattered. It bowled me over that HP thought an ASK product was good enough to run on one of their machines. It was like being asked to the prom by the golden boy who was both the valedictorian and the varsity's star quarterback.

Dick wasn't at all what I was expecting. He was relatively short, wore thick glasses, and had a flip, arrogant manner. But the brochures he produced of the HP 2100 minicomputer and the recently designed Terminal Control System (TCS) and Image Data Base Management System that would allow the use of multiple terminals and increase the 2100's capacity were absolutely gorgeous: four-color glossy paper. Not only that, but the accompanying manuals were a wonder in themselves: clear, thorough, with an answer to any question. They were everything I had always thought HP to be. He left them with me, and I read them over and over. A couple of days later I told him I'd go down to L.A. with him to help make the sale.

I spent the night before the sales call at my parents' house in West Los Angeles. As usual, they were concerned about who was taking care of Andy and what would happen if he swallowed a medicine cabinet, but I was too excited about the next day's meeting to let it get to me. Instead, I talked and talked about HP with my dad, trying to impress him with the company I was keeping. He was pleased but unimpressed. As a self-made small businessman he had little admiration for big business. Also, like most of the rest of his generation, he was dubious about this new computer technology that relied so much more on "faith" than it did on paper. Dad was tremendously organized and proud of it. He entered all his business's financial data on carefully kept handwritten ledger sheets. He knew where every receipt, every order was. At his desk he could put his hands on any paper or piece of information in seconds. "Here it is," he'd insist, pointing to his file drawers. I'd say, "But, Dad, with a computer you could put all those files, all that paper—" He wouldn't let me finish. "I'm in the construction business," he would say. "What do I need a computer for?"

It's not, finally, that he didn't believe in computers. He read all the newsmagazines, was extremely well versed in current affairs, and probably knew as much as any layperson about computers. But he believed that computers were for big companies—largely true at the time—and also that I was being strung along by HP, who'd never depend on his daughter to write a program for them.

I met Dick and Joe Pifko, HP's local sales rep, for breakfast at a small greasy spoon a few minutes from Powertec, in Chatsworth in the San Fernando Valley. It was over my melon and their overstuffed omelets that I first got the actual lay of the land. Powertec liked HP's machine, its iron, and they liked HP's reputation; but they wanted a manufacturing system, not a computer, and weren't about to buy HP unless they got the whole package, software as well as iron. Enter ASK. No ASK, no sale.

The main guy at Powertec we had to sell was Wally Silver, the VP of manufacturing. After my experiences with Evan Bakke and other manufacturing honchos, smarts and sophistication in manufacturing management never surprised me. Wally was no exception. Powertec was about a seven-million-dollar company in 1974. Most companies that size would not have had much experience with computers. But Wally, who'd worked with computers at Varian, already knew what computers could accomplish. Powertec's boss had given him a luke-warm okay to computerize, and now Wally was running with it. He knew precisely what he was looking for: more or less the same program I'd written for Tymshare, but for HP's minicomputer, which Powertec would own, so he wouldn't have to pay for the time he spent on-line. I liked him immediately.

To prepare for the sales call, I'd worked up a MANMAN demonstration using a Powertec parts list, a bill of materials, and a few purchase orders I'd had sent up to me. I wanted to give them a demo that used their own data. In that way Wally could see I'd taken exceptional interest in his situation and had spent extra time and trouble prior to the call, all of which might work for me in closing the sale. I obviously couldn't do the demo on an HP 2100—the program existed only in its Tymshare version—but Powertec had a teletype terminal, and I had my own user number to access MANMAN on Tymshare, so I ran a few simple scenarios for Wally and his small entourage.

"And you could rewrite this software," Wally began, "to run on the HP system?" Absolutely, I said. Sure, it would take a few months. Plus there were a number of new features that I couldn't include in the Tymshare version because they would require even more time on-line and make the time-share cost prohibitive. "Of course, with your own minicomputer . . ." Wally gave me a smile. Behind him Dick and Joe beamed. We all were in this together. I assured Wally that the programming would be relatively simple, a piece of cake. Wally was impressed.

Not sufficiently, however, to close the deal. In fact, it took a half dozen trips to L.A. and nearly six months to put the deal together—my first experience with the computer sales cycle versus the time-share or service bureau sales cycle—and this was with a customer who already believed he needed a computer. It was a cautionary exercise.

Nearly a decade later I found out one reason for Powertec's slow response. I was at a trade show when a former Powertec guy came up to me and said, "You know, it's nice to see that you're so successful because I remember the staff meeting where we were voting whether you should get the job and most people said that there was no way that a woman could know anything about manufacturing and make it in this business." It was the first time anyone had ever come right out and said that my being a woman might stop a company from doing business with ASK.

During the Powertec sales trips I stayed with my parents. I told my dad we were getting closer and closer to a deal, but he was sure I was being led down the primrose path by some sharp businessmen. "In the construction business," he declared, "when we decide what we want, we go out and get it!"

Finally the deal was made. Powertec took delivery of their computer from HP, and ASK received a purchase order from Powertec to develop the software. I had no idea what to charge, but I'd seen companies the size of Powertec spring five thousand, ten thousand dollars a month on time-sharing. So I asked for twenty-five thousand dollars with five thousand dollars up front. No one batted an eye.

At the time I saw the Powertec job as just another sale, plain and simple—an exciting and, of course, highly prestigious one because it involved HP. What I failed to appreciate, even though it was evident from my first meeting with Dick and Joe, was precisely how important my program was to the process and how important software was becoming to the Powertecs of the world—as well as to HP, DEC, and even IBM.

12

Unhappy Campers

The Powertec contract once again made me face something that trips up a lot of entrepreneurs: You can't do it all. I was already putting in twelve-hour days and more, and with the Powertec job starting up, something had to give. So I made a list of my strengths and weaknesses to determine where I should devote my energies at ASK and whom I should hire to help. I knew I could make sound decisions—whether it was changing our focus from contract programming to a service bureau or moving from time-sharing to batch programming and back to time-sharing again. Each of these moves had been made at just the right time for ASK's growth. I was also coming to realize that I was a good leader. People actually seemed to enjoy the long hours they spent working for me, and they produced at the peak of their abilities.

While I was good at inspiring the troops, I was not as strong at managing the day-to-day business operations. I was okay with details, but I was impatient. After I worked through one problem or challenge, I wanted to move on to the next challenge. And while I loved working with people, I didn't like having to keep after them. I was also relatively inexperienced in business. What I needed, therefore, was an experienced operations manager. I offered the job to Bob Rasmussen, who'd been my liaison while I was developing MANMAN for Tymshare. I was pleased and relieved when he accepted.

Bob was about ten years older than I. Tall and handsome, he just *looked* like a manager. He'd come from a big company—Tymshare was probably doing about a hundred million dollars at the time—and had worked at a few other companies prior to Tymshare. He knew both software development and manufacturing, and I figured he'd be the ideal guy to implement the Powertec project and see to the day-to-day operation of ASK. Meanwhile, I could continue looking for new clients and make certain the old ones stayed happy. Not that any job description in a company the size of ASK could be adhered to too strictly. We all shared in making coffee, sweeping the floor, and even tending to Andy if he found his way into the office.

Still, it was difficult for ASK to take on another employee because of the relatively large financial risk. ASK remained virtually a hand-to-mouth operation—when we incorporated, we had ninety-eight thousand dollars in gross revenues for the first six months of 1974—and Bob's salary was basically money out of my own pocket.

Yet only a few months after hiring Bob, I also hired Marty Browne, heightening the financial risk. But I was certain it would be worth it. I'd first met Marty on the Farinon project. He was tall with sandy blond hair he wore pulled back in a ponytail, a sign of the times for Vietnam era college students and graduates. Marty had recently left Stanford with a degree in math and was working odd jobs in the area when Farinon hired him to transpose onto keypunch sheets the hundreds of thousands of lines of parts numbers and other information necessary to put Farinon on our service bureau. Seven-eighths of the way through the project, I realized I'd coded the system incorrectly, and all the information had to be rewritten. Marty just took it in stride. Besides, it extended his employment. To this day, however, he has a callus on his finger from writing all those numbers.

More than anyone I'd met to that point, Marty had a gut understanding of what made a good program. Not trained as a programmer, he approached software problems more as a layman than a techie. He knew a program had to be lucid and easy to use. Again, user-friendliness may sound like a fairly self-evident concept today, but in 1974 it was downright revolutionary.

With Marty's thinking so clearly mirroring my own and his easygoing manner contrasting with mine, I knew ASK had to have him aboard—complete with his sixties ponytail, his tire-tread sandals, his Grateful Dead T-shirt, and his single pair of jeans. His first job was to write the user manual for the Powertec program. I knew that if we were successful on the HP 2100, there'd be plenty more for him to do.

The Powertec contract put ASK officially in partnership with HP. At least, that was the way I liked to think of it. Now all we needed was a computer. Since we couldn't afford the sixty thousand dollars plus to buy one, HP agreed to give us access to a 2100 at its new Santa Clara office. Assuming the actual conversion of MANMAN to the machine would be the piece of cake I had said it would, I focused my initial efforts on creating the additional features I'd pitched to Wally Silver. Three of us—Bob, Marty, and I—set up shop in our makeshift office at HP, armed with pencils, yellow pads, and HP's perfectly written user's manuals. We were young, eager, and completely unprepared for what hit us.

The HP 2100 system was about six feet high, eight feet wide, and two feet deep, with 32 K bytes of memory. Back then there were no video monitors. Instead, as with time-sharing, you interfaced with the computer via a teletype terminal. Paper tape was used to load start-up procedures into the machine. On the computer's face were rows of flashing lights, plus a series of little toggle switches and buttons. Even with all those switches and buttons, it was hard to tell if the computer was actually computing or just on and nonfunctional. The lights were supposed to be the tip-off. When they blinked, the computer was actually thinking. When they were on but not blinking, the computer had either caught up to you and was waiting for further instructions or had crashed and all the data you'd been working on had been taken to never-never land. Unsure whether we were on-line or in deep trouble, we programmed the computer to count continuously when it was on. In that way, as long as the lights flashed, we knew we were okay.

The next snag we ran into was far more serious. We'd spend a few hours writing code, all the time feeding it into the 2100 to test it on the machine. We'd be tooling along, the lights blinking merrily, when suddenly without any apparent provocation the machine crashed. Lights on but not blinking, no vital signs. At that point the computer forgot whatever we'd fed into it, and we'd have to start from scratch.

The first few times this happened we dutifully went back to the manuals and reread them to make sure we were doing everything by the book. If we were making a mistake, we sure as hell couldn't figure out what it was. So we called in HP service. HP was known worldwide for its ever-ready topflight service and support team. Naturally, whenever we needed help, they were on another service call. And since we weren't paying customers, we were last on the list, despite the fact that the 2100 and service resided in the same bulding. Finally, the servicemen would arrive, pull the 2100 away from the wall, examine its guts, and declare it healthy. Indeed, it was up and running in no time, flashing its lights for hours before crashing again. We'd call service, and the whole process would start all over. This went on for weeks.

The servicemen must have thought we were total flakes. But since upper management had given us access to an HP computer on HP premises, a privilege no other vendor was getting, they were nice to us.

Unbeknownst to service or *us*, ASK was being treated so well because the Powertec project was to be one of the very first commercial applications ever for the 2100. Up until then it had only been used to control instruments. ASK's success on the machine would be HP's first solid indication that they could become a serious player in the commercial minicomputer marketplace.

Meanwhile, the 2100 kept crashing. The servicemen came; the servicemen went. Sometimes they came alone. Sometimes they brought some technical guys from another building. There were many powwows in front of the unblinking lights. When Wally Silver and Joe Pifko, the HP rep on the Powertec account, called, I'd assure both of them things were going swimmingly.

At about this time we began to hear rumblings from some of the HP workers in the building. Our daytime use of the 2100 had extended into the evening hours. Most of us were spending the night, in fact, trying to meet our deadline with Powertec. We rolled out our sleeping bags in supply closets, then used the company showers to freshen up, appeared for free coffee and doughnuts in the morning, and scarfed down the free HP fruit and juice in the afternoon. In those days HP had a tradition of Friday afternoon beer busts, and we were there for those as well. Not only that, but we were using HP's phones and were monopolizing and demoralizing their crack service team, not to mention their technical gurus.

I sympathized with their concerns, but after all, we were there to help HP in their minicomputer campaign. And by then I had begun to suspect that the problem with the computer was not our fault at all. Still, the questions were surfacing: Why do these guys get free use of our computer when no one else does? And more important: How come we have to wear name badges and these guys don't?

Finally, one day, a bright service guy came into the office with a hair dryer. I assumed it was for us to blow-dry our hair after our showers. But no. The 2100 was up and running, its lights blinking to beat the band. We were in a hopeful mood. The guy plugged the hair dryer into a standard 110-amp wall receptacle. "Ready?" he asked.

"Sure," I said. I had no idea what he was up to.

He flicked on the hair dryer, and lo and behold, the machine crashed. Then he flicked it off, told us to boot up the machine again. We got it going, he flicked the hair dryer on again, and the computer went down.

"Aha!" he announced. I looked at Marty. Marty looked at Bob. Bob looked at the man from service. The serviceman looked at the hair dryer. "Well, wouldn't you know it!"

As it turned out, the super-high-tech company's most sophisticated computer, installed in their newest facility, was sharing a circuit with the copier machine in the hall. Whenever someone made a copy, the surge from the copier machine was enough to crash the computer. The bottom line: We'd wasted at least a month, worn out our welcome as guests, and hadn't gotten any closer to meeting the Powertec deadline. But I'd never been one to dwell on the past. I felt liberated. It was only a glitch, and now things would fall rapidly into place.

But new glitches kept appearing. We'd eliminate a minor bug in our program only to find more serious bugs in HP's nifty Image data base manager software or in the 2100's new Terminal Control System—the breakthrough that was supposed to allow more than one terminal to access data at the same time. To keep Powertec happy, I flew down to L.A. frequently with specs for new functions I was designing to demonstrate how MANMAN on the HP 2100 would be superior to the far more rudimentary version they'd seen on Tymshare.

The constant crashing of the machine plus the glitches—wherever the fault lay—put a damper on HP's enthusiasm for our project. We were behind schedule and getting desperate. The absolute low point came when I got a call from Bill Richion, HP's regional sales manager in L.A. I'd never met the man, but the second I picked up the phone he announced, "This is Bill Richion, and I want you the hell out of there! I want to sell that computer, and I want our technical people back on the job." I told him the hair dryer story, I told him about the glitches in the HP software, but he was unimpressed. He wanted us the hell out of there. Finally I persuaded him to let me demonstrate what we'd already accomplished on the program. Reluctantly he agreed to meet in HP's North Hollywood office the following week.

When I asked around about Richion, I heard he was the company maverick. He was outgoing; he was brash; he was a gambler. When he came to Santa Clara for his biweekly staff meeting, the major item on the agenda was the all-night high-stakes poker game, where thousands of dollars changed hands. Sometimes Bill Hewlett was allowed to sit in and bet nickels. Rumor had it Richion never lost. He was also a golfer and known to take his opponents' money on the greens. Finally he was the archetypal male chauvinist, so obvious about it that it was almost a joke. Things didn't look good for my demo. The only bright spots were that Bill's head for business reportedly overrode any and all of his shortcomings and that he was a salesman through and through—he'd earned his way through college selling pots and pans—and there's no one easier to sell than a salesman.

I had one week to prepare my case. Marty, Bob, and I worked

virtually every hour of it at HP to produce as much as we could of the program. There are two universal laws of demos. Law No. 1 is "Demos fail." Machines are configured differently, or you forget to include one of your files. Plus there's the pressure of the moment— people peering over your shoulder, breathing down your neck when you have only this one chance to make your case. Law No. 2 is "The probability of a demo's failing increases in proportion to the importance of the demo." If and when this demo failed, I wanted to be sure I was covered. So in addition to preparing the software, I made hard copies of all the transactions I was intending to demo.

Since this might be my only chance at Richion, I wanted to take the opportunity to do more than demo the Powertec job. I wanted to use this meeting with the highest-ranking executive I'd so far dealt with at HP to plead a case for ASK to be included in other sales situations to manufacturing companies—a joint ASK/HP selling arrangement—even if it meant adding an agenda item that Richion wouldn't be expecting or be prepared to discuss. So in addition to the demo, I prepared a full sales presentation. In it I defined the manufacturing market as I saw it and spelled out why HP was in the best competitive position to exploit this market. For starters, at the time none of HP's minicomputer competitors was actively selling applications; their focus was still on hardware. Also, the 2100 was a far friendlier machine to use than the downsized mainframe IBM was offering its manufacturing customers. Finally, I stressed that the software ASK was developing for Powertec would give HP the edge it needed to dominate this market niche. I knew if I could present this plan, it would significantly raise HP's stake in ASK's success on their machine, at the same time taking some of the heat off the ailing Powertec job.

Richion was available only near the end of the day, so I spent the early afternoon at my parents' rehearsing my pitch. When the appointed time came, I grabbed my pink briefcase, my lavender cards, my demo tape, and was on my way.

Richion greeted me looking as if he'd just ambled in off the golf course—no jacket, tan and brown golf shirt, and brown polyester pants. As was the case with Dick Breon, Richion didn't look like anyone I'd ever seen at HP and looked even less like the white-shirted sales manager I had met my one day at IBM. He was about five feet eleven inches, with gray, thinning hair. "So you're the broad who's trying to sell this manufacturing system?" He seemed both amused and earnest as he said it. "Beyond the bluster," I thought, "this guy is okay." I told him yes, I was the very broad.

Next came the demo. Luckily the 2100 in his office was configured much like the one we'd been working with in Santa Clara, and I could get it to run our tape. At first I demoed a parts list and a bill of materials from Powertec. Then I showed Bill how easy it was to enter a new assembly. When the terminal asked for "ASSEMBLY NAME," I typed in "Bill Richion; for "DESCRIPTION" I entered "a handsome man"; and for "QUANTITY ON HAND," "one." When the program asked for "QUANTITY ON ORDER," I turned and asked, "Is your mother going to produce any more of you?" Bill was smiling, and now he laughed. Next, I did a bill of materals, as if I were going to build a BILL RICHION. "PART?" I entered "legs." "QUANTITY?" I entered "2." "PART?" I entered "ARMS." "QUANTITY?" I entered "2." "PART?" I entered "HEART." "QUANTITY?" I entered "0."

"What do you mean by that?" he demanded.

"Heartless," I told him.

"Very clever," he said after the demo was over, "but you've still got to get the hell out of there." The words were the same, but the tone had softened. I figured now or never, so I produced the binder containing my joint ASK/HP sales plan.

"No time," he insisted. "Meetings." He pointed to a door where the alleged meetings were to take place.

"How about dinner then?" I pressed. "Let me buy you dinner." Bill looked me in the eye. I'm sure he didn't know what to make of it all. In any event, I'm certain he never thought that our meeting, the proposal in my binder, and my software would eventually cause him to rethink the whole way HP would sell computers. Indeed, in less than five years, ASK was to become the largest customer for HP computers in the world, and Bill Richion was to become an HP vice-president and director of its U.S. sales operations.

We went to dinner. I presented my plan, we talked about how I'd gotten into software and how he'd gotten into sales, and by the time Bill picked up the tab, he'd given us another month on the machine.

13

Leaving Home

By fall 1974 there were six of us working out of ASK's tiny two-bedroom office. Not only had space become a problem, but Andy spent much of the day toddling downstairs to visit, with Eldemira hot on his tail. When she'd tell him that Mommy had to work, he'd let out a huge hullabaloo, insisting he wanted to play with me. Guilt.

That December I decided it was time for ASK to leave home. In the six months since we'd incorporated, our revenues had nearly doubled to more than $15,000 per month. We had $12,000 in the bank and $45,000 in receivables, with monthly expenses of about $10,000. Our capital equipment consisted only of a few desks, chairs, and filing cabinets bought at discount furniture stores, plus a couple of terminals. The keypunch was rented. The real value in the business was in the software, which I calculated to be worth $250,000.

Hustling new business and camping out at HP to untangle the Powertec snarl, I didn't have much time to hunt for office space. But my requirements were simple: It had to be cheap; it had to be close by.

I didn't want to drive too far to work, and I wanted to be close enough to home to drop in on Andy during the day if necessary. So I checked the papers for an office within ten miles of the house. I found a nice, twelve-hundred-square-foot build-to-suit space in Los Altos, only a few minutes from home. With its floor-to-ceiling outer glass walls it looked more like a shopping arcade than an office, but the rent was relatively reasonable, and twelve hundred square feet seemed positively huge at the time. I asked my dad to fly up and check the space out for me. He told me to take it and sketched out a workable floor plan. I signed a three-year lease for nearly twenty-five thousand dollars, ASK's first real financial commitment.

We set Jan up behind a partially glassed-in reception area with a U-shaped Formica working counter and the floor-standing keypunch machine. On her rolling desk chair, she could pivot from the machine to the phones or to the front of the counter to greet our visitors. While they waited, they could sit on the couch left over from Arie's and my apartment in Short Hills and stare at a fake Picasso print, an office-warming gift from my parents. The whole operation looked professional, all right, but it looked more like a doctor's office than a software company—whatever that was supposed to look like. The rest of us each had our own offices.

The problem was we weren't ever in the office. Most of us were still spending all our time at HP, desperately trying to get MANMAN to run on the 2100. Even with Bill Richion's stay of execution—and a few subsequent stays—we simply weren't able to get the program to run on more than a single terminal at a time. This would severely limit the program's use in a manufacturing environment. The second we tried to go to multiple terminals using HP's super Terminal Control System software, the 2100 crashed. After this had happened enough times, it dawned on me that maybe like the earlier crashing episodes, it was not our fault.

Snooping around and befriending HP's technical people, I found out that TCS had not been designed by HP but had been acquired from an outside source and that HP's Image data base manager software hadn't actually been developed for the 2100 but for a newer-generation HP computer, the 3000. In other words, the two basic pieces of software we were building our program on, TCS and Image, had been created by two different design teams, without any thought that they would work together. I checked my glossy four-color TCS and Image brochures and the user manuals to see if they mentioned anything about this potential incompatibility. To the contrary, they promised a trouble-free union. Finally, after three months on the project, I asked what success HP's other customers were having marrying TCS and Image. "What other customers?" was the reply.

ASK, in other words, was the guinea pig in an HP experiment. Armed with this distressing news, I asked Richion to meet me along with HP's technical people, and I put it to them. The technical people sheepishly admitted that no, TCS and Image probably wouldn't work together correctly. Everyone seemed sorry.

Sorry wasn't good enough. From a technical standpoint, we were at the major crisis point in the Powertec job. We had three choices: Go with the Image software and make the system work with only a single terminal—a bad idea—write new data base management software that would work with TCS, or replace TCS with a system of our own that would work with Image. We had just hired a bright young UC Berkeley graduate, Roger Bottarini, and he was sure he could develop a polling program so multiple terminals could run off a 2100. Whichever option we chose, however, we'd have to start virtually from scratch on the MANMAN program. And we were already overdue on the promised delivery date specified in the Powertec purchase order.

We were also in dutch financially. It was obvious that if we didn't deliver, we'd be out the remaining twenty thousand dollars on our twenty-five-thousand-dollar purchase order. I also figured that we might have to return the five-thousand-dollar down payment and, worse yet, that Powertec could sue us for loss of something or other. Though I'd never been sued, I knew that lawsuits consumed money and time and created bad feelings all around.

Finally I called Wally Silver to explain the situation and give him the alternatives. Wally understood the vagaries of the computer world, and I was confident he would make the smartest possible decision, which, in my estimation, would be to extend the contract a few months and take delivery of MANMAN running on Image and ASK's own version of TCS.

Since we'd started work on the program, however, Powertec had been sold, and the first thing Wally's new boss asked was why he'd bought an HP computer. "Where's IBM? Let's go with the best!" he'd insisted. This mind-set was as common then as now. IBM was big, powerful, and impressive, and over the years Big Blue had become synonymous with quality computing. No one ever gets fired for choosing IBM. The machine may crash, the software may be inefficient, the cost may be way too high, but you don't get fired. And here was Wally, a true iconoclast, who not only bought a *mini* computer from an *instrument* company but along with it bought a program that hadn't been written yet—vaporware, as it's known—from a dinky company called ASK that was run by a woman. Of us all, Wally was in deepest. But he knew that a batch-run IBM would never give him the control he needed, and he'd convinced his former boss of it.

Still, when I called to tell him the situation, Wally was optimistic. Though I could sorely afford it, I even suggested we abandon the project and cut our losses. "No, no," he said, "you've got a purchase order, and we want you to deliver on it." Wally must have figured he'd made a good deal. Even if we delivered the product late, he was getting a lot for his twenty-five thousand dollars. We had already installed parts of our software. And even though only one terminal at a time could be running, Powertec had done an inventory count with the computer and had found more than one hundred thousand dollars of unaccounted-for inventory. Wally was convinced we should continue and went along with my idea of redesigning the system to work on multiple terminals.

The only catch was that Powertec's new president, Emmett Bradley, wasn't a man who liked to be kept waiting. Wally asked me to fly down to L.A. to sell Bradley on HP and ASK. I prepared a demo to show what we'd already accomplished. But when I arrived at Powertec, I was told I had only fifteen minutes with the boss: not enough time for a demo, not enough time even to make my case.

The second I walked into the room and saw Bradley I knew I'd wasted my airfare. He was sitting behind his desk, chunky arms folded across his chest. Plastered on his face was a look that said, "I've used IBM before; IBM worked; I'm going to use IBM again." He uncrossed his arms, fiddled with his wrist alarm, and told me my fifteen minutes had begun. So I started my pitch, and exactly fifteen minutes later the alarm on his watch beeped, and he said, "Thank you very much. The purchase order is canceled. We're putting in IBM." End of meeting, end of the deal with Powertec. I was crestfallen. Wally was mortified.

Afterward he took me aside. "Look, there's nothing I can do about what just happened. But I want you to know I think you guys have really got something here. You can do it. You're almost there. Don't give up." Coming from Wally, whom I really respected, it gave me a tremendous boost.

A few days later HP reluctantly picked up Powertec's machine. The sale had gone south with our program. In making ASK's case to Powertec, I could have trashed HP, but that would have accomplished little. We still needed them at least as much as they needed us. Besides, I didn't feel that HP had purposely misled us but that rather, like ASK, they had been too optimistic and ambitious. More important, even before Bradley's wrist alarm beeped, we'd proved that interactive, friendly, on-line question-and-answer manufacturing software *could* be run on a minicomputer. And given a few more weeks, we proved that such a program could be run on multiple terminals—better and more cost-effectively than anything on the market.

On my flight back from L.A. it occurred to me that my entire professional life had been built around resurrecting successes out of failures. My failed first experience with computers at the UCLA computer center led to my success at TRW. My failed experience at Bell Labs led to my success at Pulverizing Machinery. And now I saw that my failure at Powertec could still lead to a stronger, potentially more profitable connection with HP.

14

Bigger, Bigger

While in 1974 HP was using ASK to get their foot in the door at Powertec for a hardware sale of about one hundred thousand dollars, only a few months later the ante increased more than tenfold to where millions of dollars of computer hardware were at stake. Only this time ASK beat HP to the door. And our software made the sale.

Even as we struggled with Powertec, I had been calling on other customers and had interested Boeing's Electronic Support Division in Seattle in MANMAN. Late deliveries were damaging Boeing's credibility with customers. Also, they were using too much manpower to run their shop and had scheduling problems, all impacting on their bottom line. They'd seen MANMAN on Tymshare at a trade show that summer and decided they wanted it. In a presentation to their own people in October 1974 they claimed that MANMAN would increase the division's productivity 15 to 20 percent in the first year, decrease shop labor, cut overtime, and optimize inventory. I couldn't have said it better myself.

But Boeing didn't want MANMAN on the 2100; they wanted it on HP's other minicomputer, the HP 3000. There were a number of differences between the two machines. Unlike the 2100, the 3000 had been developed from scratch as a multiterminal, multiprocessing computer that had no need for TCS. Also, its internal design, or architecture, was different, it used a different version of Image, and it had a different operating system.

The biggest difference, however, was in the marketplace. HP had recently split its computer division into two separate profit centers, one selling the 3000 and the other the 2100. HP positioned the 2100 as a "scientific" machine for primary use by original equipment manufacturers (OEMs), while the 3000 was targeted for "commercial" end user applications. As such, the 3000 was perceived as top-of-the-line and priced accordingly, at more than twice the price of the 2100. Whatever the positioning, however, and despite the fact that the machines had totally different architectures, they were capable of running many of the same types of applications, so the two separate HP sales forces often found themselves competing against each other.

A second problem, raised not so much by Boeing's wanting MANMAN on the 3000 as by the 3000 itself, was that the initial introduction of the 3000 a few years earlier had been a catastrophe. Targeted for use in schools and universities, the 3000 had bombed. The machine simply hadn't met HP's specifications for it, and there was no ready fix. A year after the 3000 was introduced, it was redesigned and enhanced to meet customers' expectations. This was extremely embarrassing for a company with HP's reputation for quality. By the time I'd pitched Boeing, however, HP had worked most of the bugs out of the 3000 and had begun selling commercial as well as educational clients. Still, it was a relatively unproved machine. While HP had sold a few 3000s to commercial clients, they had yet to sell to Boeing, where the first sale could be an entrée to selling dozens, maybe hundreds more.

In any event, Boeing wanted the 3000. They wanted a minicomputer because that was the new technology. They wanted to go first cabin, so they turned to HP, with its reputation for quality and customer service. They wanted the HP 3000 because that's the machine

Hewlett-Packard had dubbed top-of-the-line. Consequently the contract ASK finally signed with Boeing specified that we'd develop MANMAN for the 3000. We were to be paid $50,400 for the program, with a $10,000 down payment, more than twice what I'd charged Powertec. But I figured if Boeing was willing to spring more than twice the price for the machine, the software should be priced accordingly.

The contract process was an event in itself. Once Boeing and ASK had reached an agreement in principle, it took months of negotiating with Boeing's lawyers and contracts people before the actual deal was signed. When I realized the amount of time the process would eat up, I decided we couldn't afford a lawyer, so I negotiated on ASK's behalf.

Part of the enormous amount of paper work generated by the deal involved Boeing's getting brownie points from the federal government for working with small, minority-owned businesses. In the mid-seventies companies like Boeing that did a lot of work for government agencies and the military were encouraged to hire companies like ASK. And by coming to tiny, woman-owned ASK, Boeing would earn "attaboys" that could stand them well.

Finally, in March 1975, after months of dancing around, we had a deal. I called HP, who'd been beating on Boeing's door for months and informed them I'd sold MANMAN to Boeing, which now needed a 3000 to run it on. In exchange for this "bluebird"—a sale that flies in the window—I said I'd have to have access to a 3000. By then we'd lost the Powertec job and been banished from the 2100 in Santa Clara and were back in our own offices. Arrangements, I was told, would be made.

An interesting sidelight to the Boeing contract negotiation was the cost issue. Knowing I could deliver on the 2100 a lot easier and a lot faster than on the 3000, I tried to convince Boeing to go with the cheaper machine—the 2100 was about $80,000; the 3000, nearly $150,000—but the incremental difference in cost didn't seem to matter to Boeing. On the contrary, they were eager to pay the extra money. This was my first experience with the fact that the market we were addressing wasn't highly price-sensitive.

From Boeing's point of view, both machines were cheap—particularly compared with a mainframe, nearly ten times the price of a 3000—so why not go for the deluxe model? Second, if the 3000 was the model that HP had designated its commercial machine, why question the decision of another large company? And third, when a company the size of Boeing makes a purchase of any magnitude, be it eighty thousand or three hundred thousand dollars, it has to write hundreds of pages of justification, so the department preparing the pages figures it may as well pop for the bigger number. In fact, it's easier in some companies to get an approval for three hundred thousand or more than one for eighty thousand because different levels of management are involved in the decision process.

These all were lessons that ASK was to put to use in the years to come. Back in 1975, however, we weren't thinking levels of approval. We were ecstatic with a contract that was twice the size of any we'd ever had. More than that, we were tremendously excited by the Boeing name. Working with HP was one thing; they were respected, known worldwide, but only in the circle of the scientifically savvy. However, everyone knew who Boeing was. Strategically, of course, Boeing's interest in ASK, particularly in light of HP's commitment to the 3000 as its commercial machine, put us in a far stronger position with HP than we had been.

There was a second big deal in the offing during the early stages of the Boeing project, a large sale to Hughes Aircraft in Fullerton, California. In all, the sale could include fourteen separate MANMAN systems, to run on fourteen HP 3000s. If HP got the order, it would be its Computer Division's largest ever.

Despite our failure at Powertec, Bill Richion was backing us 100 percent on this one, again seeing ASK as a way of opening doors to a potentially huge client. To make things interesting, Data General, at the time a very significant player in the minicomputer marketplace, was also eyeing Hughes—and ASK—and had begun an aggressive courtship to get us to abandon HP and convert MANMAN over to its machine. Just about every day Data General called us with a proposal—technical help, lending us a machine, everything but the kitchen sink.

I opted to stay with HP. While HP was a lot less flashy than Data General, they were the hometown team. They had the more solid engineering reputation, and they'd already gone out on a limb for us. In the end, Hughes Fullerton didn't go with anyone. But ASK's importance to the selling process was mightily reinforced.

At about the same time as all the excitement at Hughes Fullerton, ASK had a deal cooking with another, far smaller division of Hughes in Oceanside, its Industrial Products Division. This division manufactured automated laser cutters for the apparel industry and was looking for a single system to run their manufacturing operation. The stakes certainly weren't as high as at Hughes Fullerton, but unlike that nondeal, at Hughes Oceanside we were dashing headlong into signing a contract—not on the 2100 but on the 21MX, a slightly updated version of the 2100. Working in our favor was the fact that the Hughes division already was an OEM for the HP 21MX, repackaging the computer as a process controller within their laser cutter products. So they were familiar with the machine and with HP. By then, too, our young UC—Berkeley computer whiz, Roger Bottarini, had perfected an ingenious terminal polling system to replace HP's ill-fated Terminal Control System. Since Hughes was already familiar with the HP 21MX, they looked at our design and agreed that it would probably work. Bill Richion backed us. If it didn't work, he'd let Hughes return the machine. HP, of course, was extremely eager to keep out of Hughes any of their competitors—particularly IBM, which was always lurking on the fringes of any sale.

Sales to small divisions of larger companies like Hughes, incidentally, were how IBM grew. They'd install one machine, gain visibility, install a second and third, and before anyone knew it, it would be an all-IBM shop. To put this in perspective, in the seventies IBM's *growth* in a single year was comparable to the total annual sales of DEC or HP. Even now its growth is one-half of DEC or HP's annual revenues. And much of that growth has to come out of someone's hide. So at

Hughes Oceanside, HP salesmen were scampering around, willing to try anything to make the sale. ASK was their ace in the hole.

In the spring of 1975, while all these projects were still hanging fire, Arie attended a technical conference in Paris, and I went with him. It was the closest I'd had to a vacation since I'd started ASK more than three years before. When we returned, I was greeted by two surprises. Bob Rasmussen, ASK's general manager, had negotiated a contract with a company called Litronix, a Silicon Valley highflier that manufactured digital wristwatches and whose building was across the parking lot from HP's computer division headquarters. Litronix was looking for a manufacturing system, they liked what they'd seen of MANMAN, but they were not interested in the HP 21MX or the HP 3000. They wanted to go with a DEC machine. In my absence Bob had virtually closed the deal for ASK to convert MANMAN to the DEC machine. He and Marty had even attended a few DEC training sessions. All that was needed to set things officially into motion was my signature on the dotted line.

The second surprise upon my return from Europe was that I was pregnant again.

15

Over My Head

The 3000 that HP provided us access to as part of the Boeing deal was fifteen miles from ASK, at HP's Computer Division headquarters in Cupertino. The real catch was that we could use the machine only when HP people weren't using it—that is, from six in the evening until six the following morning. So we grabbed our sleeping bags and moved back to HP. Surprisingly, there was little dissension in the ASK ranks. We all were working equally hard, we all liked what we were doing, and while no one, including me, was earning much money, we had enough to suit our life-styles. ASK was paying our salaries and the rent with Tymshare royalties and the funds generated by the service bureau, being run by Jim Parker.

Once again we were camping out at HP. There was, however, a new wrinkle. By 1975 reasonably high-level HP executives and technical people were beginning to desert the ship to open or work at competing companies, often only a few miles or even blocks away.

While spin-offs from other large Silicon Valley companies were common, it was virtually unprecedented at homey HP. The most recent deserters were a group of six or seven guys headed by a former HP marketing manager named Jimmy Treybig who started a company called Tandem Computers.

Actually HP shouldn't have been too surprised by Treybig's departure. The pattern for spin-offs and high-tech desertions in the Valley had been set nearly two decades earlier when seven of William Shockley's cohorts at Shockley Semiconductor Laboratories abandoned Shockley, the Nobel Prizewinning coinventor of the transistor, to form Fairchild Semiconductor. A number of these early renegades subsequently left Fairchild to take over or create companies of their own, including Charles Sporck with National Semiconductor, Jerry Sanders with Advanced Micro Devices, and Bob Noyce with Intel. Treybig's departure from HP, then, was part of a long-standing Valley tradition—but revised for the economic times. When the relatively low 20 percent tax rate on long-term capital gains in the seventies was instituted, venture capitalists began scouring the Valley for bright middle managers like Treybig who had ideas for products they could hang a company on. Treybig's idea was for a fail-safe computer—actually a pair of computers running in tandem—for customers like hospitals and banks whose operations couldn't tolerate computer failure. The idea panned out, and Tandem became one of the fastest-growing companies of the seventies.

Still, HP was a great company to work for. They were among the best—back then as now. They've managed to keep their entrepreneurial edge—even as they grew to a thirteen-billion-dollar-plus company in 1990—by encouraging initiative and invention and by making their people feel part of the product development process. More important, HP made their people feel like part of a family. But no company could expect to hold on to a maverick like Jimmy Treybig, with his good ol' boy Texas accent, his jeans and cowboy boots, and his obsession with ham radios. Treybig, still the head of Tandem, was an original. And in the mid-seventies the money was there for him to start a company in his own image.

In the wake of Treybig's mutiny, the atmosphere at HP turned tempo-
rarily from family, motherhood, and apple pie to paranoia. The great
fear was that the Tandem guys would sneak back into the company
and steal away big secrets, not, mind you, that Jimmy Treybig would
ever do such a thing. Nevertheless, security, which had always been
good-naturedly lax and laid-back at HP, was stepped up, and recep-
tionists and guards were given photos of Treybig and his group to
display at their stations. The night guards, in particular, were told
never to leave their posts and were sworn to eternal fealty and vigi-
lance.

In the midst of all this security ASK was given virtually free run
of the place. No badges, no escorts. And whenever the guards—hired
hands themselves, who could have easily been Tandem agents—
needed to go to the bathroom, they'd ask one of us to watch the front
door. It was all kind of funny.

Not so funny, however, was that from the day we moved back to
HP and started on the Boeing job, we had problems—not with the
conversion of MANMAN to the 3000 but with Boeing. While three
or four ASK people—Marty, Roger, Bob, and I—worked nights on
the program, Boeing must have had at least ten people in Seattle
working days on software specifications. What the program had to do
kept changing. For example, we had set up MANMAN on Tymshare
to have part numbers with fifteen or fewer characters. Boeing wanted
twenty-four-character part numbers because they broke things out
into a lot of subcategories. Next, they wanted elaborate and arcane
specifications for checking and counterchecking information. And
each one of these general requests had to be broken down into dozens
of small subrequests. Most mornings, when we returned to the ASK
office, there'd be a thick wad of special delivery packets waiting for us,
with a complete revision of the work we'd accomplished the prior
night.

We should have seen the handwriting on the wall when we were
nitpicking with Boeing's lawyers during our contract negotiations.
But we were far too seduced by the Boeing name to realize we might
be getting into trouble. Corporations the size of Boeing, I was now
discovering, generated enormous paper trails. Everything was docu-
mented. And everyone was always writing memos—partially to com-

municate but mostly to cover his behind if things went wrong. The deeper we got into the project, the more people it seemed that Boeing was putting on the case, and the more paper they were generating. If one of Boeing's chief objectives with MANMAN was to cut down on man-hours, they were sure burning up enough of them in the development process.

Very quickly the Boeing project was getting out of hand. I'd go into HP and give pep talks to the ASK crew. "We can make it through this," I'd tell them. But words were cheap, and the only real way to motivate everyone was to put time in at HP myself, as I did, night after night. Soon, though, it began to dawn on me that maybe we couldn't do it—and that we would fail on the 3000, as we had on the 2100.

Around this time Paul Ely, the vice-president of HP's Computer Division, called me in to demonstrate MANMAN. A fifteen-year HP veteran and former general manager of another of HP's divisions, Ely was the one who'd been called in to work the bugs out of the 3000 and get it back on the market after its near recall. Rumor had it that Ely's power in his former division had been so absolute his co-workers had given him a coronation robe and crown at his going-away party and dubbed him King Paul.

When King Paul heard about tiny ASK's dropping the Boeing sale into HP's lap, his interest perked up. Also of interest to Paul was the fact that we'd licensed the software to Boeing for a substantial up-front fee, $50,400, plus a maintenance charge of $3,600 paid annually in advance. The common practice at the time—that is to say, what IBM did—was not to charge any up-front fee but rather a monthly license fee that included maintenance. A manufacturing program similar to MANMAN but written in batch for an IBM mainframe would cost the customer in the vicinity of $500 per month. The going rate, in other words, for what I had licensed to Boeing for $50,400 plus $3,600 a year was about $6,000 a year. At that rate it would take IBM almost nine years to make what ASK did in year number one. Paul Ely was sufficiently impressed to ask for a demo.

It had been only a few months before that I had had to talk an HP regional sales manager into giving me a chance to demonstrate my software. Now the head of the division was calling me for a demo of his own. If ever there was a big chance for an ASK alliance with HP, this was it. While I might have been a little flip in my demo with Richion, I was all business with Ely. I brought a spool of computer tape that held enough of the Boeing/HP 3000 tape to give a flavor of the program. I was in the middle of a trial run when Paul arrived with a half dozen of his people. Once again an HP honcho wasn't what I expected. Paul carried a little more weight than the average HP engineer, he didn't have a crew cut, and while his shirt was white, it was a bit disheveled. So this was King Paul, the top banana? All right, I thought. I'd convince him how good MANMAN was, everyone else would fall in line, and we'd get the order. We shook hands.

"Okay, Sandy. Show me what you've got."

We sat down in front of the terminal—a computer screen on the 3000—and I ran through the program with the others peering over my shoulder. I was able to demonstrate enough of it for Paul to get the flavor of how it worked: how simple the question-and-answer format was to use, how easy it was to get the information you needed, how well the program worked with Image, and overall, how it took full advantage of the 3000's basic design as an interactive machine.

Paul was with me all the way, firing questions. I entered a part number, and he asked, "How do I add it to a bill of materials?" I added parts to the bill of materials, and he asked how I'd open a work order against it. Then he asked, "What if the company sometimes buys the assembly outside instead of manufacturing it in house?" He was fast; he was aggressive; he was impatient. But he asked good questions. He was of the old school, more engineer than manager. And tap-tapping on the keyboard, I was coming up with the answers; the right ones, I hoped. With our intense focus on the screen, it was easy to forget the others in the room.

When the demonstration was over, I switched off the terminal, and we sat for a moment gazing at the afterglow of the darkened monitor. I knew it had gone well, but I didn't know how well, and I was nervous about what would happen next. Suddenly Paul turned to his people and announced, "If this thing is as good as I think it is, *we* should be using it. HP should be using this on our *own* machines!"

This got a rise out of his entourage, but no one said a word. Paul stood. "I mean, here we are, HP, trying to sell computers against IBM, and what do we do? We run all our manufacturing on IBM machines. If we're serious about manufacturing companies, the first thing we've got to do is get our own house in order. Throw out IBM. Put in 3000s. And customize this ASK stuff to run our manufacturing operations."

A couple of his people winced, but still not a word. On the one hand, what Paul said made sense. After all, that's what we were asking Hughes and Boeing to do. On the other hand, it was blasphemy. Was he actually suggesting that HP themselves replace their IBM mainframes (i.e., "real" computers) with minicomputers and run all of HP's billion-dollar manufacturing operations on them? Not only that, but with tiny little ASK's software running the show? As much as I'd come to believe in minis and in ASK, it hadn't really occurred to me that our software on a mini would be kicking out existing IBM installations. At best, I thought, our solution could beat out IBM's at new installations. So Paul's response was a real surprise. I was also surprised that he came up with it in front of me, an outsider. The look from the others in the room seemed to say, "Cool it, Paul, let's talk about this later."

But Paul was on a roll. He turned to me and said, "Here's the next step. I want you to meet with our corporate data processing people. Talk to the guy in charge of manufacturing, go through our system, and see if you can't modify your software to be like ours so it can handle HP's manufacturing operations on a 3000." Then he charged out the door, carrying his people in his wake. I was amazed. All I'd hoped was that HP would agree to sell MANMAN, using its connections and its first-rate sales force, and pay us a royalty. Now, suddenly, ASK was being called on to redo HP's worldwide manufacturing operations. Long live the king!

Paul was right, of course. HP could hardly go around peddling our software on the 3000 to manufacturing companies if HP didn't use it themselves. Customers would ask, "What do *you* use?" And the HP rep would have to stammer, "Well, ah, we use IBM." And even if the HP rep could avoid this embarrassing confrontation, you'd better bet that the astute IBM rep on a sales call would point out that HP was using IBM. So while I knew that MANMAN could help sell HP machines, Paul was already one step ahead of me. He knew that HP couldn't sell MANMAN on the 3000 effectively until HP put their money where their mouth was.

Appointments were immediately set for me to meet with HP's internal data processing (DP) people. My first meeting with the guy in charge of HP's manufacturing didn't go well. He didn't know much about HP computers—all he knew was IBM—and he wasn't particularly interested in running on the 3000. Also, the scuttlebutt was that I was Paul Ely's point person to throw IBM out and put HP in. Still, the data processing guy was a bright, friendly fellow who loved talking about the HP manufacturing program. He demonstrated its bells and whistles and told me he wanted to add even more. My mind boggled. It was already the most complicated, arcane, overwritten manufacturing program I'd ever seen.

Half of what it contained no one ever used. Going through it with him, I asked, "Why do you have this function if you're not using it now and can't imagine using it in the foreseeable future?" He looked at me as if I were missing the point. Another 25 percent of the program no one knew *how* to use. The remaining 25 percent was okay.

At first I thought I'd just tweak my MANMAN program to "HP"ize it. I'd add a bunch of features, forget features no one used or could define, and keep a few hooks so that other features could be added later. But I soon realized it would be more efficient to start from scratch—meaning I'd have to write a custom program.

Meanwhile, somewhere in the middle of the second trimester of my pregnancy, ASK struck a deal with Hughes Oceanside, the Hughes division wanting MANMAN on the 21MX. Four related things contributed to its coming together. First, unbeknownst to me, Powertec's Wally Silver invited Bill Richion to lunch to reaffirm his faith in ASK. "I'm not really angry with you or those kids," he said. "Besides, I'm certain they're on to something. Something big."

Second, Bill Richion himself decided to take a big chance on us. A gambler to the core, he told Hughes that HP was willing to bet on ASK despite the Powertec failure. "We'll send you a machine," he told them. "If ASK can't make it work for you, we'll take it back, no charge, no questions asked."

Third, I myself staged a campaign to win over an ambassador within Hughes to plead my case internally. This was Jack McNamee. While the final decision wasn't in his hands, as data processing manager he was in a position to support us. I knew that Jack believed in us and that if I formed a good business relationship with him, he'd level with me about his concerns and the concerns of others in the company. In that way, before I went into a meeting, I'd know who was against me, and why, and be prepared to address those issues.

Over the years I'd come to understand the importance of ambassadors. It's far better to have on your side a red-hot decision *influencer*—someone like a Bill Richion, who, after all, was only a regional sales manager, or a Wally Silver, or a Jack McNamee—than a lukewarm decision *maker*. To win over an influencer, I'd focus on what that person needed to succeed in his job. Bill Richion sold hardware, so my pitch to him was that ASK would help him sell more hardware than ever before. Wally wanted an efficient way to manage his manufacturing operation, so my pitch to him focused on MANMAN's efficiency. On the other hand, Jack as data processing manager was primarily concerned with having control over his data processing needs without having to hire a staff of support people. As part of Hughes he had access to the IBM mainframe at Hughes Fullerton, one hundred miles away. But one hundred miles away meant no control over his own destiny. So my pitch to him was the control we could provide him. Also, once the HP 21MX was up and running, it was extremely reliable and easy to operate—no need, in other words, for a lot of support.

The deal clincher at Hughes from ASK's perspective was that Hughes told Richion that they'd have no use for a machine until the software worked on it. So the 21MX was sold to Hughes but lent to ASK to develop the program. It was to be installed in our offices in Los Altos.

Fine and good. We now had the Hughes deal. But even before the ink dried, I knew I was in trouble. Every workday was already twelve, fifteen, and more hours long. Boeing was keeping special delivery in business, I was five months pregnant, and the nights at HP were getting longer and longer. Not only that, but Bob Rasmussen was pressuring me to sign the DEC/Litronix deal, and I was meeting with HP's data processing people to see whether there was any way to convert their custom-written IBM program over to the 3000. I was in over my head.

16

Bailing Out
of Boeing

By fall 1975 ASK had reached critical mass. We were expending our energies in too many directions. I'd started as a contract programmer. Seizing opportunities as they arose, ASK soon became a service bureau, then created a universal MANMAN product on Tymshare. Responding to the problem of the skyrocketing on-line costs of time-sharing, we turned to minicomputers and took on the Powertec job with the intention of developing a one-size-fits-all program that could be sold over and over. It was a logical progression, driven more by the market than any grand strategy. In the last year, however, the progression had seemed to lose its logic. Confronted with writing new programs, potentially at least, for Hughes Fullerton on a Data General machine, Litronix on a DEC machine, Powertec on the HP 2100, Boeing on the HP 3000, Hughes Oceanside on the HP 21MX, and a program for HP to use internally, I was back to being a contract programmer, albeit on a larger scale than in 1971. Somehow, in the midst of all this excitement and the lure of big-name customers, I'd lost my direction. And seemingly on the brink of success, ASK was on a collision course with failure on almost every front.

Hughes Oceanside was the notable exception. We were only a few months away from implementing MANMAN on the HP 21MX for Hughes, and success there was in sight. With our limited human resources (there were still only six of us), we were stretched pretty thin, and the other projects we were working on were just too iffy. All this stuff had been spinning around in my head for weeks when I decided to go with my instincts: to focus our energies on being successful at Hughes and get out from under all the other projects. Litronix, Boeing, and HP's internal system had to go. I called the team members together to share my thoughts. I wanted their approval and backing. Even though I was paying their salaries and the decision and responsibilities were ultimately mine, I wanted every one of my employees to feel that he or she was part of the decision-making process.

There was dissent on only one front. Bob Rasmussen was upset about my decision to turn down the DEC/Litronix deal. A few days later he asked to borrow three thousand dollars, more than ASK had earned after salaries and expenses in fiscal 1975. Being a trusting soul, I lent him the cash. It was the last I ever saw of him. He took the money and disappeared to Hawaii. Some time later a collection agency tracked him down and I got some of my $3000 back.

I was very concerned about how to spring the news to Paul that there was no way I could tweak HP's program to work on the 3000. How could I tell him without offending him and burning bridges? As it was, he wasn't going to be too happy about my abandoning Boeing. I pondered, "Should we have a meeting? Who should be there? Would the DP people get pushed out of shape? Do I subtly allow Paul to come to the conclusion it can't be done or do I come right out and say it?" etc. Then one day I passed Paul in the hall at HP. "How's it going?" he asked.

And I just blurted, "Paul, it can't be done. No way can you rewrite your IBM program to work on a 3000."

He stood there for a few seconds, then said, "I kind of figured as much. Forget the IBM program then. Just get MANMAN to work on HP hardware." I later learned that this was Paul's management style:

Throw out an idea—as he did at our first meeting—then let his underlings determine if it was worth pursuing.

Getting out of the Boeing project, I feared, would neither be as fast nor as easy. After all, if it took Boeing months to write a contract, it would probably take twice as long to cancel one. Fortunately at that point Boeing also had misgivings, questioning whether a six-person company could service a client its size. It was also a question whether what Boeing wanted could even work on a 1975-vintage minicomputer.

In any event, I felt awful about having to close down the Boeing project. Halting a project in which you and your people have invested so much time and energy is one of the tougher things an entrepreneur must be able to do. I felt terrible for Marty and Roger and the rest of the gang who had been knocking themselves out at HP, night after night, to give Boeing what they wanted. In the wake of the Powertec failure, giving up on Boeing would be doubly demoralizing. I also felt bad for HP. This was the first HP 3000 sold to Boeing, and HP was hoping it would be the first of many. Closing down Boeing would also further erode ASK's credibility with HP. Finally, I felt bad for Graeber Jordan, the project manager and our ambassador at Boeing, who'd pushed for us to get the job. At first the Boeing/ASK relationship had gone extremely well. Graeber had even signed some of his correspondences to ASK, "Love, Graeber."

In retrospect we might have been able to finish the program— but only at an enormous cost in man-hours, morale, and, ultimately, dollars. Boeing, on the other hand, was certainly happy enough with the $50,400 we were charging; to develop the same program internally would have cost them a million dollars or more. But they never thought twice about pushing our backs to the wall. They wanted the program, whether that destroyed us or not.

I called Graeber to set up our showdown. By now it was no more "Love, Graeber." Graeber had been distancing himself from ASK as the project bogged down. He was an up-and-comer in the company, and he now was trying to get his fingerprints off the murder weapon.

When I told Graeber over the phone that ASK wanted out, he yelled, "We've put all this time and energy into this system, and you've made a commitment, and you have to fulfill your commitment. Besides, we're helping you develop a system that you can turn around and sell elsewhere for millions."

While I didn't know whether he was right or not, I did know that if I agreed with him, I'd weaken my negotiating position.

"Now wait a minute," I said. "This system can't be sold to anyone else." I listed a half dozen features that only a Boeing could love.

"Are you kidding? Everyone wants those features."

"I'm sorry, but I don't see it that way."

"You don't eh? Well, I'll bring my team down and let's see what they think."

A few days later Graeber trooped his team of Boeing lawyers and contracts and procurement people into my office. The air was thick with "nonperformance." "We can sue you," they insisted. "You haven't fulfilled—"

My strategy was to play the part of the small company in over its head at the mercy of the larger company, which, of course, was precisely the situation. Besides, playing tough against Boeing wouldn't get me anywhere. They had all the money and the strength. Instead, I pointed out the unforeseen problems on the project, including the 3000's not working up to specs and Boeing's repeatedly modifiying its requirements. I also pointed out that we were not as adept as Boeing in contract procedures and the contract we had signed was too open-ended in Boeing's favor. While ASK had worked in good faith to keep its end of the bargain, finally we were unable to. Prior to the meeting I'd figured ASK would be doing well if we only had to return the ten-thousand-dollar up-front payment. No lawsuits, case closed.

Graeber and his legal team heard me out. But instead of responding to my points, they emphasized how much effort Boeing people had put into the project, and they kept stressing again and again how much the completed program would be worth to ASK, the millions we could sell it for. I repeated my reservation that the program wouldn't be valuable to anyone but Boeing. "No, no," they insisted. "A lot of companies could use this program." Still, whether they could or couldn't wasn't the issue to be discussed, as I saw it. Or was it? I knew the program was at a point that it could be finished, but we just didn't have the resources to do it.

The back and forth about the value of the completed program went on for quite a while before it occurred to me what Boeing was up to. Though the program I was writing was ostensibly for Boeing's Electronic Support Division, the contract was actually with Boeing Computer Services, which not only provided software for Boeing's divisions but also sold to other companies. Boeing Computer Services obviously wanted a completed program to sell on the outside, to make the millions they claimed ASK would make.

Then Graeber handed me a three-page agreement to sign. I read it very, very carefully, glancing at Graeber and the others over the top of the pages as I read. The document stipulated that ASK surrender to Boeing all its work to date and that Boeing Computer Services had the right to distribute the software in any way they saw fit.

On to their scheme, I said, "What do you mean, 'distribute the software'?"

Graeber and his cronies fiddled with their narrow little ties and looked furtively down at their briefcases.

"You know," one of them finally ventured, "if we can salvage what you give us and one of our divisions wants to use it." At that point they weren't yet positive I'd caught them with their collective hand in the cookie jar. And at that same point I figured, okay, not only wasn't I going to get sued, but I had something Boeing really wanted, even if it wasn't finished. I decided to press my luck.

"Tell you what. We'll let you take over the program. And instead of charging you fifty thousand four hundred dollars, since the program's not complete, we'll charge you only fifteen thousand, including the ten thousand you gave us up front. But you can use the program only within Boeing."

Again there were quick looks around the table. I'd rained on part of their parade. Still, Boeing Computer Services could make plenty of money selling the program internally. Suddenly Graeber announced, "Fair enough!" And I walked out of the room free and clear of Boeing, with nearly five thousand dollars to boot.

A few days later Boeing sent down the paper work for the mutual release. Everything seemed in order except that in the place where the fifteen-thousand-dollar payment was mentioned, the release gave Boeing Computer Services the right to distribute the software in any way they saw fit. I called them on it. "Come on, you guys. We specifically agreed you could use the program within Boeing only." We finally decided on a royalty of an additional 5 percent of whatever Boeing could sell the program for to any non-Boeing company over the next five years. It didn't make us millions, but before the agreement expired, Boeing paid ASK nearly a hundred thousand dollars.

17

Three Deliveries

On a Friday in late October 1975, Marty Browne, Roger Bottarini, and I were at ASK waiting for HP to deliver Hughes Oceanside's 21MX computer. By now the three of us were seasoned minicomputer users. Marty, the low-key math major from Stanford with his sandals, jeans, and ponytail—now trimmed to shoulder length—had been with ASK through Powertec and Boeing and had even taken a few classes at DEC to prepare for the Litronix job. Roger, who had been graduated from Berkeley during the Vietnam war period, was atypically clean cut, with all-American-boy looks. He was the technical wizard that every high-tech start-up needs. Put him in a room with a problem, and a few hours or days later he'd emerge with a solution. Along with Marty and me, Roger had also done hard time on Power-tec and Boeing. Camping out together at HP, the three of us had developed a closeness rare in business. So it was only fitting that on the most exciting day of ASK's existence, Marty, Roger, and I were waiting together for the HP van carrying ASK's first computer—even if it was only a loaner.

It was late afternoon when the van finally arrived, and the delivery guys were in a hurry to drop off their cargo and head home. When they asked where everything was supposed to go, we took them to the eight-by-ten-foot cubicle that was to house the three two-by-two-by-six-foot computer bays, a printer, two primitive terminals, boxes of manuals and paper tape, a paper tape reader, and a paper tape winder—a mechanical contraption used to rewind the unspooled paper tape that was fed through the paper tape reader. The delivery guys scratched their heads at the size of our computer room and made joke after joke at our expense. Finally they unloaded the van and instructed us to leave everything crated up. HP's crack assembly team would be by sometime next week to put it all together.

Next week! Give us a break. The delivery guys weren't even back in their van before Roger, whose father owned a gas station in San Francisco, had produced his red toolbox and was eyeing his screwdrivers like a surgeon with his scalpels at the ready.

I called Arie. "It's here!" He said he'd be right over with Andy. I ran down to the corner store for a few six-packs and a bottle of champagne to christen the machine. Next stop, the local Chinese restaurant for some takeout. By the time I returned, the computer was half out of its crate, Marty was unpacking the printer, and Andy, who was nearly two, was on the floor thumbing through one of the manuals.

"Well," Marty said taking a swig from the first opened beer, "quite an occasion, eh?" Arie freed a terminal from its packaging as Andy toddled over to help out. By now Roger was jockeying one of the computer bays into position. And there I stood, bottle of champagne in hand, six months pregnant.

"Quite an occasion," I repeated, and popped the cork.

By 1975, after having been in business for myself for almost four years, I decided I'd worked too long and too hard to throw away what was surely my last chance with HP by writing anything less than a state-of-the-art program. So I challenged myself and the others on the

ASK team to create the most efficient program possible for Hughes.

Fortunately, since the 21MX was not an entirely new machine, but a next-generation 2100, we were able to use a lot of what we had done on the aborted Powertec job. We already understood the vagaries of HP's Image data base manager. Roger had developed the terminal polling program to replace HP's Terminal Control System. We knew what we wanted MANMAN to accomplish. Now, all we needed was a few months to put it all together.

Actually the version of MANMAN we were writing for Hughes was the culmination of everything we had learned about what it took to run a successful manufacturing operation. Though as a whole it was brand-new, the Hughes program contained bits and pieces from the programs we'd already developed for Halcyon, California Microwave, Tymshare, Powertec, Boeing, and others.

The program we eventually delivered contained six modules. The first of these gave Hughes an overview of inventory. The second or bills of materials module, enabled it to track the parts that went into each product or subassembly. The materials requirements planning module helped it plan its inventory needs on the basis of its production forecast and actual customer orders. The purchasing module updated Hughes on the status of purchased parts and assemblies. The work in process module provided progress reports on the in-house production being accomplished day-to-day, including estimated completion dates. And the sixth module, management reporting and product costing, gave Hughes's management an overall look at the entire manufacturing operation, including material and labor costs, production times, and delivery commitments.

Once complete, the Hughes version of MANMAN was to be the first ASK program to operate on a minicomputer, the Powertec program never having been completed. And this same basic system with its six modules was also to be the solid foundation upon which ASK was to build its success in the years to come.

About the time we were developing the Hughes program, a number of competitors offering minicomputer solutions for the manufacturing market were cropping up. Like ASK, they were faced by an array of machines on which to run their software. But unlike ASK, most of them tried for the quick killing. To get into the market as fast as possible, they took the easy route. Instead of writing a strong program tailored from the ground up for a specific machine, they kept their old foundation—most often developed for IBM batch processing or time-sharing—and added a new wing to the house, new rooms here and there, or a second story. The resulting programs were often cumbersome and slow and ate up much of the machine's computing power. The problem was compounded by the fact that minicomputers of that time didn't have much memory, so programming them was tricky. As a result, a lot of ASK's early rivals enjoyed a brief success, then disappeared.

Aside from its significance to ASK's ultimate success, the Hughes project was noteworthy because of the exceptional working relationship we enjoyed with Jack McNamee, Hughes's data processing manager who'd stuck his neck out for us when we'd already failed with Powertec and were in the process of failing with Boeing. Jack was a retired military man with a crew cut so short the longest hair on his head couldn't have been more than an eighth of an inch. The first time I saw him, I figured him to be the last guy in the world to do business with a woman and a few hippies, particularly in 1975. I was dead wrong. In fact, I doubt that Jack ever gave it any thought one way or the other. He simply believed that we could give Hughes what it needed, and in turn, we knocked ourselves out to give him even more than he was expecting.

In the last week of January 1976, three months after we had taken delivery of the machine, we crated everything back up and shipped it down to Hughes. When the machine arrived a few days later, Marty and Roger flew down to deliver the MANMAN tape and get Hughes up and running. I didn't make the trip, however. On the day the shippers came for the machine, I was involved in another delivery: Arie's and my second son, Kenneth Alan Kurtzig.

18

Up and Running

I used to joke that when I started ASK, the only long-range plan I'd had was lunch. In a way it was true. The arena in which ASK was competing in the mid-seventies was changing rapidly. The only way a tiny company like ours could succeed was to be sensitive to the market and change course as it dictated. In fact, being a small company that could react fast enough to stay in step with the market was a real advantage at that time. IBM, for example, was not unaware of the trend toward minicomputers for the manufacturing market. But with their huge installed hardware base, their historical commitment to mainframes and batch processing, and their enormous size, they simply weren't able to move as quickly or with as much abandon as an ASK or even an HP. Before the decade was out, IBM was to concede hundreds of millions of dollars to the HPs, the DECs, and the ASKs.

Call it luck or brilliant strategic planning, but in 1976 ASK had two important revenue sources—the service bureau and MANMAN on Tymshare—that enabled us to take risks and start a program from scratch if a better idea came along. Indeed, most of the approximately $140,000 of ASK revenues in fiscal 1975—and roughly the same amount in fiscal 1976—came from these two sources. Nowadays it is venture capital that keeps you in business in the early going. But venture capital is impatient money, and I doubt many venture capitalists would have stuck with ASK as it continued to redefine itself in its first four years. Not having venture capital means never having to say you're sorry.

On a more personal level, but every bit as important to ASK's success in the early years, was the luxury of my being able to count on Eldemira to take great care of Andy and Kenny as well as the house. I'd often work at home on the weekends when Eldemira was off, leaving dishes piled in the sink and dirty laundry in the hamper. The older the kids got, the more dishes, the larger the clothes, the bigger the piles. Come Sunday evening, when I'd pick her up at her home, I'd always think, "What if Eldemira quits? What would I do without Eldemira? The whole house of cards would collapse." It didn't happen. At least not for many years.

In February 1976 ASK faced a new challenge. We'd finally succeeded in creating a program for a minicomputer, but with the delivery of the 21MX to Hughes, we no longer had a minicomputer to develop programs on. Nor did we have the money to buy one. Even after I had paid myself a minimal salary of twelve thousand dollars in fiscal 1975, ASK showed a pretax profit of only three thousand dollars. And I doubted a bank would lend on a business as shaky as ASK's. Besides, I came from a long line of folks who paid cash.

Still, I was convinced that having our own computer was essential to ASK's existence. Though I'd never liked turning to my parents for financial help, I asked my father for a loan. I was extremely reluctant about doing so. Not that Dad was imposing or formidable or that he might turn me down. On the contrary, Barney Brody was one of the warmest, nicest guys you'd ever meet. He was heavyset with wavy medium brown hair and a light complexion, though his arms and neck were always tanned from his having been out in the sun all day on construction jobs. He had a deep, deep voice and a wonderful, booming, infectious laugh. With his good looks, his manner, and the Brody name, folks in Chicago and later in L.A. often mistook him for an Irish cop. In Chicago, in fact, the local greasy spoon where he had his morning coffee was so convinced that he was on the force they refused to let him pay for his coffee. No, I was reluctant to borrow from my father because I wanted ASK to be *my* business, something I had built by myself. But we *needed* that computer.

Deciding which HP computer to buy was a lot easier than deciding whether to borrow the money to buy it. Despite HP's touting the 3000 for its commercial clients, the 21MX was less than half the price and the machine I'd resolved was the best for running MANMAN. The bill for the equipment we bought from HP came to $66,592 with HP's standard vendor discount. ASK paid $28,907 in cash, with the remainder to be traded out later in the year for a copy of MANMAN for HP's internal use. The loan from Dad was for $25,000 at 8 percent simple interest over three years, with interest payable at $500 per quarter and a balloon payment for the principal due at the end of the term.

Three years later, in 1979, when it was time to pay back the $25,000, I asked Dad if he wanted ASK stock instead of cash. That fiscal year we had revenues of $2,500,000. But it's hard to tell what the stock in a private company is worth. In 1979 even my own employees were disappointed when I gave them stock instead of cash for a Christmas bonus. So when I offered Dad stock, he just laughed. "And what am I going to do with it? Wallpaper the bathroom?" Though I was tremendously proud of what ASK had accomplished, I had to agree that taking $25,000 in ASK stock was an iffy proposition. As it turned out, it would have been a pretty good move. When ASK's stock was publicly traded and at its highest, that bathroom would have been worth $12,500,000.

But ASK's high-flying days were still a long way off. In 1976, not long after we had bought the computer from HP and started selling MAN-MAN, I decided it was time to establish some credit for the business just in case we ever needed it. I asked a customer—a well-established manufacturer—to give ASK a letter of credit for the 20 percent down payment for the MANMAN program he'd ordered instead of paying cash. Though we didn't need the money at the time, I took the letter to the bank and borrowed against it for three months. Our customer's good credit served as a guarantee to the bank that ASK could come up with sufficient funds to cover the loan. My customer paid the interest, as agreed, benefiting by not having to come up with any cash until the three months were up and the system had been delivered. ASK, in the meanwhile, established its credibility with the bank and was subsequently given its own line of credit.

With the Hughes system up and running, HP agreed to send out a press release to dozens of data processing magazines about the successful ASK manufacturing software running on HP hardware. The release was on HP stationery, featured ASK prominently, and included a photograph of the installation. I sat back and waited for the phone to ring. It didn't. Indeed, very few magazines even picked up the story. I was surprised, assuming that any press release sent out by a big company like HP would generate attention. The reason it didn't, I soon realized, was that the HP release had been written as a hardware story when in fact, it was an *applications* story. Also, the installation was a *manufacturing* story, not a data processing story.

So I rewrote the press release to make it more applications-oriented, enclosed the same pictures of the machine running at Hughes, searched a directory of newspapers and magazines for the names of manufacturing trade publications, and resubmitted the release on ASK letterhead.

It was picked up immediately by a number of publications. I figured, "May as well try to get some more," and sent out the identical press release again. Surprisingly it was picked up by far more magazines than in the first go-around. I'm certain it was because the first time around ASK was unknown. By the second time our name was more familiar. It didn't matter that it was the same story; the editors just remembered the name from the earlier release.

The data processing magazines' lukewarm response to HP's release confirmed that trying to sell MANMAN to data processing managers was a mistake. In the mid-seventies DP managers were still stoked on IBM; no self-respecting DP manager would ever write home to his mother and proudly say he was in charge of an HP or a DEC minicomputer installation. Also, in 1976 the primary concern of data processing departments was getting out a payroll, not a product. It made much more sense for ASK, then, to target manufacturing managers with our MANMAN public relations and sales efforts.

Since data processing was a staff function and manufacturing had a direct profit and loss responsibility, it sometimes even made sense to play the DP manager off against the manufacturing manager. That way, when push came to shove, the manufacturing manager could say to the boss, "Look, I can't make my bottom line unless I have control over my own tools." Going as far back as Evan Bakke and Pulverizing Machinery or to the more recent example of Wally Silver at Powertec, I knew the control argument to be a convincing one.

To distinguish ASK from its competitors during the early years, I submitted a press release to the manufacturing trade magazines for every new ASK installation, product, or product refinement. While the releases weren't always picked up, in many cases we got three- or four-page spreads, sometimes with color pictures. And not because of the novelty of a woman-run business; I rarely made any of the photos. The stories were almost exclusively focused on the customer and his application.

Other publications I'd submit press releases to—whether about a new product, a major new client, a promotion in the company, or a general-interest item—were local newspapers. Not just the *San Francisco Chronicle* or the *Palo Alto Times Tribune,* but also the smaller newpapers like Dave MacKenzie's Suburban Newspapers. Lots of executives never have the time to look at the newspapers and magazines that come to their office, but they enjoy kicking back and reading the local papers that come to their homes. An ASK story just might be the last thing an executive read before falling asleep, and the next day, when a manufacturing problem arose, we'd be top-of-mind.

Since the key to MANMAN was that it was both on-line and interactive, the best way to sell it was to demonstrate it in action. So when I heard that HP was bringing a 21MX to the 1976 American Production and Inventory Control Society (APICS) show in At-

lanta—a semiannual trade show that drew thousands of manufacturers—I asked Bill Richion to let us tag along and run MANMAN.
Since he'd convinced Hughes to bet on ASK and we'd delivered on
time, we'd become minor heroes with Bill, and he, in turn, had
become a minor hero at HP. HP gave us the okay, and Marty, Jim
Parker, and I flew to Atlanta to set up our part of the booth. It was the
first time east of the Mississippi for Marty.

If ever there was a real turning point for the company and our
image of ourselves, it was this show. Remember, at heart we were still
a crowd of slightly disaffected hippies. None of us dressed for success.
We didn't even know how. For the APICS show, however—which
was at the Atlanta Peachtree Plaza, by far the classiest hotel any of us
had ever been in—Marty not only cut his hair but bought a suit and a
pair of Hush Puppies. In awe of the hotel's huge lobby, we wandered
over to the special conference desk to check in. When we gave our
names, the check-in clerk tapped the little bell next to his desk, bing!
and a bellhop appeared and said, "Right this way, Mr. Browne." We
all looked around for Marty's father!

The next day MANMAN was running on the 21MX in the HP
booth. The three of us took turns demoing the program. When a
particularly hot prospect showed up, I took over. It wasn't so much
that I was the boss as that I was more sales-oriented than either Jim or
Marty. What we hadn't realized was that a large number of exhibitors
at APICS types of shows hire attractive women models to do demos as
a way of luring the almost exclusively male attendees into the booths.
So here I was, twenty-nine years old, in a dress left over from my high
school days—I could never throw anything out and rarely bought
anything new—at the keyboard, running MANMAN. Assuming I
was a model, the men I "lured" into the booth figured I didn't know
the first thing about what I was doing. They fired all sorts of questions
to trip me up. "Does it do a bill of materials?" A few keystrokes, and I
showed them how. "How about a where used list?" A few more keystrokes, and we were there. This went on for a while until it was clear
I knew not only the script—and some of these models were really
sharp—but quite a bit about manufacturing. As it turned out, our
booth drew a crowd and ASK got a lot of follow-up response.

Aside from big APICS types of shows, ASK also attended a

number of smaller local shows, where we didn't have a computer and had to make do with a remote terminal. We'd bring our portable booth, put out our brochures, and be friendly and helpful to anyone and everyone who stopped by. The biggest hit of these early shows was a poster we produced. At one point I'd seen a Powertec ad with some soft-edge cartoons that I loved. I found out the artist, Norm Kirk, lived in L.A., and I called him to ask if he'd be interested in drawing a poster I'd envisioned. It was a series of panels depicting the offices and work areas of a manufacturing company where everything was going haywire: an overstock of obsolete parts, out-of-date bills of materials, too many back orders, no spare parts for warranty work, shipping clerks throwing paper airplanes because they had nothing to do, etc. A simple copy line at the bottom of the poster plugged MAN-MAN as the solution to these problems. The artist took the job over the phone, sent me some preliminary sketches, and a few weeks later sent the finished product. Though we never met face-to-face, he produced exactly what I wanted. The poster was a great success, and over the years we've given away thousands. Even now people still ask for copies.

I also became publicity chair of the local APICS chapter, publicizing shows and seminars, which gave me even better access to local press. Eventually I came up with the idea of doing seminars of my own and in conjunction with HP. I'd pick a city with a lot of manufacturing companies and send off invitations, keeping the HP name prominent, to potential customers whose names I compiled from local industrial directories or from purchased mailing lists. We'd rent a conference room in a large hotel, set up a coffee urn and a tray of sweet rolls, and we were in business. While we obviously couldn't afford to ship a computer to demo our software at these seminars, we generally set up a single remote terminal for our demonstration. One of the advantages of doing these seminars out of town was that clients had no idea how big or, more to the point, how small we were. All they saw was MANMAN, the HP name, and customer references like Hughes and gradually others, equally impressive.

The bottom line was that as the year progressed, the ASK name was being seen more and more. In August 1976 *Computerworld,* a major computer publication, ran a highly complimentary piece on our

Hughes installation. This was followed by another piece about the Hughes installation in the September issue of *Mini-Micro Systems.* In October I was asked to teach a class on fundamentals of production and inventory control sponsored by APICS. And in November the Management Information Corporation, a packaged software review company, put out a major report on MANMAN that began: "Over the past year we have evaluated a number of software packages for manufacturing firms, including IBM's and Burrough's. . . . This month we present a manufacturing package which we think is the most detailed, comprehensive one ever evaluated. . . ." ASK was on the road to being recognized as an expert in the field.

19

The Big Payoff

In fall 1976 ASK entered a cooperative sales agreement with HP. This meant that ASK could accompany HP on calls to prospects interested in manufacturing management. This was a definite boost for ASK. HP had a terrific sales force, highly respected and aggressive, despite the firm's generally informal nature. It also proved to be a boost for HP. As good as their sales force was, ASK had a better understanding of the manufacturing market.

Still, I was hoping for more. Rather than a cooperative sales agreement, I would have preferred something like the deal I had with Tymshare, whereby HP would sell MANMAN under their name and pay ASK a royalty; at the time this seemed like the smart way to go. I mentioned this one day to Dick Anderson, the general manager of HP Data Systems. Following our success at Hughes, Dick had written a flattering article about ASK in HP's *OEM Journal,* which was sent to all their OEMs. In it Dick said that HP was intending to use MAN-MAN to realize significant savings in their own manufacturing operations. When I told Dick what I wanted, he said he'd see what he could do.

I was pleasantly surprised when only a few days later he told me that he'd spoken with Paul Ely, who had agreed to work up a "little something" in the way of a deal. The catch was that HP was putting increasing clout behind the 3000, and MANMAN had yet to run on that machine. So any agreement would require that the program be rewritten for the 3000. Aside from having to start from scratch, reclaiming what we could from the Boeing program, writing MANMAN for the 3000 was complicated by the fact that I didn't get along with the guy heading the 3000 effort, Ed McCracken. Ed had already made alliances with a few software companies in the education application area, but basically I felt he had little use for anyone not working at HP. He was a true golden boy, a young blond M.B.A., so blond, in fact, you could hardly see his eyebrows. He seemed to weigh every word. I could just picture him in his office going through his Boston Consulting Group types of charts, developing strategies.

By contrast, Paul Ely shot from the hip and took his chances. Lots of times he was off base. Other times his ideas were positively inspired. Paul was one of the first in the hardware industry to see the need for user-friendly commercial minicomputers, as opposed to technical tools that could be used only by scientific types. Obvious today, but not in 1976. Even more significantly, Paul was one of the first at HP to understand that computers had to be more than fast iron, flashing lights, and impressive specs, that to do the job, they needed the right software—operating systems as well as applications—and that standard, packaged software would drive the growth of the computer industry. This, in fact, is precisely what happened and what continues to happen. In the early seventies one in five data processing dollars was spent on software. In the early eighties the split was fifty-fifty. Today the ratio is nearing four to one in favor of software and services.

The trouble was, in developing the program for the 3000, I wouldn't be reporting directly to Paul, who seemed to like ASK's slightly audacious, freewheeling style. Instead, I would be working through Ed. Still, when Dick Anderson said that Paul and Ed were working on a "little something," I was excited. What would this little something be?

By fall 1976 ASK had sold at least six new companies on buying MANMAN at $35,000 a pop, which eventually brought $210,000 into our kitty. HP, on the other hand, could sell a lot more systems than we could on our own. Say we went with HP and they sold thirty systems at the same price. At a 20 percent royalty we would net $210,000—the same as if we'd stayed on our own. At a 40 percent royalty we would net $420,000. That would be three times our gross revenues in fiscal 1976, and we'd incur far less expense, I reasoned. Feeling reckless, I calculated what we'd make at a 40 percent royalty if HP sold fifty systems. Seven hundred thousand dollars! It boggled the mind. And with HP's ace sales force at work for us in the large market for manufacturing software, maybe HP could sell even more!

When I finally received HP's "little something" in the mail, my mind was more than boggled. Like all of HP's paper work, it was short and to the point, just two typed pages. My eyes traveled immediately to the bottom line. I couldn't believe it. One million dollars. One million! I was ecstatic. Really? One million dollars? Naw. But there it was, on paper, a real deal. All that was left was for HP to sign on the top line and me to sign on the bottom. According to the accompanying letter, this was to happen in two or three weeks, when Paul would be back in town.

My first few seconds as I looked at the two pages, I couldn't get over how terrific the deal was, how great I felt about it, how much I loved HP and Paul Ely and even Ed McCracken. I imagined how I'd spend the money, how much I'd save, what kind of interest I'd earn. Kid stuff, but I was only twenty-nine. Besides, I wasn't a seasoned businessperson. And a million dollars was a lot of money back then. It's still a lot of money.

It wasn't until I took a closer look at the agreement that I realized precisely what the deal was. For starters, HP wasn't going to pay a flat one million dollars up front for the program. Instead, the million was a cap on the royalties we could earn. In other words, the deal was only *potentially* worth that much. More significantly, after we had earned our million, HP would own the software, and ASK, having given HP an exclusive, would be out of business. That wasn't at all what I wanted. I wasn't looking for a buy-out. I was looking for an open-ended deal, with a royalty paid on each system sold, no cap, no maximum. Still, a bird in the hand, a very big bird . . .

I was calculating how many man-hours it would take to convert MANMAN to the HP 3000, noodling around with best-case scenarios if ASK went it alone, when out of nowhere it occurred to me: Why *not* sell ASK? Take the money and run. I wasn't even thirty; there were plenty of other things I could do. I could just finish the program, then kick back and enjoy the life of Riley.

Taking this line of reasoning a step farther, I thought back to Dick Anderson's article in the OEM *Journal* and the money he said HP was intending to save using MANMAN. "Hey, wait a minute," I thought, "if this software is so important to HP that they'd basically offer me one million dollars for it, why not more? But how much more before Paul Ely just kicks me out of his office?" After all, only a few months before, I'd told him that HP's manufacturing system was a total loss. At what point would King Paul just kiss off ASK altogether and go with one of the competitors creeping out of the woodwork?

In the weeks preceding my meeting with Paul, I had trouble sleeping. I tossed and turned, trying to decide what to do. Turn down HP's offer? Take them up on it? Bargain for more? How much more? Finally it came to me, clearly and simply, no question about it: Sell! But not for a paltry million. Two million would be more like it.

Almost all of HP's buildings were divided into little cubicles rather than offices, like carrels in a library, only larger. As a vice-president Paul had a pseudo-office, but it was hardly any more private than the cubicles. It was glassed in on two sides and shared a common wall with a conference room. So everyone in the cubicles could see into his office and know precisely what the boss was doing, whether he was working like a demon or staring out into the hills. Heading down the corridor toward Paul's office on the day we were going to sign our agreement, I saw Ed lean over conspiratorially to say something to him. The second I walked in he moved away, and they both greeted me with smiles. I should have guessed something was up, but I didn't.

Instead, I wondered if they'd still be smiling when I dropped the two-million-dollar figure on them.

But before I had a chance to say, "Hey, I want more money," Paul came at me with a whole new set of questions, questions that took us back to where we had been weeks before, when we were still talking about whether or not we'd write a program for the 3000. I tried to get back to my two million dollars, when it suddenly dawned on me from the way Paul was talking that today wasn't a final meeting to dot a few *i*'s and cross some *t*'s and that there wasn't a deal at all. "Hold on, hold on," I interrupted in mid-question. "I thought this was just about a done deal." I fluttered my two pages in front of them.

Paul ignored the papers. "How about," he said, "how about if *you* design the system, *we* supply the programmers, and *you* train us to sell it? Of course, there'd still be a royalty. It would still be worth the same number of dollars."

If seconds earlier I'd had any doubt, now it was certain that Paul didn't have a specific deal in mind. He was, in fact, still fishing around for possibilities. Having been fixated for three weeks on the pages in my hand, I was caught completely off guard. Still, I had the presence of mind for a quick gear change to weigh what he was suggesting. That was, as far as I could tell, my working *for* HP, *at* HP, with Paul's people—notably Ed—instead of working for myself, in my own office and with my own people. I couldn't imagine anything I'd rather do less. I was about to tell them both what a lousy idea I thought it to be when Ed, who hadn't yet said a word, suddenly piped up.

"Why," he said, "should we give you guys any money at all when HP's got competent programmers and manufacturing experts of its own who could clearly come up with a system as good as, if not better than, yours?" Ed glared at me with his little M.B.A. eyes.

That said it all. Of course, of course. Ed had never had any interest in the deal to begin with. He'd always wanted to do it with his own people and had, as I later found out, convinced Paul that he could. As for King Paul, he was a mere mortal, and my concentrating solely on satisfying him had been a tactical mistake. He may have ranted and raved like a dictator, but like any good manager, he listened to his own team and sometimes followed its lead.

No matter. Right now I felt that Paul and Ed both were jerking me around, and I was furious. But I had no plan of action, no idea what I was going to do. Then I remembered an adage of my mother's: "When in doubt, act confident." Ignoring Ed, I turned to Paul. "Why would I want to do that, Paul? If I'd wanted to work for HP, I would have just applied for a job."

It clearly rubbed him the wrong way because he suddenly pounded his fist on the table and yelled, "Look, we're going to write a manufacturing program for the 3000 with you or without you. And we're going to have it finished," he went on, pulling a number out of the air, "in nine months, whether you help or not."

I stood and said, "Paul, it's going to take you three years to do it." And it would, I knew, because they'd use their own manufacturing program with all the garbage in it as a base. "Three years," I repeated. "Maybe even longer. And by then we'll be three years ahead of you."

"That—that would be . . . that would be unacceptable!" Paul fumed. But it was my final word. The meeting was over. And though I'd just thrown away a million bucks, all I could think as I made my way past the cubicles was that I was going to show these guys. Damn them! I was going to show that McCracken jerk, I was going to show them all what ASK could do.

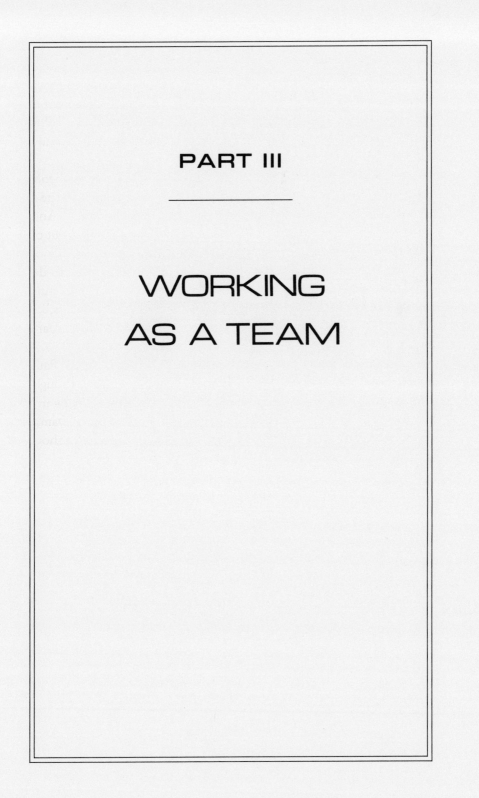

PART III

WORKING AS A TEAM

20

Advisers,
Not Insiders

In winter 1976, with the Hughes system up and running and no cushy royalty deal with HP, I focused on building a real business. I had dozens of questions. How to set up my books? How to grow yet keep control? How to compensate my employees?

I decided to form a board of advisers to guide me in running a high-tech business. Made up of myself and three others, the board met every few months at a restaurant to talk about what was going on at ASK. We brainstormed together; the board answered my questions and provided invaluable advice; I paid for dinner.

Besides myself, the original board members were Dave Leeson, the CEO of California Microwave and one of ASK's earliest customers; Wally Silver from Powertec, who'd gone to bat for ASK when his own job was on the line; and Gary Harmon, the vice-president of finance at Avantek, a microwave components system company ASK had written a program for a couple of years earlier. My appeal to them was simple: "I'm trying to make a go of this business. Can you please help me out?" I didn't invite anyone from ASK because I wanted a fresh approach. If I wanted a board of insiders, I'd just call a staff meeting.

Although none of the members had known one another, we worked together very well. Everyone brought something special to the party. Dave was an entrepreneur who'd grown his own company from zero and was excellent on organizational matters, Wally was an expert on manufacturing systems, and Gary had extensive financial experience. Meeting with the board as a group rather than individually was particularly valuable. Sometimes our interaction opened up whole new approaches. Other times bad ideas were quickly and unanimously shot down. Most often, however, the board reinforced my own gut feelings about how to get things done. Nothing builds your confidence better than three people you respect saying, "Yeah, that's the way I would do it."

Among the issues discussed at these dinners were setting salaries, incentive bonus formulas for key employees, the dangers of overcompensating a good employee in the early going, how to value the shares in a company, what to look for when hiring, and how to develop strategies over the short and long term. One long-term benefit I derived from the board was connecting up with a good law firm— Wilson, Mosher & Sonsini.

Dave Leeson recommended them, though it wasn't the firm he used but one he'd been up against in litigation and had been impressed by. The firm had a reputation in the Valley for being deal makers, not deal breakers, and for arriving at agreements where both parties were satisfied. Today, as Wilson, Sonsini, Goodrich & Rosati, they are one of the leading law firms in the country.

I met with Craig Johnson, the young lawyer who was to handle our account, and John Wilson, the senior partner in charge at the time. True to form, I asked a lot of questions—about their philosophy, who their clients were, whether there'd be any potential conflicts of interest, and if they were interested in the business ASK was in. They passed all the tests, the most important being that I trusted and liked the people I met at the firm. Shortly after establishing our relationship, I asked Craig to join my board. Now we were five. Craig had been with the law firm only a few years. He had spent several years in the Peace Corps after getting a law degree from Stanford. With his shaggy hair and fascination with technology (he was always sending me articles from a variety of technical journals), he seemed more like one of "us" than like our lawyer. Our conversations were more about business and technology than about legal issues, especially since ASK was doing nearly seventy-five million dollars in sales before we ever had a serious lawsuit to worry about.

On December 1, 1976, I presented my first formal business plan to my board of advisers. Committing my ideas to paper clarified my thinking and led me to make a few hard decisions I might not otherwise have made. One was to phase out the service bureau. Another was to focus only on manufacturing software and turn down all other potential customers who didn't fit ASK's goals or customer profile.

The twenty-page plan included a two-page summary, a description of the company, a definition of both the product and the market we served or planned to serve, an analysis of our competition, and current and projected financial statements. I stated ASK's goal as part of the company description: "To become the nation's leading supplier of manufacturing software for the small manufacturer, focusing only on minicomputer applications, and selling only a standard product." That meant no more custom programs and no more clients with data bases too large or problems too difficult, no matter how prestigious the company or how large the check it waved before us.

Defining ASK's product, I provided a rationale for MANMAN and descriptions of the six MANMAN modules. I also zeroed in on the machine we'd use, the HP 21MX. In addition, ASK's joint selling agreement with HP focused us on selling complete, or turnkey, systems—hardware *and* software, with HP participating in the sale and picking up all the hardware dollars.

As it turned out, ASK's early focus on HP gave us an edge when competitors tried to cut into our territory. Committed to HP, we wrote all our software around HP's proprietary operating and data base management systems, never changing a line of their system code. We trusted they'd keep any future systems compatible—not wanting to obsolete their existing customers—and that HP would keep the systems up-to-date. They did, and as HP grew and introduced new machines, ASK grew right along with them, creating an increasingly

more comprehensive product line. Any other software company trying to get into our market on an HP machine would essentially have
to go through all the steps we'd already taken. This would be a costly
process for a smaller company. And while a larger company could
afford the R&D time and dollars, we had a head start and were
adding new modules to complement our base products, making ASK
an increasingly formidable competitor in the HP marketplace.

In defining our market, I originally targeted the approximately
sixty-five thousand small manufacturing companies in the United
States—those with fewer than five hundred employees and with revenues between five and forty million dollars or divisions of large manufacturing companies that fitted these parameters. Smaller companies,
I knew, couldn't afford or justify the cost of our system. And larger
companies—the Boeings, for example—would be less likely to accept
a canned version of MANMAN, though in principle and in fact, it
would work just fine. Besides, the sell to a Fortune 500 company was
generally to the data processing manager, who was usually IBM-ori-
ented and, if anything, was ASK's and HP's natural enemy.

Soon we narrowed our focus even further by selling only to *discrete* manufacturing companies, those that assemble things, such as
electronic equipment or machines, as opposed to *process* manufacturers, which produce things like soap, foods, or chemicals. Still, this left
us with more than fifty thousand companies in our market segment, a
segment in which I had resolved to become an expert. I figured when
a company that fitted our tight parameters came along, it would be
relatively easy to sell ourselves because we knew that market cold.

Once a business concentrates on a finite market and becomes the
expert in that market, it is in an ideal position—as ASK soon was—to
use its reputation to broaden its focus and move into other areas.

One sobering aspect of choosing ASK's market was the realiza-
tion that we couldn't be all things to all companies. A year earlier,
when I'd closed down the Boeing job, I had blamed Boeing for asking
for too much. In fact, our troubles were as much my fault for going
after a piece of business that was beyond our capabilities. It's inevitable you'll make mistakes in business; it's fatal if you don't learn from
them. By 1976 I had learned my lesson, and over the next few months
we turned down two large divisions of Hughes, as well as Reliance

Electric, Bendix Teterboro, and a handful of other prestigious companies.

Defining our competition for the business review with my advisers was far more difficult than defining ourselves or our market. In 1976 the players in the computerized manufacturing systems marketplace were difficult to pin down. The industry was in a state of disarray and flux. There were dozens of companies looking for a piece of the action. Many offered IBM batch solutions. Of course, IBM was the heaviest hitter here, with its MAPICS, IPICS, and COPICS products. Univac, another mainframe manufacturer, was strong with its proprietary UNIS software. Others, like Xerox Computer Services, Tymshare, and Martin Marietta, were offering time-sharing services. Many competitors, too, were around for only a few months, overcommitting to get into the market, then crashing and burning when they couldn't deliver. The upshot was that ASK often found itself up against different competitors in each sales situation.

One early competitor playing in the minicomputer ball park—right in ASK's ball park, in fact—was a company called Interactive Applications, Inc., or IAI, run by a former Tymshare alum named Barry Weinman and his wife, Virginia. They were offering a basic time-share system they had clumsily modified, or kludged, over to the HP 3000. I was a bit envious of their early success. They were eventually acquired by Boole & Babbage for about two million dollars. But Boole & Babbage had problems selling their kludged software against ASK's MANMAN and, like dozens of other companies starting up at the time, soon got out of the market altogether.

Another ASK competitor in 1976 was NCA, also located in the Silicon Valley. When ASK turned down the Litronix job, NCA was there to pick it up. They developed manufacturing software that ran on DEC minicomputers and were a thorn in ASK's side for years. We eventually had to buy them.

Being part of such a confused market made it difficult for us to get a clear fix on competitors or predict what direction the industry would take. It did, however, provide the opportunity for a company like ASK to stake out a quick claim, then grow large and fast enough to make it difficult for any challengers to succeed. That is precisely what we did.

On the final page of my 1976 business review I projected the number of ASK's installations over the next three years. Despite the fact that in fiscal 1976 (ending June 30, 1976) we had only $134,000 in gross revenues, I projected that by 1979 ASK would install nearly $2,000,000 in systems—meaning that we would more than double our revenues every year. The $2,000,000 was a totally made-up figure, based on selling at least one more system each quarter than in the prior quarter. "Why not?" I thought. I hoped I wasn't kidding myself.

21

Accounting for the Future

Not long after deciding to stay away from custom programs, I called on a company named Gardco that manufactured outdoor lighting equipment for office buildings, parking lots, and shopping centers. Their best-known installation was the lights on the Golden Gate Bridge. Gardco had annual sales of about eight million dollars and was looking for a turnkey manufacturing system. Phil Hurlow, their vice-president of finance, liked MANMAN but was looking for software that could also help him solve Gardco's accounts receivable, payables, and general ledger problems. Basically he wanted MAN-MAN integrated with accounting software to provide him with a bigger picture of Gardco's manufacturing operation. "Either develop some financial software to go along with MANMAN," Phil said, "or forget the sale."

I considered Phil's ultimatum. Here was a potential buyer who fitted ASK's customer profile perfectly. Plus he liked the program and he liked the machine, which incidentally was now the HP 1000, an upgrade of the 21MX. Yet he thought our product was too limited. Fortunately he was forceful and articulate enough to convince me he was right. Not only for Gardco but for other customers, too. Only weeks after presenting my business plan, I expanded ASK's goals to include becoming the nation's leading independent supplier of manufacturing *and* financial software to small discrete manufacturing companies.

It wasn't the first time I'd listen to a customer, and it wouldn't be the last. Virtually every ASK product evolved from discussions with and suggestions from our customers. In years to come we even involved them in the design stage, asking what they thought the product should do, how it should work.

In the case of FINMAN, the name of the early versions of ASK's financial program, Phil worked closely with us in its development. He spelled out what Gardco needed in an accounts receivable, accounts payable, and general ledger system and how they all should fit together as well as integrate with MANMAN. In addition to these basic accounting modules, we developed a sales analysis module to prepare reports to aid Phil in making informed decisions about Gardco's operations. Using this module, for example, he could track sales and gross margins by product, product line, market segment, or sales agent.

Intending to sell the FINMAN program as a one-size-fits-all product like MANMAN, we listened to what Phil wanted, but we also checked other basic accounting packages to make certain we were developing a program other customers could use. Not that FINMAN was meant to be a general-purpose accounting system. It wasn't. It was designed as a financial adjunct to a manufacturing program. Still, we wanted to be sure we didn't end up with a product that only Gardco could love.

Heading the project for ASK was Liz Seckler, a recent Stanford math graduate I'd hired a few months earlier. Liz's father ran a successful swimwear company in Los Angeles, and she had worked in his accounting department during her summer vacations from college. Later in the project I hired Howard Klein, another Stanford math graduate, to help her out, though Liz claims that she didn't need help and that I was just playing Cupid. The romance didn't take in any event. But FINMAN did. Gardco's program was installed in 1977 and became part of the MANMAN family of products the following year.

Liz and Howard both were smart, young, hardworking, and dedicated. They were typical of the men and women I hired at ASK, who enabled us to grow as fast and successfully as we did. When I first started hiring, I knew I needed good people just as GE and IBM did. So along with GE and IBM I recruited on campus, first locally at Stanford and later at other universities. If IBM could register with the placement office and send recruiters to the campus, so could ASK. If GE sent literature to potential applicants in advance of their arrival, so could ASK. And if General Motors' name was on the interview schedule in the *Stanford Daily,* ASK's could be, too. There were differences, of course. I was ASK's sole recruiter, I typed the one-page description of the company and photocopied it, and I called the *Stanford Daily* newspaper to make sure we appeared on the schedule.

In the early years I was hiring primarily programmers, and the first thing I asked any applicant was whether he or she was interested in applications software. Most of the theoretical math people weren't and would have become quickly bored at ASK. They were more interested in bits and bytes than in finding nifty ways to manage inventory. I, on the other hand, was looking for the Lizes, the Martys, the Rogers, with the real-world view and the real work experience.

If an applicant was interested in real-world applications, I'd ask him or her to write a sample program. Years before, when I interviewed for my first research job at Bell Labs, I had been put through a similar exercise, the difference being the Bell Labs problem was highly complex, and that made the experience scary as hell. But it had cut through the chitchat characteristic of most interviews and quickly given my interviewer a sense of what I could do. As ASK's recruiter I wanted to know the same about my prospective employees.

I gave them ten minutes to work the problem through. I didn't really care if they finished it or whether they got it right or wrong. All I was looking for was how they approached it, the thought process. Some did it sloppily but made it work. Others were neat and orderly, and didn't. Whatever the outcome, within ten minutes I knew whether someone had an organized mind, whether he or she thought through problems systematically or was slapdash . . . and possibly terrific. It was the applicants who combined organization and invention that I wanted for ASK. We still use that same simple program today in our interviews.

I was also looking for independent thinkers and people with a sense of humor to help them deal with the pressures and long hours of working for a start-up. And most important, I was looking for men and women who'd fit into the team and help us grow. I knew of no tests for this and relied on intuition, usually going with my first impression. Fortunately I was right far more than wrong. Nothing wastes more time than hiring the wrong people.

Compared with the interviews of the GEs and IBMs, mine were informal and unorthodox. But, then, so were many of the job applicants in the seventies. The men showed up for interviews with hair down to their waists and wearing Levi's and Birkenstocks. The women, too. Long hair and Levi's notwithstanding, the men and women I interviewed were graduating from topflight universities and could have had their pick of jobs. I often wondered why these scruffy applicants accepted the jobs I offered. Part of the reason was the times, of course. Young men and women were looking to break from the mold. Still, I imagine it was difficult, particularly for a man, to go back and tell his roommate he'd accepted a job in a company with a handful of employees that was run by a thirty-year-old woman. It was a gutsy thing to do, and I've heard it said that part of what made ASK such an exceptional place to work was the men who were willing to work for a woman boss in the seventies. Times have changed, and today things are different, though I know there are still men who find it difficult to work for a woman.

Also changed along with and by the times are the job applicants. Now they show up in three-piece suits and polished shoes and ask, "What are my career opportunities?" They want to see the map, know how to move from the job they're applying for today on up to the presidency. It presents a whole new set of challenges to the recruiter. But I'm still looking for those same self-motivated, imaginative, independent-thinking team players with a sense of humor.

In fact, if I had to predict the success or failure of a company, I'd rather meet its people—whether they wear suits or Birkenstocks—than look at its product. The right team can determine whether the product is right or not. They'll know to ask their customers. They'll know to ask each other. They'll know how and when to make the difficult decisions and move on. A business doesn't have to win every game to be the leader. It just has to win more games than its competitors. And the more games won, the easier it is to attract others to the team. When you're in business with the right people, success breeds success.

Not long after starting on FINMAN, I finally closed down the service bureau. It was a tough decision. The bureau had carried ASK for years and was still generating nearly two thousand to three thousand dollars a month of almost pure profit. But it was time to get out. Though I wasn't involved in its day-to-day operation, the bureau still took up time I needed to focus on building the ASK I outlined in my business plan.

Not wanting to leave my customers—or Jim Parker, who'd been running the bureau the last few years—in the lurch, I offered to sell the bureau to Jim. I knew he couldn't afford to pay up front for it—certainly not on his ASK salary—so I sold it to him for a thousand dollars a month for a year. Selling an operation generating more than twenty thousand dollars in profits a year for twelve thousand dollars wasn't sound business practice, but Jim had worked long and hard for ASK, and I wanted to give him a chance at making a good profit.

A final move I made in the months after submitting my business review was to make Marty Browne ASK's first vice-president, a decision to which I gave serious thought. Marty had truly become the primary decision maker regarding MANMAN's functions, and for this I affectionately call him today the father of MANMAN. My advisers had warned that whenever you promote someone, no matter what the size of an organization, it makes ripples. I was concerned that the others would be jealous or that it would put Marty on the spot. After all, he hadn't asked to be vice-president. On balance, however, I thought Marty's promotion would be a spirit builder for everyone and communicate the message that ASK was finally a "real" company.

Like everyone, Marty had flaws. As a manager he wasn't hard enough on people. He was great with customers, but he'd sometimes overpromise, leaving his staff overextended. He simply couldn't bear to tell anyone anything he or she didn't want to hear. In the early days this worked in our favor because it resulted in our software having more features and functions than our competitors'. Long term, however, it sometimes became a problem as we spent too much time implementing features usable or desired by only a few customers, often without charging for them. But this was more than outweighed by Marty's incredible loyalty and his commitment to doing only the best work, no matter how long it took. Sure, he might overpledge to customers, but he was such a strong leader and generous person his people would break their butts to save his. Most important, I saw Marty as a person to build a company with. Together with the help of others equally committed and loyal, that's what we were about to do.

22

Machine Dreams

By mid-1977 ASK was tooling along nicely, calling on prospects with the HP 1000 sales force. I was about to close deals for ten MANMAN systems at thirty-five thousand dollars each and was generating interest in FINMAN at twenty thousand dollars each. Plus we were earning a twenty-five-hundred-dollar installation charge for each system and ongoing software maintenance fees totaling nearly six thousand dollars per year per installation. The problem was that in almost every selling situation we were competing head to head with an HP 3000 salesman. Not only that, but we were also bumping into IAI, the company that had kludged a time-sharing manufacturing program for the 3000.

At first I wasn't nervous about the competition. In fact, IAI's success with a less than optimal product seemed to bode well for ASK. It demonstrated how hungry the market was for a program, good or bad. What concerned me was that ASK might be missing the boat. While my initial thinking about staying on the HP 1000 versus moving to the 3000 was "Why change?," it soon occurred to me that if we didn't take the next step soon, it might be too late. We'd still sell systems, do okay, but IAI on HP's commercial machine might eventually own the market. You always have to think about breaking things—patterns, products, and processes—in order to grow.

I started thinking seriously of converting MANMAN to the 3000. There were a number of arguments in favor of doing so, aside from the fact that it was a newer, slightly more versatile machine. For one, the minicomputer market was nowhere near as price-sensitive as I'd originally assumed. At first I thought, "Well, Boeing was so huge they could just toss money out the window. That's why they went for the 3000." But since then a number of smaller companies had also opted for the 3000—and IAI's program. One lost sale that really rankled me was a local high-flying telecommunications company called Rolm. Their manufacturing VP, Dennis Pabojian, told me that he liked our software better than IAI's but that their product was on Rolm's machine of choice—the HP 3000.

Also in favor of going to the 3000 was the simple fact that HP was touting it as their commercial machine, supporting it with advertising and promotion, with some of the sales force even going so far as to tell customers that the 21MX and the updated 1000 were the wrong machines for the MANMAN program. Some of this misinformation could be attributed to the 3000's positioning by HP, the rest to an overly aggressive 3000 sales force. In any event it was hard to compete against. Whenever it got back to me, I'd call Richion and tell him to lay off. "Well, Sandy, there's an easy way around this, you know." I knew. But I knew it wouldn't be all that easy.

What it came down to was that ASK was not going to be able to buck the trend to the 3000. As a small company with a single product we had to listen to the market, even if it was misinformed. To position ourselves for the future, I decided ASK had to change machines.

Looking back, I believe it was my ability to grasp the business realities of the times and make strategic decisions such as the one to go to the 3000 that kept ASK moving in the right direction. Fast-growing businesses are always reaching important junctures, and the good leader has to steer the course, even if it is unpopular with the team.

I assembled the troops to discuss the conversion. I knew the decision wouldn't be well received, though with fewer than ten employees, we were small enough that everyone was aware of my frustrations from banging into HP 3000 salesmen and losing sales to IAI. Still, we were just beginning to reap the benefits of all our hard work in developing MANMAN and FINMAN on the HP 1000. I didn't want to blunt everyone's excitement. I wanted to keep morale high. Coming to a strategic decision was one thing. Keeping the team behind me was another.

So when it came time to share my thinking with the others, I didn't present going to the 3000 as a *fait accompli.* Instead, I laid out the pros and cons and allowed the team to come to the decision collectively. I listened to everyone's opinions, concerns, and objections. I was even willing to be swayed back to sticking with the HP 1000 if someone could make a strong enough case to do so. There was a lot of moaning and groaning at the meeting, but finally it was unanimous: "Let's go for it!"

The first thing we had to go for was a machine to write the program on. For this I went straight to Dick Anderson, the HP Data Systems general manager who'd earlier written the glowing review of MANMAN. At the time HP was juggling titles in the Computer Division, and it was difficult for an outsider to determine who was reporting to whom. But everyone finally reported to Paul Ely, and I was convinced that despite our disagreement in his office a year before, Paul was on my side—if for no other reason than he knew that MANMAN was the best product for HP's commercial machine. After some back and forth, HP agreed to lend us a 3000 for a year, with an option to buy it at a discount at the end of a year.

We picked up the option on an additional thousand square feet of space next to our office, and with the help of my father and my brother, Greg, who had gone into business with my father, we built ASK's second computer room. Since I'd be bringing customers through, Greg designed the room to look like a miniature IBM mainframe installation, complete with raised floors for the computer cables to go under, and a wall-to-wall, floor-to-ceiling glass showcase so visitors could look in and see us work.

All through the building of ASK, my family was an enormous help to me, and I truly believe I couldn't have made the success of ASK that I did without them. Beyond the normal support, advice, warmth, and acceptance they provided, my father, mother, and brother were always there to lend a hand. As ASK expanded and moved into new offices, my mom oversaw the color design and interior decoration. And if I ever had a question about a lease, a building, a bearing wall, or anything to do with real estate, my dad was on the next plane up from L.A.

I used to kid Greg, who was seven years younger than I, that his parents were richer than mine and that they loved him more because they took him on trips to exotic places they had never taken me. The truth of it was that it wasn't until I was out of the house and married that my mom and dad could afford the time and money to travel extensively. By 1977 I was thirty-one and my baby brother was twenty-four and a pillar of dependability. In the years to come he came through for me again and again. When ASK needed a second building, Greg not only helped out on the design and construction but handled the relocation of our expanding staff, saving me a lot of headaches and ASK a great deal of money.

Even now Greg and I talk on the phone nearly every day, bouncing ideas off each other or just kidding around. He has a terrific sense of humor and can always make me laugh. Often he'll just utter a single word that will spring a memory of some experience we've shared, and the two of us will be roaring with laughter. And the second I need him, like our dad, he's there. I've never even had to ask.

For the conversion to the 3000, we were able to use some of the basic design work we'd done for Boeing. But HP had since modified the 3000's operating system and improved the hardware. That meant every piece of code had to be rewritten. Again, we had the option of kludging our existing program and getting into the market faster. But that would have resulted in a product not much better than IAI's. And with their head start, we would have a difficult time catching up. We decided to risk the time and the manpower and start from scratch

. . . again. It was worth it. We were finally on the right machine.

To pay our bills for the year it would take to develop the program, I continued selling software for the 21MX/1000 in tandem with HP's sales force. The rub was that it took me a lot more time and effort to sell my thirty-five-thousand-dollar software than it took an HP salesman to sell his hundred-thousand-dollar-plus machine once I had laid the groundwork. Sure, he had to spend some time but nowhere near as much as I did.

What's fair is fair, I figured. If ASK was doing most of the work involved in selling the hardware, plus incurring the greater sales costs, then we should be given a piece of the hardware action. Instead of our current joint selling agreement with HP, ASK should become a full-fledged systems supplier and an HP original equipment manufacturer. That is to say, we should be able to purchase HP hardware at an OEM discount and resell it as part of a total hardware-software solution.

While OEMs were common in the computer industry in 1977, virtually all were companies that would add hardware to an existing computer to make it perform a specific function. A typical OEM, for example, was the Hughes Industrial Products Division, which manufactured laser cutting systems controlled by HP computers. Hughes bought the HP computer at a healthy discount, packaged it as part of their laser cutting system, slapped on the Hughes name, and sold it. It was a rare software company, on the other hand, that in 1977 enjoyed as cushy a deal. Certainly none did with HP.

I made my request for HP OEM status through the appropriate channels, which meant starting with Bill Richion, by then the national sales manager for HP's Computer Systems Division. At first HP said ASK couldn't be an OEM because we weren't modifying or adding hardware. I pointed out the definition of an OEM in HP's own contracts: An OEM had to "add value" to the hardware to qualify for the discount. Without the added value of ASK's software, HP would have had as much chance selling a 1000 or 3000 to a company looking for a manufacturing system as they would selling it to a customer looking for a laser cutter without Hughes's laser.

Using HP's contract was an appropriate tactic because the company prided itself on playing by the rules. Since HP was extremely sensitive to equal opportunity issues, I also pointed out that selling to a Hughes and not selling to an ASK might make it appear that HP was discriminating against us because of our size.

Besides, I had two other sound business arguments in my favor. First, unlike most OEMs at the time, who mixed and matched hardware from various vendors, ASK's system of choice, including the computer, printers, tape drives, and monitors, would be 100 percent HP. Granting ASK OEM status would boost sales of the entire HP computer product line.

Second, ASK would save HP considerable sales and overhead expense. We'd sell the machine as part of a total solution, arrange with HP to have the machine drop-shipped, carry the burden of accounts receivable, and take responsibility for payment.

After a few months of wrangling, ASK was granted OEM status. Within two years ASK became HP's largest 3000 OEM and one of the largest purchasers of HP computers in the world.

On the heels of our move to the 3000 and the subsequent OEM agreement, we had to decide how to price ASK's software and the overall package. When I first started ASK, my pricing philosophy had been simple: Charge whatever the market would bear. In business parlance this is value pricing, but at ASK we called it the flinch method. We'd sit across from a customer and tell him the software cost thirty-five thousand dollars. If he didn't flinch we'd add, "And the financial package is twenty thousand dollars. Still no flinch: "Per module." And if he still hadn't flinched, we'd say, "And the updates are ten thousand dollars." Still no flinch: "Per year." The second we detected a flinch we backed down one level.

Moving to the 3000, we decided to set a standard price. I figured that since the 3000 cost more than the 1000 and was perceived to be a better machine, the software should also cost more. Invoking no higher math, I decided on a price of fifty thousand dollars.

ASK had early established payment terms that were unique in the industry. From my days as a struggling contract programmer, I was a staunch believer in getting as much money up front as possible. So when ASK started selling systems, we required a 20 percent deposit upon the signing of the contract and the remaining 80 percent on delivery. This was unheard of in the systems business, but we had a product people wanted, and I saw no reason not to take advantage of the demand. And that was 20 percent on the *entire* contract, software and hardware. HP, on the other hand, didn't require their money from us for their hardware until thirty days after they delivered the system to our customer, which was sometimes months after we had signed the contract with our customer. Naturally we paid exactly on the thirtieth day. In the early years those 20 percent deposits often kept us going. And over time the interest we made on the float earned a great deal.

Once ASK had graduated from the flinch method and set a standard price, I was determined to stick by it. Dealing with other vendors, I'd learned that once you start negotiating price, the customer always wonders, "How much lower will they go?" and "Am I getting as good a deal as Joe Blow?" Besides, there's no such thing as a street price that isn't known. The minute you start negotiating price everybody's going to know your lowest price and won't pay a penny more. So if that's the price you want it to be, set it as your standard.

Also, if you want to give discounts, fine, everyone loves getting a discount, but make it an established discount. We gave a 10 percent discount to customers who paid within ten days of final delivery, thereby providing us with more working capital. Still, we didn't take it out of our own hide. Instead, the discounted price was the price we'd wanted all along, the price we believed our product was worth. Since a 10 percent discount on a few hundred-thousand-dollar purchase was significant, most customers paid quickly. Everyone won!

23

ASK Goes Global

I never set out to do things backward, set new trends, or change the way the industry was run. And I had every intention of increasing our sales effort in the United States as soon as possible. But as it turned out, ASK was in England before we were in New England and in France before we got to Paris, Texas.

Throughout 1977 I worked hard at getting ASK's name in the media, sending out product announcements, application articles, and press packets to manufacturing trade magazines, doing interviews for local newspapers, and going to every trade show and exposition where I thought MANMAN could be hyped. As a result, by that fall ASK was getting offers and queries from all over the world—not so much to buy the product as to sell it. Everyone wanted to make a deal. Someone wanted to sell MANMAN in Spain (HOMBREHOMBRE?). And there were dozens of offers from Joe and Bob's garage-type operations wanting to be our Wyoming sales representative. Out of every ten deals that crossed the transom, I'd turn down five with a note, turn down four more after a phone call, and follow up on one.

The most interesting offer we received was from a computer consulting services group in England named Scicon, a division of British Petroleum, one of the U.K.'s largest corporations. Scicon management was beginning to realize that selling software products could be a lot more profitable than selling computer services and consulting, and the managing director of the division, John Ockendon, and the assistant managing director, Warren Werblow, were making an exploratory trip to the United States to find some good software products to sell. They'd heard about ASK through Joe Schoendorf, an HP marketing manager who saw Scicon as a way to sell a lot of HP iron.

Scicon's interest in MANMAN in 1977 was particularly noteworthy because back then the Europeans were generally a few years behind the United States in the software business. This was in part, because their approach to problem solving differs from ours. Europeans tend to be more analytical and precise. For example, if an American sees water seeping out of a wall, he chops the wall apart until he finds a leaky pipe, fixes it, and replasters the wall. The European, on the other hand, gets out the blueprints and spends hours figuring where the pipe would most likely break. He then makes a small incision in the wall, fixes the pipe, and reinserts the small square of plaster—arthroscopic plumbing.

Canned software like MANMAN is like the quick American fix. Consultancies such as Scicon, on the other hand, represent the surgical European approach. They'd come in for weeks or months and analyze a company's needs, then develop a custom program to satisfy that customer perfectly. It turned out that there was room for both approaches in England as Scicon's success with MANMAN proved.

Waiting for the British to arrive at ASK, I was dubious. I was expecting stiff and proper. Instead, I got Monty Python. John, the top banana, was a roly-poly guy with a thick beard, an umbrella, a three-piece suit with a watch chain spanning his belly, and a wonderful accent. Warren was tall, slim, and expressive. They were quite a team. Maybe I was just in a good mood, but it seemed that everything they said was hilarious—if not out-and-out funny, then edged with an affable sarcasm. They were also each other's best audience. Neither could say five words without the other's cracking up. Right away, though, they included me in. Within five minutes it was as if we'd known one another all our lives. At one point Warren turned to me and said, "You know, I think we should sell this product," and I said, "You know, I think you should, too." We exchanged a few telexes, and on September 11, 1977, ASK entered a licensing agreement with Scicon.

A few weeks later I flew to England, all expenses paid by Scicon, to train their people in how to sell to manufacturing companies. While Scicon's old buildings had cold linoleum floors, everything else about the company was comfortable—and organized. Scicon had someone meet me at the airport in an elegant car, saw to my hotel accommodations, let me sleep for two hours, then collected me for dinner. In the car I was handed a list of who would be at the dinner and what each of their positions was. At dinner I was given a minute-by-minute agenda for the next day.

The next morning at Scicon I was asked by Mary, the tea lady, how I took my coffee or tea, whether I wanted scones or not. The beverages were served in fine china cups with saucers. We ate lunch in the executive dining room, where I was introduced to the chef, a toothless guy who'd been part of the Scicon family for years.

By the time the visit was over I felt more like a friend than a business partner. And though I was snowed by the way I was wined and dined, I was most impressed with the warmth and respect that I and that everyone in the company was treated with.

Our relationship with Scicon turned out to be one of the most successful in ASK's history, contributing millions in gross revenues over the years. By 1987 the Scicon MANMAN group was operating more like an ASK office than a Scicon office—that is, it was selling primarily product, rather than consulting or custom programming— and the group approached us to buy them from Scicon. We obliged, and today the group continues to be a significant contributor to our bottom line. The key reason for this success, I'm certain, was that the chemistry between us was right from the start. I trusted the people and their judgment without question. Whatever they did, whatever they wanted, I approved because I knew they wouldn't be asking for a contract concession unless it was absolutely necessary.

At one point Warren suggested I trademark the MANMAN

name in England, and he put me in touch with a hotshot firm of British patent attorneys. On July 27, 1978, I received the following correspondence: "Dear Madame: Re ASK Computer Services British Trademark Application. . . . We are pleased to advise that the official examination of the above-mentioned trademark has now been completed, but the registrar of trademarks has raised objection to the application on the grounds that the mark consists of two surnames cojoined, and is also the abbreviation, MAN, and the surname, MAN, cojoined which he considers to be descriptive of, for example, goods that are manufactured by a person or a firm named MAN. . . ." The letter went on to say, ". . . we understand that the surname MAN is in the New York telephone directory, and have been able to ascertain that it appears 23 times in the Queens directory. . . ." This rejection was the only blight in our entire relationship with Scicon.

By contrast, I wrote the U.S. trademark application for MAN-MAN myself. After a few months of correspondence with the U.S. Patent and Trademark Office, I received an approved trademark for MANMAN that is still in effect. The Queens directory wasn't ever mentioned.

Unfortunately, ASK's French connection—which I made on a side trip during my first visit to Scicon—was not as successful as the British. At the same time we teamed up with Scicon, we signed a marketing agreement with an organization called CISI, a consultancy that was part of the French Atomic Energy Commission and owned by the French government. They translated MANMAN into French and over the years sold only a dozen or so systems. Still, it was better than we would have done in France without them and better than we've done since then, selling directly in France. ASK's relative failure in France—both with CISI and subsequently with our own direct sales operation—was not because of the software, I'm convinced, but because we didn't have the right people directing the sales effort. The Scicon team, on the other hand, was perfect for ASK and for the product from the outset.

24

The Suit

When I returned from Europe in fall 1977, I was more excited than ever about ASK's possibilities. Buoyed by my experiences at Scicon and its obvious appreciation of our product, I was now convinced that significant success was a matter of making a concerted, professional sales effort in the United States—more than I alone could provide.

I was doing a reasonable job. By the end of the year we'd have three MANMAN systems up and running in Southern California, one in Puerto Rico, one in Arkansas, one in New Jersey, two in Florida, and two in Northern California, all on the HP 1000. I was also working on closing sales on the soon-to-be-completed 3000 version of MANMAN at companies in Utah, Texas, California, Colorado, and Iowa. But each sale required that I make at least one visit to the prospect's plant. Plus there were plenty of calls that never turned into sales. All of them had to be squeezed in while I ran the company, tried to keep morale high, and signed every check that went out. I rarely had any time to be with Arie and the kids, and there was almost never a day when I wasn't working. I simply couldn't keep up the pace.

Late in 1977 I established relationships with three independent sales reps: two in the East, where I believed that ASK desperately needed a physical presence, and one in Southern California. I would have much preferred to start with a direct sales force, one that worked exclusively for ASK but coming off a year when ASK had only thirty-three-thousand-dollars pretax income, I couldn't afford it. The disadvantage of having reps instead of your own sales force is that reps generally carry a variety of products from different vendors and favor the products that are easiest to sell. There are definite advantages, though. Unlike a direct salesperson who usually gets a guaranteed base salary plus commissions, the rep isn't paid unless he sells something. With a rep, too, there's no office overhead, no secretarial costs, no insurance, and minimal start-up costs. For running his own business and taking the greater risk, the rep earns higher commissions.

ASK's risk was the time it would take us to get the reps up to speed on the product. I knew that if they didn't know the product cold, there'd be no easy sales and the reps would quickly lose interest. So we had to provide them with a good education. Also part of the risk was that a bad or uninterested rep can damage your reputation and make it harder for you to sell down the line.

After only a few months on the job it was clear that our East Coast reps weren't going to work out. Our Southern California rep, on the other hand, Jim Bensman, looked like a real comer. He was bright and aggressive and had built his whole business around representing MANMAN. In exchange I gave him an exclusive for the entire L.A. area, a notoriously difficult market because it is so spread out geographically.

Jim eventually made a lot of money for the company and for himself, but he ran into a problem with ASK in the early going, and it wasn't of his own making. Prior to taking on reps, ASK had always been technically focused. Our company heroes were our programmers—meaning almost everyone at ASK except Jim. Suddenly there was a new sales guy taking up a lot of Marty's and Roger's time. And Jim had yet to make a sale.

I'm certain it was less a case of resenting Jim's questions than the team at ASK's sensing that like it or not, our little operation was changing. Up until then ASK was still like a club, a continuation of college for most of the people on the team. One or two were married, but no one except me had children to support, and only a few had mortgages. Also, in 1977 no one thought we'd ever make it big. Almost everyone was happy with the way we were.

Part of me, too, wanted to keep the family intimate. But I was the one spending my days in Toledo and my nights in airports, and I knew that the only way to move was forward. We had to change, whether we wanted to or not. Something had to give.

Finally, on New Year's Day 1978, the travel, the time spent away from home, the frustration of trying to do too much all came to a head. While doing my books, I realized that after six years of twelve-, sixteen-, and twenty-hour days I'd never earned more than twenty-four thousand dollars a year—less than half that for the first five—and that ASK had never shown more than a thirty-three-thousand-dollar pretax profit. Not that I had ever intended to become rich at ASK, but I had intended to make a good living. And I wanted to have fun doing it. Lately, however, there was simply too much work, too little fun. So I made a New Year's resolution: One more year or bust. Either ASK would turn a reasonable profit in 1978 and I'd earn a reasonable salary for the time I spent, or I'd sell the software, close up shop, and work for someone else.

In early 1978 I decided to hire a direct salesman for Northern California to help me. In his first week on the job he called the phone company to have his phone moved from the right to the left side of his desk. If he did more than that, I wasn't privy to it. After I fired him, I hired another guy. He was happy with the phone where it was but couldn't quite get the hang of how to sell what we had, so I let him go as well.

Like so many major chapters in ASK's history, the next step in building the company came unexpectedly. In March 1978 I got a call from a guy named Tom Lavey at Itel. Itel had become a billion-dollar company only a few years earlier, having created a niche market manufacturing and leasing computers that were plug-compatible with IBM mainframes. The market was drying up, however, and Itel was trying to get into other markets by buying up companies. One of their strategies was to buy applications software companies to penetrate specific industries, or vertical markets. They'd acquired companies with products in banking, stock block trading, and wholesaling and had identified manufacturing as another large market. Tom, who was Itel's manufacturing products manager, had heard about ASK and figured he could use our software to open the manufacturing door for Itel.

"Are you interested in selling?" he asked. While mindful of my New Year's resolution, I just wasn't ready to give up my birthright when push came to shove. Not just yet. I told him ASK wasn't for sale. But I didn't discourage him when he insisted on coming out from his Itel office in New Jersey for a visit.

A few days later I picked him up at the airport. He was six feet tall, a burly guy with a thatch of blond hair on top of a big jug of a face. He smoked like a chimney, had a fast wit and a great sense of humor. We talked business in the car, saw eye to eye on virtually everything except my determination to hold on to ASK. "Now wait a minute," he insisted as the car idled at a stoplight, "we're prepared to offer you one million dollars."

I batted my eyelashes. "Only one million? I've already been offered that."

Tom insisted on seeing an ASK installation, and our best at that time was still Hughes, so the next day we flew down to San Diego. It was pouring when we arrived, the streets were flooded, and at one point we had to pull to the side of the road and wait for the tide to go out. Finally, soaked and bedraggled, we got to Hughes, having had a bit more time to get to know each other.

At Hughes Tom was a quick study, and for good reason. A few years back he'd worked for Xerox Computing Services, selling a manufacturing program that competed with MANMAN on Tymshare. Before starting at Itel, he'd run a manufacturing facility for a lighting company. So Tom understood what he saw at Hughes and knew precisely how good our product was.

On the way back to the airport he revealed another aspect of his character. He put off leaving Hughes until there was no way we could get to the airport in time for our flight, even if the roads weren't flooded. Then Tom got behind the wheel and drove like a madman.

The gangway was being pulled away from the plane as we jumped aboard, Tom's tie and my pink briefcase flying. The method to his madness, as I discovered after getting to know him better, was to show he could make the flight despite the odds. He loved taking chances, going down to the wire, trying the impossible. I figured he was a natural for building ASK's national sales organization. As for his being a wild man, perhaps ASK was a little too laid-back for the growth it needed. And Tom Lavey with his experience in sales, manufacturing, and management might be just the ingredient to liven things up.

Back in Los Altos, I told him, "I don't want to be bought by Itel. But I want to buy you. How much are you?" I knew he wouldn't come cheaply, but this was my make-it-or-break-it year, and I believed with Tom Lavey on the team, ASK would definitely make it. He said he wasn't looking for a job.

Fortunately for ASK, Tom hated winter weather, so when spring came to New Jersey and brought snow with it, Tom gave me a call. He told me what it would take for him to make the move. I was right. He didn't come cheaply. I told him to send on his references.

I was really high on Tom and thought his references would say he was the greatest thing since sliced bread. But they didn't. They were lukewarm, and it concerned me. I'd already hired and fired two salespeople. I began to think that maybe I was good at picking programmers but had a blind spot about hiring salespeople. But then I figured that Tom had a unique personality. He could easily rub someone the wrong way. Who knows? Maybe he had driven his references to the airport.

After the reference check I ran hot and cold on Tom. I wanted to trust my gut and hire him. But hiring Tom, unlike my first two salesmen, was a major, major decision. Tom wanted a vice-president's title and a guaranteed salary of fifty thousand dollars, substantially more than I or anyone else at ASK was making. He also wanted stock options on 5 percent of ASK's shares. Plus I had to move him and his family three thousand miles to California. What if he liked the job, but his family was homesick for New Jersey? What if he was too wild to handle? What if he didn't get along with the others? I was worried, and I was scared.

Finally I decided to talk to him again, not to make an offer but just to discuss some of the issues. I called on a Sunday afternoon. Three hours later, after discussing everything from a compensation plan to the moving policies of big companies to how much ASK would pay for the toiletries and towels in his California apartment until he and his family were settled, Tom said, "Well, I guess that means I start next Monday?"

"What?"

"Monday. Week from tomorrow. There's nothing more to say."

He was right. I'd run out of objections. The guy was terrific. And he'd just sold me the most expensive thing ASK had ever bought.

A few days prior to Tom's arrival at ASK in May 1978 there was a minor insurrection when I told the team Tom would be vice-president of sales. I clearly hadn't understood how important titles were to people—not only to the ones who had them, like Marty, but to those who didn't. Titles, I subsequently found, played a far greater role in separating people out than salary. Salaries were supposedly confidential, while everyone knew who the vice-president was. And while Marty never said, "Gee, being a VP is a really big thing for me," giving Tom a similar title cheapened Marty's in his own eyes as well as in the eyes of the others. They thought I'd slighted Marty. Besides, naive in the world of business, they thought that a company was like the U.S. government, one president and one vice-president.

For my part, I thought that having two vice-presidents was another step in becoming a real company, though back then, in my heart of hearts, I believed that titles were to be earned and not given as a hiring incentive. But realistically I had no chance of getting Tom to come to ASK without giving him the title. More than the money, the title was his opportunity to step up in stature in the business community, even if it meant leaving a billion-dollar company to go to one that would gross less than a half million in 1978. Ironically, in 1979 Itel was to lose $444,000,000 to become one of the largest business disasters in the computer industry. Maybe Tom'd seen it coming; maybe he hadn't. In any event, he decided to take his chances with ASK.

When it was clear how pushed out of shape everyone was about Tom's hiring and his title, I called the team together in my office and said, "Look, I know you're uncomfortable about my bringing Tom in, but I think we need him. We've got a really good product that you've all developed, and now is the time to grow as a company. But my loyalty is to you. You've proven your value to ASK. I don't know if Tom will do the same. But if he doesn't work out, for whatever reason, he'll go." Aware that Roger was the ringleader of the anti-Tom movement, I singled him out after the meeting and repeated my reassurance.

This quieted the grumbling until the day Tom actually arrived for his first day on the job, all decked out in a three-piece suit. It immediately earned him the title of "the Suit," which stuck for months. In fact, whenever there was talk of Tom, his name was never mentioned. It was always "the Suit." Tom could have griped about it, but he didn't. He was no fool and knew he'd have to prove himself to earn the title I'd given him and shed the one he'd gotten from the others.

25

Back to School

By the time Tom Lavey came on board, the tide was turning for ASK. I'd been working on closing a number of 3000 sales, and suddenly within a few days' time three of them closed: Valtek in Utah, B. K. Sweeney in Colorado, and Therman in Texas. And not long after, Jim Bensman closed two large orders back to back. ASK was on its way. Whereas on New Year's Day I was concerned ASK would never make a reasonable profit, now just a few months later I was worried I didn't know enough about running a company to handle our success and keep us growing in the right direction.

After all, it seemed that most of what I'd accomplished at ASK was by gut feel. I had a good technical background, was strong in sales, but had no management experience. This was both good and bad. If I'd had experience, I might have avoided many of my early pitfalls. On the other hand, I might have done a far more comprehensive survey of the marketplace, seen IBM, Xerox, Burroughs, and Univac looming over the horizon, and decided I couldn't compete with the heavy hitters. Instead, I attacked the market with tunnel vision and stumbled into something big.

In late spring 1978 it was time to stop stumbling. Leaving Tom Lavey to handle sales and Marty to run R&D—I was still in charge of paying the bills and signing the paychecks—I went to Massachusetts to attend the Harvard Business School's Smaller Company Management Program (SCMP). It was the ideal program for me. It was exclusively for owners and CEOs of smaller companies, enrollment was limited to one hundred, and it was taught in three-week sessions, one each summer for three years. The program gave me the opportunity to be with men and women facing many of the same problems as I. The sessions were short enough so that I could break away from ASK. And the three-year time span meant I could apply what I learned one year, then come back the next for a refresher and new information.

The program format was to read and discuss small-business case studies, first in small study groups and then in the classroom with Harvard Business School professors leading the discussions. The major areas covered were human relations, finance, marketing, management control, strategy, and operations. Going to class my first day, binder and books clutched to my chest, purse hanging from my arm, I was nervous and unsure. ASK was probably the smallest company represented. Everyone seemed so much older and more seasoned than I.

The first thing I learned was how little I knew about running a company. I hardly knew how to read a financial statement. I didn't know much about strategic planning. I had no idea how to leverage financials and borrow against them or even that companies did so. I also learned that I was right about the other students in the program: Most were far more sophisticated about business than I. They'd been at it longer and had bigger businesses, though many were family businesses started by their fathers or grandfathers, complete with hornets' nests or problems involving brothers, sisters, and other warring relatives.

But when it came down to the nuts and bolts work itself—discussing the case studies—I did fine. Though I was unfamiliar with some of the jargon, when it came time to solve a problem—whether

financial, dealing with people, marketing, whatever—nine times out
of ten my gut feel led me in the right direction—in the direction, at
least, that was seconded by our professors. It was a great confidence
builder. Every bit as important, I realized that my inexperience wasn't
necessarily a handicap. My only problem was I was a slow reader.
While everyone else finished the reading for the next day by ten or
eleven at night, I'd be up till two in the morning poring over the
material.

The high point of the initial session was a class I had with a
professor named Keith Butters. Prior to the first class meeting, we
were to read a business plan that had been prepared a few years earlier
by a small company—Company X, an actual firm that manufactured
lawn sprinkler systems, as I recall. The plan justified a new market the
company was intending to move into. I read the plan and studied the
numbers. It all looked pretty straightforward. It was a good, well-
thought-out plan, and the company seemed solid. I assumed Butters
had given us the assignment as an example of how to write a good
business plan.

When Butters made his appearance on the first day of class, you
could just about hear the collective moan go up. He looked to be
about seventy-five—fragile and hunched over, the archetypal absent-
minded professor. "So," he said, suddenly straightening up, looking
over his domain, and losing about twenty years in the process, "so,
would you move into the market Company X moved into?" He fixed
on my name tag. "How about you, Sandra? Would you?" I said sure,
and from the nods around me, I could tell that everyone agreed.
Butters asked a few others, and it was unanimous. "Well," Butters
went on, "within three years Company X was bankrupt. Why?" Almost everyone thought it was bad luck, a water shortage, or something fluky that had blind-sided them. Butters listened, then grabbed
a piece of chalk from the chalk rail. He went one by one through the
assumptions of the plan, the numbers on the appended financial
statement. "What was really the size of the market? How large a share
could Company X actually expect? Look at the cost structure. What
about the debt service? Were they overextended?" A half hour later
everyone in the room was wondering how Company X could have

been so dumb as to have gotten themselves into this fix. By the end of the class Butters looked young and energetic, and the rest of us were the ones hunched over.

I walked out of the room scared to death. Were there land mines in my own business strategy waiting to blow up in my face? And would I have to wait until ASK went belly up to find them? The answer was, sure, it's easier to see your mistakes in hindsight, as Butters demonstrated. But he also showed that a deeper analysis going into the project could have averted failure—or would have at least provided a better picture of the risk involved.

When I returned to ASK, I immediately put some of the things I'd learned to work. The first thing I did was to set financial goals and incorporate them into a strategic and tactical plan. For 1979, I stayed with the two-million-dollar goal I'd set in my 1976 business review. For 1980, nine million; 1981, thirteen million; 1982, twenty-two million; and 1983, thirty-six million. For 1984, I projected sixty million dollars. Once again I had set extremely aggressive goals for ASK, projecting we'd nearly double our revenues every year.

As part of the plan, I focused on the products we needed to develop, knowing that the steep growth I was projecting could be driven only by selling a combination of the products we already had and new ones. To determine which products our R&D should go to work on, I first studied ASK's strengths and weaknesses vis-à-vis the competition. Next, I determined where the holes were in our own and in our competitors' product lines. Finally, I assessed the risks and rewards I'd face in filling those holes. For example, I decided we should develop a program called GRAFMAN that would graphically display reports because I ascertained it to be a low-risk, high-reward product. But I decided against developing a medium-risk, high-reward distribution program because that wasn't an area ASK was familiar with at the time. On the other hand, I did decide we should develop a fixed assets program that, though low-reward, wouldn't take much to get into and would be a nice complement to our product line.

The second major revamping I did at ASK as a result of my Harvard education was of our financial structure. My professors had taught me that a corporation's numbers talked, and I wanted ASK's numbers to tell as strong a story as possible.

To do so, I decided to model ASK's numbers on a company I respected. I studied the financial sections in the annual reports of a number of manufacturers: HP, DEC, IBM, ADP, and a few others. I finally focused on Hewett-Packard, widely regarded as a topflight company with an excellent reputation and a commitment to R&D. I saw that over the years HP showed a gross margin—total revenues minus cost of goods sold—of approximately 50 percent. So I decided that's what ours should be. I also knew that an aftertax profit of 10 percent was considered substantial, so I set that as a second goal. Working backward from these two figures, I then established a financial profile for ASK that mimicked that of HP.

Next, I applied this formula to my projected revenue goal of $2 million for 1979. Our gross margin would be the $2 million minus the cost of goods sold; in ASK's case, this consisted primarily of the HP computers we resold plus the $10 reels of magnetic tape on which we put our software. To show a 50 percent gross margin would mean that the cost of goods to me from HP in 1979 would have to be less than $1 million. Fifty percent was an excellent gross margin for a company that didn't do its own manufacturing and had no fixed manufacturing costs to maintain. Profits, obviously, would have to come out of the other million. A 10 percent aftertax profit on $2 million would be $200,000. To achieve this, we'd need to make about a $320,000 *pre*-tax profit based on ASK's 40 percent tax bracket. This left $680,000 for R&D, administrative costs, fixed overhead, and sales and marketing expenses.

Using the HP model also gave me a fix on how much a topflight company spent on R&D: 8 percent of gross revenues. On the basis of my $2 million goal for 1979, that meant I would budget $160,000 for R&D, leaving slightly more than $520,000, or 25 percent of total revenues, for sales and general administrative costs.

We were proud of making a profit and pointed this out to potential customers as well. Making a profit should be a selling feature, not a point of embarrassment. Very few customers will begrudge you a profit if they see themselves benefiting over the long term—for example, by your reinvestment in product improvement or customer service. Besides, they know that profitable companies stay around to be accountable for their products.

With a financial plan and some clear-cut goals, I felt ASK had a better shot at the future. I told all the people in the company the target we were shooting for and gave them progress reports along the way. It was like a telethon, with the red line chugging from plateau to plateau as the months and years passed. And it was a long way from the $2,000 I'd started with. In the end, we beat our 1982, 1983, and 1984 projections, doing $24,800,000 in 1982 against the plan of $22,000,-000; $39,400,000 in 1983 against the plan of $36,000,000; and $65,-000,000 in 1984 against the plan of $60,000,000.

26

The Suit Delivers

That first summer at Harvard I was worried about Tom. I'd taken him on a number of sales calls, and while he understood the product, there was a good chemistry between us, and he was terrific with prospects, he had yet to close a sale. Figuring that maybe I was making him nervous, I suggested he go on calls without me. One particularly hot prospect he was bringing along on his own was Cushman Electronics, a Northern California manufacturer of test instruments for FM radio systems. When I left for school, Tom assured me Cushman was close to signing a contract. Three weeks later Tom said they were closer, it was nearly a done deal.

Now I knew our sales cycle wasn't an overnight process, but by then Tom had been with ASK for nearly three months, and I was anxious for a result, and soon. I was still insecure about him—not only because the last two guys I'd hired hadn't worked out but because I'd committed heavily to him in dollars, in time, and in emotions. I needed Tom to succeed.

Cushman didn't make it easy. Every time it looked as if the sale were going to close, there was a new wrinkle to the deal. Finally, in October 1978, they signed on the bottom line, and we had their 20 percent deposit on the two hundred-thousand-dollar deal. The Suit had delivered.

Tom turned out to be the ideal salesman not only on sales calls or in meetings but after hours, too. He would stay out to 3:00 A.M. and drink with customers, shoot pool and billiards with them, let them win at poker, and be up the next morning at 7:00, bright and ready to go. And love every minute of it. Also, like any great salesperson, he was a real chameleon; he could be anything the customer wanted him to be. When I took him to Valtek, a Utah company run by Mormons—and ASK's first customer on the 3000—he was the model of abstinence, no booze, no cigarettes, a suit in lamb's clothing. Most important, he was quickly accepted by the others at ASK and in short order became one of the family, Papa ASK.

Tom was also an excellent complement to me. While my strength was in taking the 90 percent producer and making him or her into a 110 percent producer, Tom could turn the 75 percent producer into a 95 percenter. In starting a company, you can go only so far with demanding the best from the best. Then you need a Tom Lavey to bring others along.

Another area where Tom complemented me was in human relations. Although he, I, and the other ASK officers all were team players and always mixed well with ASK employees, my skill, as it developed, was in building a team, making strategic decisions, and getting along with head honchos, CEOs, and members of the board. I think back then there was something both disarming and appealing about a knowledgeable woman who could laugh at herself yet was gutsy enough to go right to the top to make her case.

Although Tom started out as the Suit, he soon mixed well with his equals and the line troops. Whereas I drew seating charts for every meeting I'd attend to remember who everyone was, Tom heard a name once and remembered it forever. He always found something he shared in common with everyone he met, quickly putting him or her

at ease. When ASK was considerably larger and fielded its first company softball team, Tom took an active part. Not only did he make it
to every game, but he always played a major role—captain, pitcher, or
cleanup hitter. Even if he'd just come back from a sales call dressed in
a suit and tie, he'd trot out onto the field to play. As a result, almost
everyone in the company thought he was a god, while the people
above him—notably ASK's eventual board of directors—were less
inclined to grant him deity status.

Another of Tom's strengths was that he was always coming up
with ideas—many of them outrageous. He always had ideas for new
products or ways of dealing with difficult customers and negotiating
thorny contracts. Initially he sprang his ideas on me whenever they
popped into his head, but after a while he realized that I was most
receptive to them on Fridays, when the week was just about over and I
was loose. By contrast, on Monday, having had the weekend to cogi-
tate, make new lists, drop memos into everyone's in box, I was all
business. Anyhow, out of every ten of his ideas, nine of them were
flaky and I quickly discounted them before anyone got too carried
away. But there'd always be that one. . . .

A few weeks after the Cushman sale I decided Tom had things sufficiently well in hand for ASK to go nationwide, meaning we'd open a
New York office. Tom said he had just the guy for the job, one of his
old cronies from Itel, Jim Manion, whom he'd evidently planned on
hiring all along. In fact, before Tom left Itel, he'd called Jim and told
him, "I've got some good news, and I've got some bad news. The good
news is I've found a great product we can sell. The bad news is I'm not
buying it for Itel. I'm leaving to sell it on my own. But hang tight. In
six months I'll have a job for you."

I met Jim at a coffee shop at Newark Airport. We shook hands,
sat down, ordered. Almost the first thing out of his mouth was "My
father's a salesman, my brother's a salesman, and I'm a salesman.
That's what I do. I sell, and I'm proud of it." There was nothing he
could have said that would have impressed me more. In the computer
business, in particular, a lot of people, especially those with math or
engineering degrees, are embarrassed about selling. They figure sales

are what you do if you can't cut it in research or product development. What Jim said, however, put things in a very clear perspective. He knew what he did; he liked what he did; he respected what he did. On top of that I liked him. So I hired him.

Always looking to spend as little as possible in those relatively lean years, we set Jim up in a one-room office on the second floor of a union hall in Long Island. Every morning he climbed the back stairs to his office and got on the phone. And sometimes in the background—particularly if he called us from New York after 5:00 P.M., when the rates were lower—you could actually hear the singing from the union hall downstairs.

Of course, he wouldn't have to remain there forever. The deal we cut with Jim—and the way we opened most of our early sales offices—was that once he had sold a few systems, enough to support an office, he could hire a secretary and then a technical support person. Until then he'd have to do his own secretarial work and his own technical support. In an emergency we'd fly someone in from California to help out. This arrangement cut down on his selling time, but in the long run it made Jim and our other early sales reps extremely knowledgeable about the product. I'm convinced this hands-on experience made them more effective salespeople and, later, better managers. Jim was out of the union hall and into a suite in a new office building within the year.

With the New York office cooking, all we had to do to qualify for being a real national sales force was to bring ASK to the Midwest. Bob Stosz, the computer services manager at one of our early customers, Prodelin, in New Jersey, wanted to move to Chicago to be a technical manager with ASK. We were apprehensive about hiring from a customer, but it worked out fine when Bob's boss and the VP of manufacturing for Prodelin, Paul Caffrey, said Bob could go if we also hired *him.* So Paul became regional sales manager in Chicago, and Bob became regional technical manager.

After that there was no stopping us. We just kept opening offices, with virtually everyone we hired in Tom's image—mavericks and risk takers, most of them men and women who didn't quite fit in at the button-down companies they came from but were perfect for a boss like Tom and a company like ASK.

The one early employee who wasn't perfect for a boss like Tom was Ann Rehling, my secretary. She was my mother away from home—a real grandmother, in fact—and our oldest employee by about twenty-five years. I never asked her how old she was for fear of finding out she was past retirement age. Until her arrival I'd had a frustrating history with secretaries. I'd hire bright young women (no man ever applied) who caught on to the job quickly and did good work. But ASK was growing so fast, there were so many job opportunities I had no choice but to promote them to higher-paying, more prestigious jobs. I loved watching them develop and contribute to ASK's success. But then I'd have to hire and train another secretary. The cycle ended with Ann.

Ann had initially interviewed as Tom's secretary, not mine. He'd hired her after I told him that she was exactly the type of secretary I'd want—a real pro, with twenty years' experience. But she wasn't Tom's cup of tea, nor was Tom hers. Tom wasn't ready for a grandmother, and Ann, well, she was used to someone a little more organized. So I inherited her. With Ann on the job, my productivity doubled. I'd get a letter or a phone call and ask her to handle it, and she would. Perfectly. I'd never have to check up on her. And if a similar situation arose, I never had to ask her to handle it. She already had.

As ASK was beginning to make a real impression in the manufacturing marketplace, offers from companies to buy us or entice us onto their computers were heating up. Xerox Computer Systems made a pass. They were looking for a minicomputer product to complement their sagging time-sharing service. Comsat, flush with satellite systems dollars, tried to put us together with Computervision, a computer-aided design (CAD) company, to form a company aimed at the computer-integrated manufacturing (CIM) market—a concept that involved using computers to link factory floor automation devices, knowledge workers, and manufacturing control systems. Comsat thought the CIM market would hit one billion dollars in a few years. My instinct and Harvard education said it wouldn't, at least not then. Had we gone for it, we would have been at least a decade too early. Even today the market for complete CIM hasn't fully developed. We also got a proposal from DEC, seeking to put MANMAN on their machine, with DEC handling sales and marketing. But the deal had all the earmarks of Paul Ely's HP offer, so I passed on that as well.

Of all the offers, the only one that made sense came from Sperry Univac, a huge mainframe company. Univac, now known as Unisys, had just swallowed up the small minicomputer division of Varian—a Silicon Valley company started at about the same time as HP but far less successful—called Varian Data Systems and was shopping around for software applications to carve out a piece of the minicomputer market. In the fifties the name Univac had been virtually synonymous with computers, and the company had remained a major producer of mainframes through the sixties. But by the late sixties an aggressive IBM sales and marketing effort had left Univac in the dust.

No longer able to compete successfully on hardware alone, Univac focused on selling software solutions, concentrating in the manufacturing area where they were widely respected. Univac was, in my mind, the only major hardware company at that time with a true commitment to manufacturing software, and a deal with them promised more potential than the unconsummated Paul Ely and HP deal. Their UNIS software was by far the best mainframe manufacturing software in the industry. Also, Univac had thousands of sales reps worldwide knowledgeable in manufacturing, and the company supported their products with terrific documentation and sales literature. Finally, they'd proved they could sell turnkey solutions to manufacturers. We were a perfect match, it seemed. So when Univac called Tom Lavey, our sales VP, to ask about making ASK's software available on their new machine, Varian's V77, and Tom presented it to me as one of his flaky Friday ideas, I went for it.

On the face of it, the deal we cut with Univac was a good one. We'd convert MANMAN to run on their mini for an up-front fee of $125,000, to be credited against future royalties. Unlike the phantom HP deal, there was no ceiling on royalties, and to keep the contract active, Univac would have to maintain an annual royalty minimum to ASK of $500,000. The potential downside for us was that if Univac maintained considerably higher minimums—$1,500,000 in year one, $4,000,000 in year two, $7,000,000 in year three, etc.—they would have a perpetual limited exclusive on MANMAN. In other words, if these more aggressive minimums were met, ASK could be barred from putting MANMAN on any machine other than Univac's and HP's. At the time, however, I figured that ASK's small sales force would have their hands full selling MANMAN on the HP 3000 and that anything Univac's enormous sales force sold would be gravy. The deal looked like a smart, low-risk way for us to grow.

When we negotiated the contract with Univac, no one from their team mentioned anything about our financials package—FIN-MAN was about to be introduced on the HP system—so I kept my mouth shut. I figured that I didn't have enough leverage at the time to get much more for the four FINMAN modules than I was getting for MANMAN and that Univac would just want me to throw them in. I decided to hold that card in my hand to play at a later date.

As expected, when Univac began preselling the MANMAN/ V77 system, savvy customers asked for financials to be integrated into the MANMAN program. By now, however, Univac had its brochures printed, their sales training was in full swing, and their initial sales effort was under way. They were committed to MANMAN and ASK. So when they came asking for FINMAN, I had leverage on my side and was able to establish an aggressive pricing scheme for the financials. By then, too, I had changed my pricing strategy to reflect the way the mainframe guys did it. They priced software by the module rather than by the entire package. Going into the initial Univac deal, I was pricing MANMAN with its six modules at a flat fifty thousand dollars. The price I subsequently established for FINMAN's three modules was fifteen thousand per module. So the entire add-on financial package would actually bring in almost as much as the core program. Also, I didn't jump into closing the deal with Univac on the financials. Instead, figuring the financials would become more and more important and Univac would be more inclined to pay a premium to have them, I dragged my feet until they had the manufacturing program in hand and were actually installing it.

The agreement on the financials was never concluded, however. Only months after we had delivered MANMAN to Univac, the entire deal started to crumble, culminating in an eleventh-hour negotiating coup two years later that became enormously important to the success of ASK . . . and was worth many millions.

27

On the Sales Trail

In 1978 ASK's total revenues were $470,000. In 1979 they were $2,500,000. In 1980 they were $8,300,000. How did we grow nearly 1800 percent in two years? The answer is simple. We sold a lot of systems. We worked like hell. And we kept morale high.

First, we sold ourselves. We'd cut our teeth at Hughes when we didn't have a product, didn't have a track record, didn't look like a winner. Still, we'd sold Jack McNamee on our personality, our ideas, our energy, our hard work, and our commitment to his success. Three years later, with a topflight product and a growing reputation, personality, ideas, energy, hard work, and commitment counted every bit as much. The sell was the same.

Next, we worked at the grass-roots level. We were very active in local APICS and American Electronics Association chapters. We went to meetings, attended seminars, and helped out where we could. We knew that good word of mouth was our best chance for success. For example, one of our early Boston customers played poker on

Thursday nights with a number of other manufacturing VPs and told them all about MANMAN. Within a year three of his poker-playing buddies had bought ASK systems. One of those customers was Apollo, the high-flying workstation manufacturer, whose very first order was entered in through MANMAN.

In the early going, before we had a lot of regional offices, we actually found it advantageous to sell to customers from out of town. As it was, we were cherry-picking, responding to queries from all over the country, rather than concentrating our efforts in one geographical region. When a call came, we asked enough about the company to make sure they fitted our target profile, then invited them to Los Altos to see the system. If they took us up on the invitation, it was already a commitment on their part. Impressed, they flew back home, thousands of miles away—far enough so that when we installed a system, they quickly became proficient in its operation, invariably a lot quicker than the customer in our own backyard. There's an old saw that an expert is anybody more than fifty miles from his home base.

Going into a selling situation, we found out as much as we could about our potential customer. Before calling on a company, I asked for product literature and an annual report, if available. I went through the material, pulling out company buzzwords and carefully studying the "Message from the President" for lines I could use in my sales pitch. The president of Scientific-Atlanta in Georgia, for example, said in his 1977 message: "Profits weren't enough. We had to control inventory." I used the quote in my meeting with his people.

We also knew our product. Virtually every sale turned on this knowledge. One that didn't was to an Oklahoma company called Lowrance Electronics that manufactured marine depth finders. Two of us were on the sales call, I and our local rep, Van Purdy, now ASK's southern regional manager. Lowrance already had a system on a Univac machine—not MANMAN—but was extremely dissatisfied and was shopping for something better. Since Van had the good ol' boy accent and we were in his territory, he gave the presentation. Attending were the president of the company, a few VPs, and some others. They were seated at a long table, a very somber bunch. Dissatisfied or not, they looked as if they were going to be a tough sale.

I handed Van the presentation slides, forgetting there were some new ones covering our just-introduced financial software. Van zipped right through the old manufacturing part of the presentation, doing a great job until the first financial slide appeared on the screen. Though it was dark in the room, I could see him blanch. At first I was unsure why, but then, as he read the bullet points off the slide verbatim, clicked up the next, and did the same, I figured it out. It was clear he didn't know what he was talking about. But now it was too late to take over for him graciously. Instead, wishing I could crawl under the table, I just listened as he read slide after slide. When it was finally over and the lights came on, Van had a sick, hopeless smile on his face.

"Are there any questions?" he asked. Dead silence.

Finally the president, Daryl Lowrance, leaned over to Bill Elliott, the controller, and asked, "Well, do you think the system will give you what you're looking for?" I couldn't tell if he was serious or if there was a slight chuckle in his voice.

Elliott looked at Van, then me, then back to the president. "You know," he drawled, "when you're in the gutter, the curb looks great." They bought a system.

Selling as well as we did, we had to know the competition. We studied their products and their position in the marketplace. On sales calls we played down their strengths and played up their weaknesses. In describing MANMAN, I'd always stress the importance of the features we had that my competitors didn't, which inevitably sent prospects scurrying to my competitors' brochures. In making these comparisons, I rarely mentioned my competitors by name, however. I'm always amazed when someone trying to sell me something tells me who his competitors are. Usually he'll mention at least one name I haven't heard of, which I will then quickly check out. Often it's the product I'll end up buying.

The one name I always mentioned when asked who my competitors were was IBM. "Of course, there's IBM," I'd say, "but you *already* know IBM's software doesn't really compete with MANMAN." This was only partially true. IBM competed with everyone. Still, the company stoked on IBM wasn't going to buy ASK, so I had nothing to lose by mentioning them. Besides, everyone knew IBM, so I wasn't giving the prospect any new information. And by mentioning IBM's name, I'd dispel the specter of Big Blue. Of *course,* there was IBM.

We were also smart enough to sell what made the company the most money, which in our case was canned software programs. That was our company goal, and I supported it by paying a higher commission on software than hardware—except in years when I wanted to increase our revenues. Then I'd pay the same commission on both. I discouraged our sales force from selling custom programming, which was labor-intensive and slowed us down, by not paying any commission at all on it.

We also knew when to hold 'em and when to fold 'em. You hold 'em when a new guy comes in to "revamp the company." It doesn't make any difference whether the company's already got a great system; the new guy is looking to leave his mark. One of our earliest sales on the 3000, in fact, was a revamp at B. K. Sweeney in Colorado, an old-line company that made manufacturing tools for the transportation industry. They already had a system installed, but the new boss, Joe Bergeon, was intending to take the seventy-seven-year-old eight-million-dollar company and make it into a twenty-million-dollar company and was looking at anything that would get him there, and fast. ASK's MANMAN was the answer. The old system went.

You fold 'em when your competitor's major investor or brother-in-law is on the board of directors of a company you're trying to sell to. We learned this the hard way. We were pitching a company called Altos, competing head to head with an extremely aggressive newcomer called MADIC. MADIC had good salespeople, but so did we. By then we also had a large number of successful reference customers, something MADIC didn't have—and never would, crashing and burning within a few years when they'd promised more than they could deliver. Still, Altos went with MADIC. As it turned out, MADIC was largely financed by a venture capital firm called Sequoia Capital, which also had a piece of Altos. Don Valentine, the managing partner of Sequoia Capital, sat on both companies' boards.

Another major reason for our sales success was that we weren't afraid to ask for an order. I can't tell you how many salespeople I've encountered who do a fantastic job impressing the customer and presenting the product but can't close a sale. They're simply afraid to ask. Me, I'll ask at the drop of a hat or whatever it takes to get the order. A while back we were trying to wrap up a big deal with a company called Spectra Physics. The contract was for $1.8 million over a two-year period, with an initial order for $430,000—a very big deal for ASK at that time. Of course, they knew how important the sale was to us and were asking for the moon. I was trying to get them to settle for maybe just a few stars.

At about that time ASK was hosting a large party for its customers at our annual users' conference, and I invited Spectra Physics' chief financial officer, Mike Gaulke, to attend. We'd rented a robot as part of the festivities. It had a little microphone to "talk" through and a receiver to "listen" with and was controlled remotely by an operator standing inconspicuously away from the robot. We told the operator whom to accost and what we wanted the robot to say, usually semi-innocuous or funny lines about their work or their personal life, things like "Oh, I hear your wife just had a baby," or, "How's that football hero son of yours doing?" I figured we were paying for the robot, we might as well get a return on our investment. I decided to have the robot ask for the Spectra Physics order and sicced him on Mike.

Mike was a tough cookie, however. He had the perfect poker face, and when it came to business, he was in complete control, never letting on what he was thinking. So it was hard to tell how he felt about being followed around by a robot. At one point he asked the robot why he was so interested in him, and the robot replied, "I just want to get near a prospect to see what he looks like before he's a customer." Mike turned and walked away, but the robot took right off after him. It was pretty funny watching Mike, trying to be cool and businesslike with the robot hot on his trail. Finally the robot cornered Mike. "I hear Spectra Physics is going to give ASK the order," it said, to which Mike responded coolly, "We're still negotiating." This was followed by some back and forth, and then the robot said, "Well, it doesn't sound like there's a lot left to negotiate," to which Mike said, "There are still some details." Again Mike made his escape.

A little later on, however, just when Mike thought he was safe, the robot cornered him again. "Okay," it said, "I think we've discussed this deal long enough. Time to sign the contract." And out of the robot's mouth popped the contract and a pen. Mike was floored. He didn't sign that night, but three days later we got the order. Ultimately Spectra Physics purchased more than seven million dollars of hardware and software from ASK.

After closing a sale, we also gave our customers terrific service. For example, when Collins Avionics in Florida installed their system over the Christmas holidays, their goal was to have it running by the start of business on January 2. On New Year's Eve it ran into some technical problems and they called me New Year's Day at 5:30 in the morning (it was 8:30 in Florida). I didn't know the answers but figured Marty would, so I called him at 7:00 A.M. He also didn't know but thought Roger would. We waited till 8:00 to call him, but he hadn't gotten home yet from New Year's Eve festivities. We finally reached him a few hours later. He got in touch with the customer, and the problem was solved.

Another reason for ASK's sales success was that we used the goodwill we generated with our customers to get more customers. One way of doing this, unique in our industry, was to provide every prospect with a complete list of all our installations. I remember a customer once telling me, "I couldn't believe it when your salesman gave me the list and urged me to call anyone on it. I thought he was either incredibly cocky or incredibly naive." By contrast, our competitors in that deal had preselected three customers for him to call—one local, one in Maine, one in Idaho—and all three in industries totally unrelated to the prospect's. Picking and choosing from ASK's list, the prospect called a dozen similar businesses, got an idea of what we were like to work with, how to implement the system best, and what pitfalls to avoid. "It was your customers that really sold that system," he told me. Another prospect in the refrigeration business in Minneapolis contacted every single name on the list before he bought. Years later, when I was trying to impress the financial community, I'd invite him along. No one knew more about our customers than he did.

We also used our goodwill in one division of a large company to provide us entrée into other divisions of the company. That's how ASK grew at Foxboro, at General Signal, at FMC, at Emerson, at Mars, to name a few.

Finally, as part of our sales effort to grow from $470,000 to $8.3

million in two years, we motivated our customers to become cheer-leaders for ASK by showing them how important they were to us. In our lobby we created a gallery of framed photographs from the annual reports or product brochures of every ASK customer. We also held regular users' conferences that were as much fun as they were serious business get-togethers. We had seminars at which customers presented technical papers and discussed how they used the MANMAN product, and ASK talked about products in the pipeline. There were also less formal sessions for customers to exchange ideas and suggestions.

Every bit as important as motivating our customers to work for us was keeping our own team motivated. Taking our cue from HP, we had Friday afternoon beer busts and parties at the drop of a hat. And whenever possible, I'd single out employees for individual recognition.

The most successful motivational event in ASK's early history was a trip the entire company took in 1979. We'd had an incredibly good month, and Tom suggested we all go to Las Vegas for the weekend. I agreed. There were about ten of us at the time, and everyone was allowed to invite a friend, spouse, or "significant other."

A few team members, not certain whether ASK would spring for a hotel, arrived at the airport with sleeping bags. Indeed, some of our latter-day hippies had never even stayed in a hotel. All doubts were dispelled when we checked into the glitzy Caesars Palace. We spent our days in the sun, lounging around the pool, and our nights in the casinos, taking in shows and gambling. ASK picked up the entire tab and even bankrolled everyone with fifty dollars of lucky money to start him or her on a winning streak. Tom, who'd been to Vegas dozens of times, was the role model for the trip. He played high-stakes poker and ordered every exotic drink on the bar menu.

Back in Los Altos, he challenged me to commit to a trip the following year if we did eight million dollars in sales. I agreed. This time the entire company went to Puerto Vallarta—fifty-five of us in all. Almost everyone got *turista* except Tom, who could eat or drink anything. The guy was amazing.

28

In a Man's World

Tom Lavey was once asked, "What's it like working for a woman?" He paused, as if surprised by the question. "You know," he said, "I almost never think about it. I just think of Sandy as a businessperson who happens to be a woman." To me that was the ultimate compliment. I've always tried to make being a woman a nonissue. I worked hard because I wanted to succeed, not to prove I was better than a man. I never felt I was competing with anyone but myself. And I think the men whose paths I crossed respected, rather than resented, me for it. I'd also like to think that ASK never got or lost a deal because I was a woman, but that would be naive. I just hope we got more than we lost.

When I was a student, much of my world was dominated by men. I often found myself one of the few women in the group—at UCLA in math and at Stanford in aeronautical engineering. Later, when I was at GE, and then when I tramped around the country for ASK, most of the people I did business with were men. Sure, by the mid-seventies there were women in business, but rarely in the manufacturing area and rarely in the upper reaches of the management I was dealing with. And sure, there were women selling, but more often they were in inside sales, not taking the red-eye to Gary, Indiana.

While I was generally successful at making being a woman a nonissue for myself, I was aware that other women didn't have it as easy. My first face-to-face confrontation with sex discrimination came when I was working for GE. I was one of two professional women in the office. The other one was a former schoolteacher, Mary Ellen Romain. I had no complaint about my own pay—I was making as much as anyone—but Mary Ellen was doing the same work and being paid considerably less because before joining GE, she had been a teacher, a lower-paying, traditionally female-dominated job. It really rankled me. Fortunately we had an enlightened manager, Dennis Casazza, who bucked the system and gave her raises at a higher percentage than the company's suggested increases until she was at a par with everyone else.

Another experience I had cut the other way. Not long after leaving GE to go into business for myself, I got a call from a woman in a Southern California GE office, asking if I had quit the company because I'd been turned down for a two-level promotion and new position I'd been in line for. It was the first time I'd even heard I had been considered. She'd also been in line for the promotion, she said, but it had been given to a man. She was convinced it was sex discrimination and asked if I'd join her in a lawsuit against GE. When I turned her down, she was furious. I didn't know all the particulars of the case, though I eventually found out that the guy who got the job was highly qualified—certainly more qualified than I'd been at the time. Still, the assumption was that I would join up with her to slug it out with GE. Like Mary Ellen's poor pay, it rubbed me the wrong way.

Of course, there were many times I *could* have taken a stand: the hundreds of times I was asked or heard, "What's a nice girl like you doing in a business like this?" and, "Well, if you'd brought in the pretty girl when we started, we'd already have a deal," or the dozens of passes I deflected. It almost never got to me, though. And I rarely thought that taking a stand would accomplish anything other than alienate people. In fact, in the seventies, if someone called me a pretty girl, I was flattered. I didn't see it as a put-down.

Put-down or not, to most of the inane remarks I smiled and thought, "I'm soon going to have your business and your respect." As for the passes, I usually had a clever comeback, never cruel, letting the man walk away with his dignity. What it usually boiled down to was that after the guys, particularly the roll-up-your-shirt-sleeves manufacturing guys, realized I knew what I was talking about, I gained even more credibility than if I were a man. Once they recognized that I was good at what I did, they figured I was probably better than most men because of all the BS I had to put up with.

For the most part, I thought that being a woman gave me an advantage in business. If I were competing against four guys, I was the one remembered. In the barrage of phone calls received by an executive, mine was often the one that had the best chance of being returned.

An example of when being a woman worked for me was the day I was late for a meeting at ASK with Tom and a half dozen representatives of an out-of-town company we were pitching. By the time I arrived, everyone was sitting around the small conference table in Tom's office. Before Tom had a chance to introduce me, one of the guys asked me for a cup of coffee. "I'd be happy to oblige," I said, "but I'm not sure whether the coffee would be any good." At that point Tom introduced me, and the guy got all flustered and apologized. "No, no," I insisted. "I *want* to get your coffee. In fact, if you close the deal right now, I'll get you sugar. Cream? Little cookies? A pen to sign the contract? Can I make you dinner?" The way I saw it, the guy's minor faux pas immediately put us at an advantage. Not long after, they signed the contract.

Another time I made the identical mistake. Three of us, Marty, Ken Fox—our VP of R&D—and I were at a company called Britton Lee that had a data base system we were thinking of using. They had just moved into a brand-new building with all-white walls. I was sitting in the president's office, gesturing with a cup of coffee in my hand, when I sloshed most of it onto the wall behind me. Ken and Marty ran out to get some paper towels. Seconds later a woman walked in, leaned over, and said something to the president. I held up my empty cup and asked for a refill. It turned out she was the vice-president of sales and marketing, and I was quite embarrassed. We didn't use Britton Lee's system, however.

The most obvious instances of sex discrimination I see in a man's world are on the airlines. If first-class seats are unused, the gate airline agent has the prerogative to upgrade coach or business-class passengers. Invariably, if there's an upgrade available at the gate, it'll go to a man. One time Tom, Jim Manion, and I all were flying to San Francisco from New York but had arrived at JFK at different times. I was the first at the airport and asked for an upgrade. Next, Tom arrived, then Jim. The two of them were upgraded, and I flew where the airlines deemed that women belonged: a few steps and a little drape behind the men and those who paid for first class, of course. I realize that upgrading isn't a right but a gesture of good faith on the airlines' behalf. Still, I figure they should spread that good faith around to women as well as men. It's gotten better over the years, especially on United Airlines.

Working in a man's world is about more than discrimination, however. For me, particularly in the early years, it was about fear. There were dozens of times I landed at a strange airport late at night to make an eight o'clock meeting with a prospect the next morning. Manufacturing plants are usually on the outskirts of a city, and I'd spend the hours until morning at a nearby motel. To get there in ASK's leaner days, I took the airport van along with a half dozen others, almost always men. One by one we were dropped off at our destinations. For some reason, I was always last, or so it seemed. I remember one time in particular the van stopped at a huge housing project to let off a passenger. The guy told the driver he had to go upstairs to get his fare. We waited and waited. It was freezing out, so the driver kept the engine running to keep the heater on. When the passenger didn't show up with the money after ten minutes, the driver went in after him, leaving the door to the van partially open, the engine still running. A few denizens from the neighborhood peered in at us through the windows. One guy asked me to come out and spend some time with him. Without thinking, I turned the small diamond of my wedding ring—the only thing I had of value—in to the palm of my hand, leaving only the thin platinum band visible. Suddenly the door of the van flew open. It was the driver. He glared at us, as if we were the reason he'd been stiffed. Cursing, he wrenched the van into reverse and pulled back on the road. The grimy little motel I finally checked into a half hour later sure looked good.

PART IV

WORKING, GROWING

29

In a Hurry

I've always been in a hurry. On the day I was born, October 21, 1946, my mom awakened with the alarm clock. It was 7:00 A.M. "The baby's ready to be born," she told my dad.

Dad called the obstetrician, Bernice Rosen, a college friend of Mom's, and she said, "Can't be. Just tell Marian to relax, go back to bed. First babies simply don't get born that fast."

Dad looked over at Mom. "She says first babies don't get born that fast."

"Maybe not," Mom said, "but the contractions are only a couple of minutes apart."

Dad relayed the message.

"Get her in here then. And fast!"

We made it to the delivery room just in time. Like catching a plane with Tom Lavey.

Early in 1980, when it was clear that ASK was going to grow faster and larger than even I had hoped, I was in a hurry again—this time to augment my part-time board of advisers with a full-time board of directors. I thought I had to find very skilled and seasoned people to help steer ASK through this dynamic but potentially treacherous period in our growth. ASK was a real business now, and a valuable one. We all could feel it. Even Howard Klein, the most irreverent of us, took down the ASK stock certificates and stock options he'd pinned to the company bulletin board and used for dart practice.

The first person I asked to be on my board of directors was Paul Ely. Right or wrong, I'd always blamed Ed McCracken, not Paul, for the HP deal's souring. After the three of us had our showdown, Paul and I remained friends, and I held him in the highest regard. In fact, years later, after Paul had left HP, I finally convinced him to become an ASK director. In 1980, however, he turned me down. He believed that ASK's OEM relationship with HP could create a conflict of interest. But he gave me two other names to call.

The first was Ken Oshman, the CEO of Rolm, a highly successful Silicon Valley company. Oshman and three others had founded Rolm in 1969 to build fail-safe minicomputers for the military, a lucrative, but limited, niche market. When Rolm's sales hit three million dollars five years later, Oshman convinced the team to invest one million to diversify into building microprocessor-based telephone exchanges, putting Rolm in the office automation business, where they quickly became a major player. When I called Ken in 1980 to ask him to be on my board, he was gracious but said he wasn't interested. I convinced him to meet with me anyhow, to introduce myself. Perhaps, too, he'd hear me out. The soonest he could make it was in a month.

The second name Paul had given me was Burt McMurtry, a director of a company called Triad. Triad sold an inventory management system to automotive parts distributors, so they were in the same type of business as ASK, though not a competitor. Paul said that Triad's history was similar to ASK's and that Burt had guided the company through the same critical period ASK was about to go through. Burt sounded ideal for the board, and when I called, he seemed eager to get together.

We met for lunch a few days later. Burt was a tall man who stood straight as a stick. He had thinning gray-white hair. I told him about ASK and showed him our numbers. When I finished, he set his fork down. "I think that's all very interesting," he said, "and if these numbers are accurate, I'd like to invest in the company."

"What do you mean, you'd like to invest in the company? We don't need any money." In fact, by this time we had a lot more cash than we needed. We had two million dollars in the bank, and with sales going so well, I couldn't imagine needing more cash than we could generate internally.

Burt gave me a quizzical look. "I'd love to go on your board, Sandy, but venture capitalists don't have a lot of time. So unless I can invest in the company, it really wouldn't be appropriate for me to be a board member."

For a few embarrassing seconds I didn't get it. Paul hadn't actually described Burt's role at Triad, only that he had guided the company through challenging times. Still, I didn't know how to respond to Burt's revelation that he was a venture capitalist because back then I was so out of everything but my own small world that I honestly knew very little about how a venture capitalist operated. All around me, I knew, companies were starting up, but since ASK had never needed money—other than the twenty-five thousand dollars my father had lent me—I'd never bothered to learn much about how others got their financing.

Nevertheless, the notion of people like Burt volunteering their expertise and money was an interesting new wrinkle. "Well, how much money would you like to invest?" Burt appeared pleased by the question. We were back on track.

"No less than a half million dollars. But I'd prefer something more—like a million."

"Wait a minute! You want to give me a million dollars? In cash? What do I have to give you?"

"In exchange for the million dollars, you'll give me stock."

"Hold it. Two years ago my own father wouldn't take ASK stock for the twenty-five thousand dollars I owed him. Now you want to give me a million dollars? For stock?" The concept of a stranger offering me money was totally foreign to me. We hadn't gotten to that chapter yet at Harvard.

Now it was Burt's turn to be embarrassed. Aside from offering strange women scads of money, he was quite charming, a humble man. "Yes," he said, averting his eyes, "well, that's my business."

I pressed on. "How much stock?"

"About twice as much as if you went public."

"Went 'public'?" We hadn't gotten to that chapter either. Knowing what I do now, I can't believe I was so naive, but I was.

Burt spent the rest of our lunch explaining the process. He told me about how venture capitalists—or VCs—operated, how VCs spotted a "good" company. Most important, he told me that a good company—and he put ASK into that category—would never have any trouble finding money. "A *very* good company, however," he went on, "wants more than money from venture capitalists. It wants their contacts, their insights, their background . . . and their time. Constructive time. And that's what I have the least of." He knew that I didn't need his money and that I'd be a fool to take it. I'd have to look elsewhere for a board member. But before I did, I made a major detour.

Now that Burt had planted the seed, I was convinced that the next logical step to making ASK a better company, the next challenge for me personally, was to take ASK public. On my way back to the office I stopped at the library for a book on initial public offerings (IPOs). I checked out the only one the library had—actually a loose-leaf binder—and read it from cover to cover. What I learned supported my conviction. As a public company ASK would have greater credibility and status, enabling it to compete better with the big boys for business and employees. Plus it would give greater liquidity and meaning to my stock and the stock and stock options I'd already given to ASK employees.

I also learned that ASK was a particularly strong candidate for going public, that we were what the investment community saw as a "good" company and a "clean" deal: good, because we would soon be a ten-million-dollar business with a sought-after product, in a growing market with a number of years of solid earnings under our belt; clean, because we had lots of cash, no debt, no venture capital, phenomenal growth—all from retained earnings—and no hidden skeletons in our financial closet.

Over the next few days I also did a quick study on investment bankers, the firms that handled IPOs and corporate financing. Basically I learned that investment bankers made millions for handling your deal and that certainly most of the first-and second-tier companies, of which there were about a dozen, were equally qualified to take you public. So why, I wondered, when you're a good, clean company like ASK, do you choose to dump your millions into one investment banker's pocket rather than another?

I saw four reasons. One, your investment banker sets the price of the company's stock. Even in a small offering, a dollar-per-share difference can quickly mount into the millions. Too low a price means less money for the company. Too high a price can result in too few buyers and in buyers' losing money when the stock price tumbles to where it should have been priced. A good investment banker, then, understands your company and its value and has contacts with the right potential investors for your kind of company.

Two, the commission you pay your investment banker is negotiable, though usually in the vicinity of 7 percent. The smaller the offering, the higher the commission.

Three, some investment bankers are genuinely interested in your business and try to do what's best for you, while others are in it only for the deal.

And four, some investment bankers will have a business philosophy you're comfortable with. Others won't.

Call it Kismet—I call it Burt McMurtry—but not a week after our lunch, I got a call from the manager of the San Francisco office of L. F. Rothschild, Unterberg and Towbin, the New York-based investment banking firm that had taken Triad public a few years back. We met, and a few days later she invited Tom Lavey and me to attend a presentation to the San Francisco financial community by a company Rothschild was taking public called Auto-Trol Technology—a road show she called it.

L. F. Rothschild, Unterberg and Towbin, incidentally, was a relatively new entity that had been formed by the merger of the brokerage firm of L. F. Rothschild and the investment banking firm of Unterberg and Towbin, founded by C. E. Unterberg and Belmont Towbin. As a brokerage L. F. Rothschild, with nearly a thousand employees, focused primarily on retail sales of stocks and bonds, while Unterberg and Towbin were financial deal makers, though on a much smaller scale, with only about sixty employees. By the time Rothschild got to me, the company was being run by C. E. Unterberg's son, Tommy, and Belmont Towbin's younger brother, Bob. Both men were in their mid to late forties.

A day before the Auto-Trol road show, I had lunch with Paul Ely to tell him of my plan to go public. He was amused when I told him my reasons. "You've forgotten the most important one," he said, "or at least the most personal. If you stay private or just sell the company, very few people will know about your success, or they'll think it was just a fluke. But once you're a public company in the public eye, everyone will know. Everyone will know everything. And you'll be evaluated on the same scale as every other public company."

While studying and asking about IPOs, all I heard was about men taking companies public. It was the macho thing to do, men measuring themselves against other men. Why not women, too? At that point no other woman had ever taken a high-tech company public. In fact, very few women had ever taken *any* company public, as I soon discovered. Being the competitor that I was, I thought, "Sure, I'd like to compete in this league."

When the Auto-Trol road show came to town, Tom Lavey and I were there. Auto-Trol was in the final stage of going public and had already been on the road for a week, selling themselves in major national and international markets. Preceding their formal presentation was a forty-five-minute cocktail party where institutional investors—mutual fund managers, insurance company, college endowment fund and pension fund representatives, etc.—rubbed elbows with stock analysts and Auto-Trol's executives and investment bankers. While the cocktail party had the veneer of suits and ties and good manners, it was actually a frantic information-gathering session, with every investor trying to ferret out the scuttlebutt that would help reveal whether Auto-Trol was the next DEC or the next Itel.

In the midst of this maelstrom was a guy who stood out precisely because he didn't appear interested in talking to anyone. He was a fairly tall, distinguished-looking man with a drink in one hand, winding his fingers through a few strands of his hair with the other. He seemed separate from the entire scene. It was Tommy Unterberg. When Tom Lavey and I were introduced to him, I was immediately struck by how shy Tommy suddenly became. He refused to make eye contact. He looked down at the floor while we talked. I noticed he wasn't wearing a belt.

After cocktails the entire crowd was escorted into a large room for an hour and a half presentation by Auto-Trol's executives. It was slick, complete with color slides, and a number of different speakers: the CEO, the CFO, the VP sales. Halfway through, I was struck by how obviously important this particular part of the going public exercise was. Sure, investors bought on the numbers, but they also bought on an image or perception of the company. If there were like numbers, it seemed, the difference between a good offering and a great one was in the presentation skills of the company's executives. The idea both intrigued and intimidated me. I was pretty good in a small group. But a group this size with millions of dollars on the line?

Afterward we met with Tommy at Rothschild's San Francisco office. He'd clearly studied up on ASK and knew what we were about. I was amazed by how well he knew our financial numbers, our product, our market and was impressed by the thoughtfulness of his questions. "If you'd like to go public," he said in closing, "we'd like to do the deal. Why don't you come to New York and see our operation?"

Immediately after attending Auto-Trol's road show, we began getting calls from other investment bankers. The word was out about ASK. Everyone, it seemed, wanted to get together—"just to talk." The only company that didn't seem to want to talk was Hambrecht and Quist, H&Q, the hotshot regional investment banking firm that had handled virtually all the offerings in the Silicon Valley, Intel and Tandem Computers being two notable exceptions whose offerings were sole-managed by Rothschild. In the hot high-tech market of the late seventies and early eighties, almost everyone going public in the Valley did well, and H&Q had developed the reputation of being *the* road to take to overnight millions.

Actually, the most common road taken was to have H&Q co-manage the offering with a larger East Coast brokerage. But it was H&Q that got the press in California; it was H&Q whose name was magic. However, H&Q hadn't called me yet to talk about the ASK offering, and my calling it would compromise any leverage I might have in negotiating commissions. Still, I felt I should have some contact with H&Q, so I asked Gary Harmon, one of my board of advisers who knew Bill Hambrecht, to let him know of ASK's intention to go public. Finally, right before I left for New York to visit Rothschild, Hambrecht called. I was cool on the phone but agreed to get together when I returned.

Rothschild's reception area on the twenty-sixth floor of 55 Water Street, just a block from the New York Stock Exchange, was nothing to get excited about: some paintings on the wall, a small reception desk, and a constant flow of people tramping through from one wing of Rothschild's offices to the other. Not what I'd expected from what at that time was a major investment banking firm. "Another day, another office, another meeting," I thought. "No big deal. No need to be nervous." Still, I was. I wasn't a New Yorker; I wasn't used to the crowds or to the push. "No need to be nervous," I repeated.

Seconds later, however, on my way to Tommy's office, I found myself on Rothschild's trading floor—the bullpen, as it was called, an enormous room with windows on two sides, probably five hundred desks, and at least that many people. Papers were piled everywhere, phones were ringing, teletypes clacking, men and women jumping up and screaming, "Do I have a sale for Intel?" or, "IBM's up a quarter!" Then, piercing the din, came an announcement blaring from a half dozen loudspeakers: "We're doing a Tandem offering this week, and it should go at sixty-six and one-half." Everywhere men and women were frantic, their collars open, their ties at half-mast and perspiration flowing. They looked as if they'd been at it for days. It was 10:00 A.M.

Tommy shared an office with his partner, Bob Towbin, at the far corner of the bullpen. While fairly small, the office had a panoramic view of New York Harbor. Tommy's desk was stacked with papers. On Bob's desk were dozens of miniature company prospectuses that had been shrunken down to the size of large postage stamps and encased in Lucite—his trophy case. Bob was out of town, however. Tommy was in his shirt sleeves; still no belt. "Hi, how are you?" he said. We shook hands. Then Tommy took me around to meet some of the others.

I'd come to New York via a short ski trip to Colorado, so I looked like the figure of health, with a great tan except for white circles around my eyes where I'd worn goggles. Actually I looked like a raccoon. Coincidentally the first person Tommy introduced me to, Mel Lavitt—the Rothschild managing director in charge of marketing—had similar markings. "Where'd you ski?" he asked even before Tommy finished my introduction.

"Aspen," I said, and we started chatting about the merits of Colorado versus Utah skiing.

I was just relaxing when Tommy, who'd been standing and listening for all of a minute, said, "Enough, let's get back to business." Tommy, as I'd later learn, was a man of very few words. Story had it that at a company Christmas party he once gave a speech to all his gathered employees. "Happy holidays," he said.

Later we had lunch in a small executive dining room, and Tommy and his people continued the line of excellent questioning that Tommy had begun in California. But I was only half listening. So much of me was still a kid, thrilled to be there, thrilled to think that at some point ASK's name would be the one flashing on Rothschild's bank of computers, that it would be our offering announced over the loudspeaker.

30

Too Soon

The day after I visited Rothschild, I went to Kidder, Peabody, another New York-based investment banking firm. While I liked what I had seen at Rothschild and was impressed by Tommy, I felt I owed it to myself and ASK to check out at least a few more investment bankers. The meeting at Kidder had been set up by Larry Sonsini, a senior partner at ASK's law firm.

Surprisingly, Kidder's operation was nothing like Rothschild. In place of a single large, incredibly loud, and active bullpen, Kidder had a number of minipens, each with its own wall of monitors tracking different stocks. There were about twenty brokers or less to a room, and they had their ties snugged to their collars. The decibel level was way down, too. Unlike Tommy's and Bob Towbin's Spartan office at the end of the bullpen, the Kidder executives' wood-paneled, elegant offices weren't even on the same floor as the trading action. Also, the men *and* the women looked as if they'd just stepped out of Brooks Brothers. They all wore belts, their pinstripes were lined up from head to toe, and their faces were well scrubbed and eager.

The Kidder people I spoke with were bright and affable, but the questions they asked were perfunctory. They'd read the material I'd forwarded and showed a good grasp of the financials, but they didn't seem to know a lot about software. While this was understandable—a software company going public in 1980 was still a little-known quantity—I thought that if Kidder had wanted us to put ourselves in its hands, it should have made more of an effort to find out what ASK did and what its prospects were. On Kidder's side, it had layers and layers of good, smart people, while the show at Rothschild seemed to be run by Tommy, Bob Towbin, and just a few overworked others.

Beyond these primarily superficial impressions, the most important thing I learned about Kidder was that they believed in taking advantage of what they called windows of opportunity and that *now* was the time for ASK to go public. Tommy, on the other hand, believed that a good company could always do a successful deal.

On the plane back to California, I pretty much decided to go with Rothschild, though I had yet to talk to Hambrecht and Quist about the possibility of their co-managing the deal, the *pro forma* way of doing Silicon Valley offerings. The next day I called Bill Hambrecht and said, "I've been to New York to see Rothschild, and I really like them," the implication being that if H&Q wanted a piece of the action, they'd better get on down here. The way I saw it, if they really wanted the business, Hambrecht could have come, Quist could have come. Instead, they sent a guy named Roy Rogers.

Secure in the knowledge that every company going public in the Silicon Valley was using H&Q at least to comanage their offerings, Roy ambled into my office. He was very tall, lanky, casual in a studied way. He maneuvered his frame down into a chair across from me. "Normally," he said, his voice coming from some big, important place, "normally the way we do these things is we invest in you with our venture capital group, give you some money, and maybe in six months or a year after we get to know you, we take you public."

In other words, H&Q first wanted a chunk of our stock at a relatively low prepublic price in exchange for venture capital, or mezzanine financing, as it was called. They'd also probably ask for a seat on our board of directors. Then, as a board member or at least a shareholder, they'd use their leverage to assure their selection as investment bankers. So when you went public in the superheated market of 1980, H&Q would make money on the deal as well as on their investment. It was greedy, and right off the bat, it antagonized me. It may also have explained why H&Q was so slow to call on us. One look at our financials, and it was clear we weren't after a sugar daddy with venture capital.

His introductory piece of business out of the way, Rogers started bad-mouthing Rothschild: how they'd let you down in the crunch, how when their deals went sour, they hightailed it back to New York City. It seemed precisely the wrong thing to say since I'd already made it clear to Hambrecht I was impressed with Rothschild and the best H&Q could hope for was a comanagement position. If I had been Rogers, I would have talked up how well H&Q and Rothschild had worked together on the deals they'd done.

I listened courteously to the rest of his spiel and decided that I didn't care if everyone else in the Valley was letting H&Q comanage his or her deal. I wouldn't. Rogers was an open book. He walked into the room trying to make me feel that I'd missed the boat for not letting H&Q get a larger piece of the action, then bad-mouthed his competitor. He told me everything I didn't want to hear.

Five minutes after Rogers left my office, I called Tommy to tell him I'd decided I didn't want H&Q as a co-manager but wanted Rothschild to handle the entire deal. If Tandem Computers and Intel could have Rothschild as their sale manager, so could ASK. Our conversation was short. Tommy said he was extremely pleased.

Not an hour later Tommy got a phone call from Rogers. "Well, I guess you know we'll be working with you on this ASK deal—" Roy began.

"Oh, is that the case?"

Tommy realized I hadn't told H&Q yet of my decision to go solely with Rothschild and felt it wasn't his place to break the news to them. Still, he must have left Rogers with the impression that H&Q's co-managing the ASK offering wasn't really a done deal because the next phone call about the matter came from Hambrecht, asking me what I'd decided. I told him I was going with Rothschild as sole manager. Hambrecht insisted I needed a "regional presence." I said I didn't think so.

Next thing, Hambrecht called Tommy and harangued him for bad-mouthing H&Q to me. Tommy told Hambrecht that he'd never done any such thing, that ASK had made a choice on its own. Hambrecht responded that Tommy should go back and tell me that Rothschild didn't do deals in the Silicon Valley solo, that they only co-managed deals with H&Q. I guess Hambrecht's assumption was that I was a dummy over whom Tommy wielded enormous power.

Sometime later I got a call from Tommy to clear the air. He told me that Hambrecht had accused him of bad-mouthing H&Q, and he just wanted to make sure I didn't think that was the case. After all, H&Q was involved in a lot of business in the Valley, and Tommy didn't want to close the door on any future deals with them by antagonizing Hambrecht. "Ha!" I said. "I'll tell you what clinched the deal. It was that cowboy coming down here and bad-mouthing *you.*"

I soon found that in the world of high finance it ain't over till it's over. In the time between my decision to go with Tommy and the actual offering, I was invited to a number of conferences sponsored by other investment bankers or to listen to companies about to go public give their presentations. I felt I could learn from watching others and accepted. At one such conference given by Alex Brown, a major old-line investment banking firm out of Baltimore, I was wined and dined and given the full-court press to dump Tommy and go with them or at least co-manage with them. When it was obvious I wasn't going to desert Rothschild, one of the Alex Brown honchos came up to me and said, "We've decided that we're going to do your deal. Unterberg owes us, and we're calling in a chit."

"Excuse me," I said. "That's nice, but do I have any say in this?"

With the public offering scheduled for October 1980, only a few months away, I now had to hustle to assemble a board of directors. The first place I turned was to my existing board of advisers: Dave

Leeson, the CEO at California Microwave; Craig Johnson, our lawyer; Gary Harmon, the finance VP from Avantek; and most recently, Ron Braniff, a Tymshare sales executive who'd taken Wally Silver's place. Sadly, Wally had died of cancer the previous year.

I thought that Craig would be an excellent director, representing our legal interest, and asked Ron to stay on because of his experience in our industry. I would have also liked Dave Leeson to stay on, but he told me he didn't have the time to be a director of a public company.

The only difficult decision was who would represent the financial side. I wanted Gary Harmon on the board. He was a sharp financial mind whose help as an adviser had been invaluable. I also wanted Tommy on the board, though I hadn't asked him yet. I liked and trusted him and wanted to avail myself of his expertise after the offering was complete. In the interest of keeping the board small and productive, however, I felt I couldn't ask them both. In the end, I decided to go with Tommy—*if* he would accept. He sat on very few boards, so I figured I'd probably have to talk him into it.

Once I had decided I wanted Tommy on the board, I couldn't let the idea go until I had his answer. It ended up taking days. He was out of the office or I was, and we never seemed to connect. I finally reached him from a pay phone at a gas station. "Now, Tommy, don't say no until you hear me out," I said. "I want you to be on our board. . . ." He said he'd be flattered to. No arguments, no discussion, no "I'll think it over." An immediate yes. I was delighted.

My pick to take Dave Leeson's place was Ken Oshman from Rolm. He'd already turned me down on the phone a month before. But everyone I mentioned his name to said Ken would be perfect. Besides, he had the reputation of being a guy whose judgment calls were right 98 percent of the time. I would have been happy with 75 percent. So armed with a battery of convincing arguments, I went to my appointment with him at Rolm. Still, I was less than optimistic.

Working with HP, I'd grown accustomed to nice buildings and pleasant landscaping, but nothing could have prepared me for Rolm. The campus was terraced with ponds, waterfalls, winding paths, and verdant little nooks. While the buildings were obviously brand-new with large expanses of glass, they managed to appear very solid and established, not at all like the "tilt-up" buildings that were popping up all over the Valley. Rolm also had a gym, a basketball court, a racquetball court, and an indoor/outdoor pool.

Ken's office was enormous, with a huge walnut desk on which a photo of his wife and children was displayed. He stood to greet me. He was about forty and was short and slight, an impression exaggerated by the size of his office. "Can I get you an espresso?" he asked. An espresso? This was definitely a first.

"Sure," I said. I followed him to the little kitchenette adjoining his office and watched as he brewed my drink. When I asked him to be on my board, much to my surprise, he agreed. I don't really know why, but I wasn't about to ask what changed his mind or why I was so lucky.

"But I will be tough, and I will be honest," he warned. That was fine with me. It was exactly what I wanted. We shook on it. Quite unexpectedly I had my full board.

A few weeks later I returned to Harvard for my third and final session. By the second session, the year before, it was clear that ASK was taking off. Now, June 1980, ASK was growing faster than any of my classmates' enterprises. While there was still plenty of basic material for me to digest, my real interest was in talking to classmates who had taken their companies public. What were the pitfalls? What was it like in the public eye? What lessons would I still have to learn?

In midsummer ASK had its first full board of directors' meeting. The major item of business was to approve the plan to go public. I had written a draft prospectus and was prepared to discuss and defend every fact and number in it. It was to be an all-day meeting, with the morning devoted to discussing ASK's R&D program, and the afternoon the public offering. Tommy had a long-standing commitment and couldn't make the meeting, so he sent a guy from Rothschild's San Francisco office. Tommy's stand-in was in his mid-fifties and during lunch told me that he jogged every morning, rain or shine. The afternoon meeting was held in ASK's boardroom, a comfortable, pleasant, well-ventilated space. Still, the morning's jog must have done Tommy's surrogate in. As I was running through the numbers—quite brilliantly, I thought—he started to snore. It made me angry, but I was determined to press on. Everything else that day was falling into place perfectly.

That night we all had dinner at a local restaurant to cast our votes to go public and then to celebrate. The "sleeper" had gone home, and Tommy now joined us. It was a slightly raucous, comfortable, clubby crowd. The only one not sharing in the hilarity was Ken Oshman. Throughout the meal he appeared distracted and chewed his food very, very slowly, as if something were stuck in his teeth. Finally, after dessert, when the good times and laughter were at their peak, Ken puffed slowly on his cigar, took his napkin from his lap, folded it carefully, and laid it on the table in front of him. "You can go public if you want to go public. Everyone else is going public." There was not another sound at the table. I leaned back, put my wineglass down. Ken went on. "I know you want a unanimous vote, and I'd be willing to resign from the board. But I simply don't think ASK is ready to go public at this time." He turned to me. "Sandy, you just don't *need* to do it. You control the stock; you've got people begging to give you money. Why go public? Most important," Ken went on, "I don't think you're ready. You don't have the management team; you've barely got the sales. My recommendation is to wait."

Wait? I was crestfallen. What about the superheated market? How long would that last? And what about all the work I'd already done? And what about, what about . . . the goddamn windows of opportunity? But I didn't say any of it. I remained outwardly calm, though holding back tears. I was so damn frustrated. Quietly, in a voice that seemed to belong to someone else, I asked the others at the table what they thought. Tommy admitted to a slight conflict of interest but said, yes, he could see Ken's point. The others concurred. I told them I'd give it some thought.

That night when I got home, I was disappointed and angry. A few months back I'd set my mind on going public, taking that next step. Still, I had quickly grown to like and admire Ken, and more significant than that, I trusted his judgment. I believed the good PR on him and had seen what he'd accomplished at Rolm. Indeed, the more I thought about what Ken had said, the more I saw his point.

Sure, we could have made the offering and done well. But Ken was right. We didn't have a strong enough management team, we didn't need the money, and just concluding an eight-million-dollar-plus year, we were shy of the ten million recommended for going public. Early the next morning I called Tommy to tell him I'd decided to delay the offering.

The punchline didn't come until later that morning. The prior day the "sleeper" and I had made a plan to meet for breakfast to discuss the details of the offering. By the time I'd decided to delay the offering, it was too late to cancel, so I showed up for the breakfast bright and early, a little hung-over and very unhappy. When he started discussing the timetable for the offering, I interrupted him and said we had decided to put it off. He gave me a really thoughtful look, as if he'd been thinking the very same thing. "You know," he said, "you've made the right decision. Your numbers simply weren't that good, and I think—" My numbers? How the hell would he know? The guy had been fast asleep. And in fact, the numbers were outstanding.

31

A Stronger Team

Many companies with eight million dollars in annual revenues are selling thousands of items and have hundreds of employees. ASK, however, was selling a two-hundred-thousand-dollar-plus product, and by the end of June 1980 we had sold a total of only 160 systems and had just thirty-nine full-time employees. Of those employees, fourteen were in sales and field service in our New York, Chicago, Boston, and Southern California offices. So the home team in Los Altos was still small, the ASK family intimate. Up to 1980 the collective thinking was that we'd continue to thrive and that early team members like Marty Browne, Roger Bottarini, Liz Seckler, and Howard Klein would rise to the top of the organization. Until Ken Oshman rained on my parade, I believed that, too. Sure, I needed a Tom Lavey to head the sales effort. But Marty could always handle R&D, and I could always handle the finanaces.

Yet after careful consideration, these two areas were precisely where ASK needed more experienced management. I was a good negotiator, I knew the value of a dollar, and I could now read a profit and loss statement. But I was hardly the strong financial mind a fast-growing company like ASK had to have, the type of person who, when faced with a multimillion-dollar commitment or a million-dollar problem, knew exactly when to say yes or no and could support that decision with numbers.

In the R&D area Marty's strength lay in applications. He knew software, and more than anyone else at ASK, he was responsible for making our product user-friendly. But he didn't know hardware, nor was he a recruiter of top talent—skills I knew ASK would require in order to reach the sixty-million-dollar goal I'd set for the company by 1984 and the hundred-million-dollar mark by 1986.

In fall 1980 I decided to build the management team Ken Oshman had chided me for lacking. ASK needed a chief financial officer and an R&D vice-president. Whereas in the past I'd hired most of my team right out of school, I was determined in this instance to hire people who knew more and were more experienced managers than I.

I knew of Ken Fox from HP, where he was the head of the R&D team for the HP 21MX/1000, although I hadn't worked with him. He had an excellent reputation. He knew what he was doing, his people liked working for him, and he had an outstanding technical knowledge of both hardware and software. In a company of topflight people, Ken stood out: He was feistier and had a better sense of humor than his peers. Also, he had the grit and the imagination of an entrepreneur. I wanted him as our R&D VP. Through my contacts I'd heard he'd accepted a job at Rolm a year earlier, but HP had talked him out of leaving. I figured that meant he wasn't a lifer but would move on if the right offer came along.

I arranged to meet Ken for lunch on a Saturday, so I'd have plenty of time for my pitch. Beyond the obvious sell of the company, the team, and the employment "package," I mentioned that Ken Oshman, whom I knew Ken Fox held in high regard, was on our board. The clincher, however, as Ken tells it, was that I pointed out the time was now or never for leaving HP. As an eleven-year veteran he was at his peak value to other companies. Much longer on the job, and he'd be perceived as being too ingrained in the HP corporate culture to make it anywhere else. True or not, he seemed to buy it. Before lunch was over, I made him an offer.

Once again HP tried to talk him out of leaving. His boss, my old pal Ed McCracken, even went so far as telling him that ASK wasn't going to make it and that HP would bury us with their own recently developed manufacturing system for the 3000. Telling Ken, who loved to rise to a challenge, that ASK would fail was precisely the wrong move by Ed. That day Ken accepted the job.

Ken had first arrived at HP in 1969 sporting a Fu Manchu mustache, granny glasses, long hair, and a tie-dyed T-shirt. By the time he got to us, however, he was thirty-five, drove a Mercedes, owned a sailboat, and wore expensive Italian suits and Gucci loafers. Though ASK had graduated from sandals and Birkenstocks, we had yet to go "designer." So I was truly panicked on Ken's first day at ASK when he cruised into the parking lot in his Mercedes, fastidiously drew on his suit coat, pulled a car cover out of his trunk, and covered his car. A bunch of the R&D people were glued to the windows like kids.

My panic extended beyond Ken's image. He was the second vice-president I'd sprung on Marty in as many years. There'd be another before too long. Even more difficult for Marty to take, I knew, was that as vice-president of software development—Marty's new title— he'd be reporting to Ken, not me. Ken had accepted my offer on Friday, and now it was Monday. Over the weekend I'd talked to Marty, told him ASK needed Ken to help us grow to the hundred-million-dollar mark. Marty seemed to take it in stride at the time, but I knew that once it had sunk in, I ran the risk of losing him. But it was too late to worry. Ken dusted off his suit, checked his reflection in the gloss of a nearby car, then made his way to the lobby.

Fortunately Ken quickly fit right in. While Tom Lavey was known as the Suit for months after his arrival, Ken's low-key style and his dry, easy humor almost at once ingratiated him with us all. Also, he was the perfect complement to Marty, and after a few tense weeks Marty was astute enough to realize it. Like it or not, we were no longer kids camping out at HP.

The leading candidate for the CFO job was Bob Riopel. He'd been recommended by Arthur Young & Company, a major accounting firm that was vying for ASK's business. Bob was a former CPA with a solid manufacturing background and was currently working for a high-tech start-up called Advanced Electronic Design that looked as if it might not make it. Still, getting Bob to come on board turned out to be a tricky proposition. For starters, he thought the software industry wouldn't be a challenging place to work. Also, though he was only thirty-seven, he was a little more old-fashioned than the rest of us. He couldn't imagine what it would be like working for a woman; he was concerned what his peers would say and was unsure whether to carry my briefcase, pull out my chair, or hold doors for me. After we'd interviewed him—he was a slightly bookish-looking guy with a mischievous smile and a relatively conservative yet still aggressive view of how a company should grow—Tom, Ken, and I agreed he was our man. I offered him the job the morning after the meeting. He turned me down. I gave him my sales pitch, but it didn't work.

Fair enough. I can take rejection. Still, I thought I owed a courtesy call to Arthur Young, just to let them know that the man they'd spoken of so highly had decided to look elsewhere. I also called Larry Sonsini, at Wilson, Sonsini, who was another of Bob's references, and told him the same thing. Finally, I called Bob's third reference, his mentor, John Rado from Reticon, and repeated the story. Evidently my innocent courtesy calls triggered an avalanche of calls to Bob, all telling him that he was making a big mistake in not taking the ASK job.

Late that afternoon I got a call from Bob, who said, "Listen, Sandy, no one's given me a new piece of data today, but I can't get anything done over here with my phone ringing off the wall. So I may as well come over there and work."

Bob was just what the doctor ordered: smart, hardworking, a good negotiator, organized, and a good friend to us all. And he was just conservative enough to keep us from spending all our millions—or our dollars and cents—in one place. Only the sales force found him too stingy (a common sales force gripe) and nicknamed him Dr. No.

At the same time I was strengthening my team, however, ASK lost two key players. By the time Ken and Bob joined ASK in 1981, Jim Bensman, our L.A. rep, was the only one selling for ASK who wasn't directly employed by the company. As a rep Jim was still in business for himself and doing a good job for us in L.A. When his contract with us expired, we could have stopped selling to him, brought in our own sales force, and ostensibly closed him down. Instead, I offered to buy out his company and make him a regional sales manager, putting him on a salary and commission plan. That was fine with him, but he didn't want cash for his company; he wanted stock. By that time the tide had turned, ASK had been conservatively valued at a worth in excess of twenty million dollars, and everyone wanted a piece of the action. Jim and I had agreed on the value of the stock and his business, and we were about to close the deal when I made the decision to delay the offering. This was initially okay with Jim, but then he got suspicious. Was I trying to put something over on him? Why wouldn't I go public if I could? So he asked that I guarantee the value of the stock and that if the value declined over the next twelve months, I'd make up the difference. "Jim," I told him, "we're all betting on the come. No one else has a guarantee. I can't give you one." Again I offered him cash. He wanted the stock for its upside potential, yet he refused to take the downside risk.

He turned down the offer, spirited away Gene Cranford, the manager of our direct sales office in Orange County, and set up shop as a competitor under the name Western Data Systems—not on an HP machine but on DEC. They secured a chunk of venture capital and hired some technical people to develop their own software. But it didn't work out. Both Jim and Gene were good salesmen, but neither was a manager. Also, they didn't get along with each other in this new working relationship. After a few months they split up. Jim stayed on at WDS but had trouble getting the product off the ground. Venture capitalists are not known for their patience, and it wasn't long before they hired a new CEO. Jim lost control of his own company.

In quitting ASK before we went public, Gene gave up his stock options, which were worth quite a bit. And Jim turned down a good deal and a good job that would have netted him millions. The irony was that when we finally went public, the stock was worth substantially more than the guaranteed price Jim wanted. It's not a happy story, and I relate it only as a cautionary tale about mistrust, misjudgment, and missed opportunity. As well as ASK has done, I think we would have done even better with Jim and Gene on our team.

32

ASK Nets
a Winner

ASK drove into the eighties with a tremendous head of steam, and by 1981 we were as well positioned as any company in the country to capitalize on the multibillion-dollar manufacturing software systems market. Just as we were hitting our stride, however, a recession hit and interest rates soared into the high teens and higher. Manufacturing companies became unusually cost-conscious and were putting off any major capital expenditures until interest rates dropped and the economic climate was healthier. Decisions to buy turnkey systems were put on hold, and with it, some of ASK's growth potential.

What was really happening on the manufacturing software sales front was at least as much a psychological reaction by companies as a sound fiscal response. It didn't take any financial flimflam to demonstrate how MANMAN could save companies money, even if they had to borrow at inflated interest rates for the system. The system would simply pay for itself in three or four years instead of one or two. Still, many companies thought it was better to make do with the inefficient system they had or, in some cases, to turn to a time-sharing manufacturing program at a costly per minute usage charge. At the time both alternatives seemed safer to many companies than springing two hundred thousand dollars for a system of their own. The thinking was that a capital expense locked you in but that you could always walk away from an expensed item paid monthly with no lock-in. Companies were simply reluctant to make the commitment that was costliest over the near term, whether it made sense or not.

The challenge for ASK, as I saw it, was to lock these companies into ASK until the economy loosened up. We'd already put in a lot of sales time with many of these potential customers, and I was concerned that we'd lose our momentum while they waited out the recession, or worse, that when the high-interest scare blew over, they would go with more insistent competitors than ASK. Both scenarios were unacceptable. From the potential customers' point of view, I wanted to be the vendor who saved their tail when the going got tough. I wanted to get these companies using MANMAN in some way. Anything was better than sitting around.

At the same time that I was trying to protect our flank during the recession, I was considering a second business opportunity. A few years back ASK had targeted discrete manufacturing companies and divisions of larger corporations in the five- to forty-million-dollar range, with more than one hundred employees. In doing so, we were missing a potentially lucrative market of thirty thousand manufacturers doing less than five million dollars—notably, the fast-growing smaller companies doing two million dollars today and possibly ten million dollars plus tomorrow. If only there were a way of locking them in as well.

The obvious technology-rooted answer to both the problem befalling ASK because of the recession and the opportunity presented by the under-five-million-dollar company was to provide MANMAN on a time-sharing basis. But with the potential for companies to incur runaway costs, time-sharing, on the face of it, didn't appear to be the right solution.

Convinced that we could solve our problem, Tom Lavey and I brainstormed one night until 3:00 A.M. When we were through, we had developed a unique time-share model, one that charged a flat monthly fee per terminal, or port, for usage, with the only additional costs to the customer being a relatively low charge for data storage and phone connect charges. Unlike GE and Tymshare, who used expensive mainframes as the bases for their time-sharing services, we'd start with a relatively inexpensive HP minicomputer and add more minis as our time-share service grew. We already had the MAN-MAN program, so there was no software to develop. In this way, once we had X number of terminals on the machine, the rest was gravy. Tom and I dubbed our model ASKNET.

The ASKNET solution was not quite as simple as it sounded. How to make the telephone network affordable to the user brought up a number of technical and hardware challenges. There were also financial considerations, not the least of which was pricing. We didn't want to make ASKNET so affordable that customers wouldn't buy turnkey systems when the economic climate was more favorable or when they were large enough to justify the expense.

The next morning Tom and I presented our ASKNET model to Ken Fox and Bob Riopel to explore and refine from a technical and financial standpoint. The information they returned with was extremely encouraging. Ken had come up with a number of ideas of how ASKNET could be implemented. And given recent developments on the hardware front, he figured it could be accomplished for even less than Tom and I had estimated. Bob figured we could make the network available for as little as a thousand dollars per port per month and still run an extremely profitable operation, with the break-even per HP machine being about thirty ports.

From the point of view of the two-million-dollar start-up or the five-million-dollar company nervous about making a large capital expenditure, ASKNET looked very appealing: Monitors or modems could be leased through ASK or purchased outright for a few thousand dollars, and we'd provide on-site installation support. For most users average monthly charges would come to approximately fifteen hundred dollars.

After further study of the market, I presented the ASKNET package to the board. I was expecting unanimous approval. The timing was right for ASKNET, and it turned a potential problem into a business opportunity. Surely, they'd see its potential.

Surprisingly I ran into opposition to the idea. Ron Braniff, the Tymshare executive who'd taken Wally Silver's place on the board, came out strongly against time-sharing. "Setting up a network will cost you millions," he warned. "It'll burn up lots of R&D time, and you'll be looking way down the line for a good return, if at all."

Ken Oshman, also in the communications business, disagreed with Ron and concurred with Ken Fox's reasoning: Today's hardware made it far simpler and cheaper to set up a network than when Tymshare had set up its TYMNET network. Ken Fox and Ron went back and forth for a while, but finally the dust cleared, and the vote was to go with ASKNET.

ASKNET was an immediate success. And the market was even larger and more varied than we'd envisioned. Venture capitalists were recommending ASKNET to all their investments, and local start-ups were signing up for the service before they even developed their products. Companies buying turnkey systems were using ASKNET to train their people and to set up their data bases in the three months it took for HP at that time to deliver and install their hardware. And larger corporations seeking to standardize on MANMAN throughout their organizations were using ASKNET in their smaller plants.

In fact, the only problem we incurred was that fast-growing start-ups stayed on ASKNET far longer than was necessary or cost-effective for them. But they had so many other things to worry about that they didn't want the hassle of running a program in-house. Instead, they added terminals, increasing their bills from a few thousand dollars a month to twenty-five thousand dollars and more. Still, had they been on a standard time-sharing service or hired a service bureau, it would have cost them at least a hundred thousand dollars. So everyone came out a winner.

The biggest winner was ASK. Only a few months after we had installed our first terminal, ASKNET became the fastest-growing, most profitable segment of our business. Over the years ASKNET has brought in more than seventy-five million dollars in revenues, with a very small initial capital expenditure and almost no R&D effort. With ASKNET, we confronted the problems that faced us and successfully turned them to our advantage.

33

The Heart
of the Deal

In the months prior to our public offering, ASK was involved in two crucial negotiations: one, to make a deal; the other, to get out of a deal we'd already made. The deal we wanted was with DEC. The deal we wanted out of was with Univac.

To get in or out of a deal, there are four things necessary for a successful negotiation: *good sense, guts, diplomacy,* and *leverage.* You need good sense to know what to ask for, guts to ask for what you want, diplomacy to know how to ask for it, and leverage to get it. I also believe that it's important always to leave something on the table. I don't like walking away from a negotiation knowing I've taken advantage of someone. The difference in dollars between a deal that's equitable to both parties and one that's not is never worth the bad feeling. Besides, my value system says I don't have to get everything to win, and I can win without someone else losing.

For example, when ASK renegotiated its one-year OEM agreement with HP in 1978, good sense dictated I ask for deeper discounts than normal on HP's hardware. At the time we needed the higher margins to build our sales force and enhance our products. Negotiating for HP was Bill Richion; I was negotiating for ASK. In the face of HP's one-OEM-discount-fits-all policy, guts allowed me to demand a better deal. Diplomacy had me reassuring HP that a stronger ASK sales force would generate even more hardware sales for HP, improving their margins as we improved ours. My leverage was that it was clear ASK had the potential for selling more HP hardware than any other OEM.

Knowing that HP would have preferred to have ASK exclusively on their machines, or sole-sourced, early in the negotiation I'd made it clear to Bill that DEC had expressed interest in MANMAN—as they had—and that DEC had offered deeper discounts than HP—as they had, at least on some elements of their hardware system, notably the computer's central processing unit (CPU).

The resulting deal gave ASK the deeper discounts it was looking for but required us to sell a large number of systems to earn them. Also, the new OEM agreement was written for three years, rather than the standard one or two. HP figured that if we could sell that many machines, we'd have merited the deeper discount and that to do so would require all our energy, keeping us off DEC for at least three years, until 1981.

As HP had hoped, ASK had not gone to DEC in the intervening years, but we did sign a licensing agreement with Univac in 1979. By the time 1981 rolled around, the Univac deal was coming home to roost. As I mentioned earlier, the deal gave Univac the option of a perpetual exclusive to MANMAN—on any machine other than HP's—as long as Univac met fairly aggressive minimum yearly royalties. The bottom line was if Univac exercised its option, we could not implement MANMAN on DEC. More important, Univac's perpetual exclusive could diminish our value as a public company, particularly if Univac wasn't doing a good job selling the system. That, in fact, was the case.

The Univac contract was signed in 1979, and the MANMAN conversion to their machine was delivered the following spring, right on schedule. Univac was so pleased that they turned us on to their division in Germany, which wanted to use some of our setup software routines as part of their manufacturing job-scheduling software package they were developing in Europe. We didn't have to write any new code, and we were paid $315,000. We were also asked to write programs for a new Univac machine called the Chameleon, for which we were to receive an up-front payment. But the deal kept changing colors, and the program was never written. Still, by June 1980 Univac was into us for nearly a half million dollars.

By July, however, with Univac's crack sales force scouring the countryside, things started falling apart. For one thing, our sales force kept bumping into Univac's. While I'd hoped—maybe naively—that Univac would expand our sales reach, it didn't. In fact, when prospects found out that Univac's software was made by ASK, they figured, "Why buy from Univac when we can buy directly from ASK?" Surprisingly, Univac's name carried virtually no weight. Also surprising is why a company the size of Univac didn't marshal its considerable resources and just say, "MANMAN on Univac is as good as MANMAN on HP. We've got a good product. Let's go out there and sell it."

Instead, Univac sent a nasty little letter to one prospect, AM Varityper, that bad-mouthed MANMAN on HP. It was also full of glaring inaccuracies, among them the claim that "test runs by ASK Computer Systems have proven that response time throughput can be three to ten times faster with MANMAN from Sperry Univac versus HP."

Then we ran into another problem. In July 1980 I learned that Univac had months before installed a MANMAN system at Morrow Electronics in Nashville that Univac had neglected to mention, despite owing us a royalty on it. A few days later I received notification that Univac was "ready to ship" sixty-eight systems. That should have cheered me up, but Univac had yet to pay a royalty on the first system.

After that things started really deteriorating. With sixty-eight systems reputedly ready to ship, there were still no royalties and no follow-up on when or where the systems were installed. Instead, Univac began bombarding us with correspondence with lawyers' fingerprints all over it, accusing us of bad-mouthing MANMAN on the Univac machine—precisely what they themselves had been guilty of doing *in writing* about MANMAN on HP.

By late 1980, however, I was far more concerned with getting out of the Univac contract than with being their pen pal. Almost two years had passed since our initial discussions. Since then, and independent of Univac, ASK had more than quadrupled its revenues, with a fourfold increase in employees and salespeople. We no longer needed Univac, nor did we want to be beholden to them. But as long as the contract with the exclusivity clause existed, we couldn't go anywhere else except HP. Whether they knew it or not, Univac was holding us hostage. And all it would take to keep holding us through 1981, at least, was to meet a minimum royalty payment of $1,500,000, which according to our agreement, they had to come up with by July 25, 1981. If not, we were home free.

By March 1981 Univac had paid us a total of $282,500, a good chunk of money, but a long way from $1,500,000. I had no idea what had happened to the sixty-eight systems ready to ship the prior July. Giving Univac the benefit of the doubt, I assumed the number to be a rosy sales forecast that had gone south. By spring 1981 I didn't care. I just wanted out—out of the contract and, if at all possible, out of having to support the few systems Univac had installed.

By April, however, just when I thought Univac had forgotten about us, it started making noises about exercising their exclusivity option. I'd figured that for one reason or the next, they'd bombed with the system and would be happy to wash their hands of it—even taking into account what they'd already invested in marketing, promotion, and sales force education. Instead, they were saying they just had to turn the corner and sales would skyrocket. Now I was really nervous. But when April came and went and there was still no offer to exercise the option, I decided I needed a strategy of my own to get rid of both the exclusivity problem and the problem of having to support the existing ASK/Univac installations.

Good sense dictated that I extract myself from Univac altogether and that I move fast. A company Univac's size can always come up with $1,500,000. But they can't do it *quickly*. With time running out and the potential future of ASK on the line, now was not the time to be gutless.

My leverage, such as it was, was my understanding of where I thought Univac was coming from and how I could use it in my favor.

Seeing the deal from Univac's point of view, I figured they were reluctant to part with the remainder of the $1,500,000 until at least a few more systems had been installed. I also knew from their correspondence that they were under the impression they were about to sell a lot of systems and that they wanted to keep ASK involved in some capacity. So I proposed that Univac forgo the $1,500,000 payment for an *exclusive* license and instead make an additional up-front payment to ASK of $217,500—petty cash for Univac—which, added to the $282,5000 they had already paid, made for a grand total of $500,000. In exchange, Univac would have to pay only 50 percent of the royalty per system that had been agreed upon in the earlier agreement and they would get a perpetual *nonexclusive* license for MANMAN on Univac V77 machines. Again, knowing Univac wanted us involved, I also offered to provide telephone consulting for existing installations for one year.

It wasn't a bad deal from their point of view. And it was perfect from ours. Somewhat to my astonishment, layer after layer of Univac management signed off on it, and on June 16, 1981, ASK received $217,500 more from Univac and put the deal to bed. To my knowledge, Univac never sold another system.

As successful as we were with HP, and as much as I liked doing business with them, it was dangerous having HP as our sole source of computer hardware. Not only did it leave us too little leverage in dealing with them, but it left us vulnerable. They could cut our discount, for example, and undermine our whole high profit-high margin-high R&D investment strategy. So, confident that we'd somehow escape Univac, by spring 1981 we were already negotiating with a number of other minicomputer vendors with the hope of signing a second OEM agreement.

At that time there were four or five major contenders: IBM, Tandem, Data General, Prime, and DEC. We quickly eliminated IBM. For one thing, they weren't in the OEM business, and I wanted that hardware margin. But more important, they wanted control of their end users—moving them from smaller to progressively larger machines—and at the time I wasn't cocky enough, nor did I have the leverage, to convince IBM they needed ASK. Also, I thought the IBM mainframe was the wrong machine to be on at this point, and IBM didn't have a competitive, easy-to-use minicomputer offering—at least not in our estimation.

Tandem was a good company, but not well enough known, especially in the manufacturing market, and we thought we'd have to sell their name along with ours, rather than use their name as a way of opening the door to new accounts. It was a similar story at Data General. Although they were better known than Tandem at the time, their name didn't carry the class or the reputation we were looking for.

That left Prime and DEC. Of these, DEC was larger and the undeniable market leader. So we chose DEC but kept low-key negotiations going with Prime and Data General in case the DEC deal didn't pan out. We also didn't tell DEC they were our first choice until we had the contract nailed down. In this way we kept maximum leverage throughout our negotiations.

In negotiating with DEC, it was obvious they were playing with a full deck—some of the best salespeople and managers in the business. Not only did it run against DEC's grain to leave something on the table, but they wanted to take the table home. It was our job to make sure they didn't.

Fortunately, unlike HP, DEC had a lot of flexibility in their pricing. They had a street price, a list price, a discounted price, a Valentine's Day price, you name it. For a company like DEC, that made sense. HP was more accustomed to selling computers to end users than to resellers or OEMs like ASK. They were also used to selling only a few machines to each customer. In fact, I'm certain HP was more surprised by the number of machines ASK sold than we were. DEC, on the other hand, looked at ASK and saw hundreds, maybe thousands of potential sales and knew they'd make up in volume anything they'd lose by offering a deep discount. Indeed, DEC saw us as a big money-maker for them. They knew our track record with HP and wanted an OEM agreement with us as at least as much as we did with them. At one point, just to show what straight shooters they were, they even offered to fly us by DEC helicopter to Data General to make an afternoon appointment. A storm came up, and we had to go by DEC limo instead.

The major sticking point in the DEC negotiation was their data base management software, which sold for about fifty thousand dollars over and above the cost of the DEC machine. HP threw in their data base manager for free. With both DEC's and HP's hardware costing about the same, this made the DEC system about fifty thousand dollars more expensive than the comparable HP system. I told DEC that manufacturing companies were buying a solution to their manufacturing problems and in most cases didn't care what hardware they ran it on and that they wouldn't pay an additional fifty thousand dollars to be on a DEC machine. DEC conceded the problem. We went around and around. Of course, there were other issues that we played off against this one, but it always came back to this fifty thousand dollars differential—*per system.* Eager as teenagers on a date when we began our negotiation, we were getting bogged down.

So I came up with a plan. Gambling that DEC wouldn't change their data base management software, I offered five hundred thousand dollars up front for the right to make five hundred copies of their data base software—one thousand dollars apiece—renewable indefinitely for five hundred thousand dollars for each five-hundred-batch increment. It was an appealing offer from DEC's point of view. They got five hundred thousand dollars up front for a single reel of computer tape. They didn't even have to do the duplicating. In short order, we had our deal.

The true beauty of the deal became apparent only when the selling began. DEC was more popular as a supplier than even we had thought, and as it turned out, customers *were* willing to pay a premium for the data base software. We discounted it some but still managed to charge a substantial price for what cost ASK only one thousand dollars per copy.

Negotiating to buy the fifty-thousand-dollar list price data base manager for one thousand dollars on the grounds that it would make the DEC system price too high for the marketplace, and then selling it for a great deal more, might have made DEC an injured party and ASK the one that walked away without leaving anything on the table. But since the signing of the DEC OEM deal, ASK has grown to be one of DEC's largest customers.

34

Almost Grown

At about the time the Univac negotiations were drawing to a close, ASK took part in a financial conference in Monterey along with fifty or so other small nonpublic companies, seeking to show their financial wares to an audience made up primarily of venture capitalists and investment bankers. On the opening day of the conference each company gave a ten-minute minipresentation to all those attending. The audience then picked those companies it wanted to know about in greater depth. The companies selected then gave a number of hour-long seminars to interested VCs and investment bankers over the remaining two days of the conference. Seagate, a disk drive manufacturer, and ASK were by far the most sought after. Virtually every dance card had our names. We were the king and queen of the ball.

It was at this conference that I met Bob Towbin, Tommy Unterberg's partner and Rothschild's designated party animal, a part he played to the hilt. While Tommy was shy and looked at the ground when he talked, Bob Towbin was immensely sure of himself and certain you wanted to be with him. Right before my ten-minute presentation he came up and introduced himself. With blown-dry hair, elegant suit, and a perfectly ballooned pocket square, Bob was known for knowing everyone, as well as for being a ladies' man. But around me he was always the model of decorum. He sat in the first row during my presentation and taped it for no reason other than that he wanted me to have a copy. "I know you'll be a star," he said as he handed me the tape.

By July 1981 ASK was on a collision course with going public that not even Ken Oshman could prevent. Not that he wanted to. We'd met all his requirements: put together a stronger management team, increased sales 56 percent, to $13 million from $8.3 million, and strengthened our product mix as well as introduced a number of enhancements to MANMAN.

Rothschild was to do a guaranteed offering. That meant Rothschild, representing the syndicate of underwriters, committed to take and pay for all the shares in the offering at a set price, whether or not they had buyers. Rothschild also had the option of buying an additional 10 percent of the stock from us at the same initial offering price within eight days after the offering. If the stock went up after it had begun trading, Rothschild could turn a tidy profit. This was in addition to the $1,143,450 it made in discounts and commissions on the $16,335,000 stock sale.

For someone like me, accustomed to watching every penny, the cost of going public was a trip into the fiscal twilight zone. Expenses were astonishingly high. Part of what made it so expensive was that once a date was set for the offering, everything had to happen quickly. The printers ($137,500), the lawyers ($70,000) and the accountants ($25,000) were all racking up billable hours.

For example, to prepare the preliminary prospectus—called a red herring, for the red banner emblazoned on its front page that essentially proclaimed, "What you are reading here may be totally wrong"—required an all-day all-hands meeting. In attendance were the underwriters, the accountants, the lawyers for the company, the lawyers for the underwriters, and the officers of the company, along with their sidekicks and their support people. I counted twenty-five people at this meeting. Its purpose was to ferret out any financial skeletons, hidden risks, or undisclosed liabilities at ASK. Everything should be out in the open. No one wanted the Securities and Exchange Commission (SEC) or misinformed shareholders breathing down his or her neck.

Since ASK was so squeaky clean financially, the primary topic of discussion at the meeting was whether anyone was hyping the stock, a practice frowned on by the SEC. While no one was hyping the stock intentionally, the offering had caught the media's eyes. More to the point, the media had found a female CEO of a fast-growing high-tech company newsworthy, and hardly a day went by when ASK wasn't mentioned in a national magazine, in a major newspaper, or on network or local TV. We even made *National Geographic*. And there was plenty more publicity to come.

The major problem confronted in the second almost-all-hands meeting was whether using color to highlight the preliminary prospectus's charts could be construed as hyping the stock. I'd seen some prospectuses with color pictures of company products, and since our reel of tape looked roughly the same in black and white as it did in color, I wanted to use color to jazz up the bar charts that showed ASK's revenues, income, and earnings growth over the three previous years. There was also a question about whether to go with dull or shiny paper. And part of the meeting was taken up with how the L. F. Rothschild, Unterberg and Towbin name would appear on the cover. Centered? Type size? These were not things to be taken for granted.

On a more substantive level, since after the offering I would still own more than three million shares in the company, the underwriters requested that I promise not to dump any of them on the market for ninety days following the IPO. SEC regulations limited subsequent sales to a certain number of shares every three months. Beyond that, the document was read and reread by everyone at the meeting to make certain it didn't contain anything that could be misconstrued. Even the ages of the officers—legally required information—were double-checked to make sure no one had had a birthday since the prospectus-preparing process had begun. Finally, in the beginning of August, the red herring was submitted to the SEC.

A few weeks before we were to go on the road to present ASK to financial communities in Europe and the United States—the road show—Ken Fox and I traveled to New York with the slides for the presentation: the past, present, and future of ASK in thirty images. A great deal of time had gone into the preparation of the slides. Their content represented the best thinking within ASK as well as the broader view that Regis McKenna, the local PR guru who had helped put Apple and a number of other Silicon Valley companies on the map, brought to the table. I was very proud of the slides.

On a warm Manhattan morning, my carousel tray of slides in hand, Ken and I took a cab to Rothschild. The plan was that we'd do a dry run with the slides, get everyone's feedback, hash out whatever changes were necessary, and go home.

Getting out of the cab, I told Ken I was nervous. "Don't worry. Just go with the flow," he said, spoken like a true Californian, though Ken had come to California via a small farm in Maine and Harvard. This was his first time in New York. Ever. The press of people took us through the doors at 55 Water Street and to the bank of elevators. As we were whisked to the twenty-sixth floor, I held tight to my precious slides.

Tommy's desk was the usual mess; Bob's, neat as could be. Tommy was in shirt sleeves; Bob looked ready for a night on the town. But that was to come later. "How are things at the mall?" Bob asked, referring to ASK's low-slung single-story offices.

All business, Tommy cut short the small talk and walked us to Mel Lavitt's office. Mel was the amiable marketing VP I'd talked to about skiing on my first visit. "Mel will review your slides," Tommy said.

"Relax," I told Ken, walking along the perimeter of the bullpen, "you're going to like this guy."

Mel's office was much smaller than Bob's and Tommy's—a desk, a chair, a few square feet of floor space—but it also had a limited view of New York Harbor. A cushioned window ledge ran along the wall on two sides of the room. "Okay," he said, relieving me of the slides, "let's see what we've got here." He looked at Ken and me. "Sit," he commanded. Quickly he set up a home movie type of screen, slapped my slide carousel on the projector, flicked it on, and monkeyed around with it until the first slide was more or less straight.

"Why don't I just talk you through them," I volunteered, "and then answer any questions?"

But Mel had no time for talk or for questions. He clicked through all thirty slides in less than a minute. Then he fixed Ken with a quick, grave look, opened the door, and yelled out into the bullpen, "You! You! You! In here!"

I looked at Ken. "Just go with the flow," he repeated. Soon there were about a dozen people in the tiny office, squeezing onto the cushioned ledge, standing in the corners.

"What we got here is a little company from California. Software," he added by way of explanation. "I want you to check out these images." Once again he went through the thirty slides—bar graphs, pie charts, nifty graphics, bullet points—in less than a minute. When he finished, everyone was deadly quiet. All I heard was the projector fan and the muted screaming from the bullpen. Finally, into the silence, Mel said, "These slides are terrible. Awful. Terrible," he repeated.

"Why terrible?" I could taste the Danish, the grapefruit, the coffee I'd had for breakfast.

Exasperated, he looked me straight in the eye. "The whites aren't white!" he announced. "The whites *are not* white."

Around me some people nodded. He spun the tray back to slide number one, and went through at a slower clip. "See," he said, walking to the screen, pointing at the slide's background, "you've got your good whites *here*. But"—and he clicked on the next slide—"but *here*, look at the whites here. That's not *white!* That's cream, that's eggshell, that's ecru, but that's not white!" I stared at the screen, but for the life of me I couldn't tell what he was talking about. By now, though, all of Mel's people were nodding in agreement.

Tense, nervous, disappointed, I didn't know quite what to say when suddenly I found myself on my feet. "Wait a minute. Wait a minute! This is the most ludicrous thing I've ever heard. We spend weeks preparing these slides, and I come three thousand miles, and all you can say is that my whites aren't white!" I glanced over at Mel, but he seemed unfazed by my outburst. The others looked on. Ken avoided eye contact. "Okay," I went on, "how many of you think that my whites aren't white?" Like school kids, a bunch of them raised their hands. "And how many of *you* work for Mel?" The same hands went up. "Aha!" I exclaimed. "Aha!"

Mel shrugged. "Okay, everyone back to work!" he announced. There was a stampede for the door. Even before they were gone, Mel had the West Coast Rothschild employee who had produced the slides on the phone. "Awful," he repeated to her. "Terrible. The whites . . ." After a few minutes he slammed down the phone and looked up at Ken and me. "That oughta do it," he said, handing me back my slides and gesturing us out of his office. "Otherwise they're fine."

35

On the Road

In early September Marty Browne, Tom Lavey, Bob Riopel, and I finally went on the road to peddle ASK's wares to the European financial community. I had asked Marty rather than Ken Fox, figuring that the European part of the road show would be the most fun, and I wanted to reward Marty for his loyalty to ASK and me through the lean times.

Our jumping-off point was Rothschild's New York office. Though I was embarking on the most critical trip of my business life, I was surprisingly calm. I was standing alone at the edge of the bullpen when Mel Lavitt appeared. "Come with me," he commanded. He led me into a tiny, dark room next to his office and sat me down at a desk. "It may not hurt your multiple," he began, referring to the relationship between the price of a share of stock and the company's earnings per share, "it may not hurt your multiple, but it's certainly not going to *help* your multiple." I had no idea what he was talking about. "Those fingernails." He pointed to my hands on the desk. "They're too long; they're too red. I want you to cut them down and paint them a very pale, nondescript color."

I glanced down at my nails. They certainly weren't *that* long, nor were they *that* red. I wasn't the Dragon Lady of the Late Show. "A lot of people are going to be coming to this road show just to see you because they've never seen a woman do it before. And you just have to be prepared for that." The entire event had taken about thirty seconds. Mel was gone before I could say a word.

It was hardly worth arguing over. Besides, maybe it was precisely this kind of advice that justified the enormous fees charged by investment bankers. Perhaps a manicure *would* net ASK millions more. So I cut and repainted my nails on the plane, and by the time we arrived at the Hôtel Beau-Rivage in Geneva on Saturday morning, I'd put the incident behind me. I was determined to have a good time. Marty slept in, and Tom, who never slept, asked me to join him to shop for a fur coat for his wife, Judy. I was to be his model. I felt punchy from the flight but went along. We went to a few furriers until Tom found the perfect coat. Exhausted, I went back to the hotel and passed out while Tom made the rounds of Geneva's night spots.

By the next morning, Sunday, I was over my jet lag and decided to work on my presentation. I set up my slide projector in a small room adjoining the hotel lobby. I clicked on the first slide and started talking, but there was no sound. My mouth was open, but nothing, absolutely nothing came out. This was a first. After a few minutes of being totally mute, I considered calling a doctor. Finally, however, I managed to croak out my talk. It sounded terrible. I'd never had such a bad case of butterflies in my entire life. I was really panicked. What if this happened tomorrow at the real presentation? At least my nails weren't too long.

On Monday, just prior to the presentation, Rothschild hosted a "simple little lunch" at the hotel for the hottest shots of the Geneva financial community. It was the most elaborate meal I'd ever seen. Course after course crossed the table. Nervous about my voice and my table manners in this classy crowd, I didn't eat more than three bites of anything. The *pièce de résistance* was dessert. It was served on small plates each holding a miniature spun sugar birdcage sitting atop a layer of cake and containing a single, wildly colored marzipan bird and three perfect scoops of sorbet in pastel hues. The others at the table dug in. Knowing that right after this course I'd have to give my presentation, I lost whatever appetite I had. Tentatively I touched a perfect silver spoon to the birdcage. It collapsed, half on the plate, half on the tablecloth.

In fact, there was really not that much to be nervous about, at least as far as our multiple was concerned. The Swiss financial institutions usually invested only in companies with a capitalization a lot greater than ASK's. So most of the all-male audience that showed up came for the meal—Rothschild was known for putting on a great feed—and, as Mel had so tactfully put it, "because they'd never seen a woman do it before." Still, there were a few investors there who indicated their intention to buy ASK stock by asking to be "circled" for so many shares.

This was also the case in France, where a similarly conservative capitalization minimum was observed. So the presentations in both countries were more interim quizzes than final exams. Still, I wanted to do ASK proud, and when we made it through the Geneva presentation without any major gaffes, I was pleased. Not only did I find my own voice, but Marty, Tom, and Bob each did an excellent job talking about their areas. As CEO I could have given the entire presentation, but even with my confidence back, my ego didn't require it. Besides, these guys had contributed so much to our getting there it would have been ridiculous to deny them a turn in the spotlight.

After the presentation was over, I was starved. I looked around for what remained of my birdcage, but it had been spirited away. And no time was allowed for unscheduled eating. We were due for tea and another presentation in Zurich in just a few hours. As the room emptied, Rothschild's representative packed us into limos and whisked us to the Geneva airport, where a private Lear jet sat waiting. This was the first private jet any of us had ever been on, so to say we were in awe of the whole experience was putting it mildly.

Zurich was a blur. Prior to our arrival all the bankers, investors, and analysts waiting for us at the Hotel Baur au Lac received continuous updates on our progress from Geneva: "They are in the limo now. They are at the airport. They are loading the baggage. . . ." When we arrived, it was to an audible sigh of relief and spontaneous applause. I felt like a rock star. We were out of Zurich and on the way to Paris before the sun went down. I don't remember a thing about the presentation.

By the time we arrived in Paris, I was exhausted. Instead of limos, we were crammed into Citroëns and unceremoniously dumped at the Hôtel Crillon, another twenty-star hotel, compliments of ASK's hard-earned money. After checking in, Tom, Marty, and Bob wanted to take in the Paris night life, but I begged off. I didn't think they wanted me along anyway. With our next presentation not until noon the following day, I decided to go to my room and unwind. But I was so hyped I couldn't relax and instead went out for a walk.

The hotel was on the Champs-Élysées, which I figured was a perfectly safe place to be walking. I didn't get very far before I realized I was wrong. Guys were whistling and calling out to me in deep, throaty French. I didn't know what they were saying, but I knew it wasn't the "May I have the pen?" or "The boy goes to church" that I'd learned in high school French class. Frightened, I walked into a fast-food place. There were no chairs, only high, round tables where people stood and ate. I ordered a burger and fries. While I ate, a guy standing at the next table gave me the eye. When I left, he tagged along behind me. Like an old French movie, I walked faster, my heels tap-tapping on the pavement. He walked faster, too. This went on for a couple of blocks until I finally reached the hotel. The last I saw, he was talking to the doorman.

The next morning I checked the room where we were to give the presentation. It was magnificent, with a towering inlaid ceiling, elegant tapestries, ornate gilded sconces, and an enormous chandelier. There to greet me was Rothschild's man in charge of international sales, John Demirjian. He was yelling out orders to underlings and scanning the guest list while he fondled a cigar. He had a swarthy complexion and looked as if he'd just stepped out of the pages of GQ. He was one of the most stylishly dressed guys I'd ever seen. Still, there was something wrong with this picture. As natty and perfectly turned out as he was, it was obvious he was a New Yorker knocking himself out to be a European. He confided that the room's acoustics were lousy but that I shouldn't worry.

By now, with two presentations complete, I was worrying a lot

less. Everyone on the team was doing a good job. The anxiously antic-
ipated road show was turning out to be a piece of cake. Even though
no one seemed to understand a word we said—our man John was
right about the acoustics—the Paris presentation turned out fine.
Fine enough, anyway.

As much as I liked to share the spotlight with the others on the
team, it was soon clear that John had little use for anyone below the
CEO level. Toward me he was attentive, solicitous, even fawning;
about the others, he couldn't have cared less. As soon as the Paris
presentation was over, he hustled us to the front of the hotel to catch
two cabs to the airport. He slipped in beside me in the first, leaving
Tom, Marty, and Bob to fend for themselves in the second. As we
pulled away, I looked out the rear window to see the three of them still
jockeying with their suitcases. When they finally caught up with us at
the gate, John managed to lose them again.

On the plane John sat next to me. We had things to talk about,
he said. As it turned out, we talked about shirts. All his shirts were
custom tailored by Turnbull and Asser in London. Each was made to
show precisely one and one-fourth centimeters of cuff. Not one, not
one and one-half, but precisely one and one-fourth centimeters. If
mid-season the styles had changed to show less or more, no doubt
he'd have shredded his existing wardrobe. By the time we reached
London, I'd learned more than I ever wanted to know about shirts.

We took limos to the Berkeley—pronounced Bark-ly—a super
fancy new hotel disguised as an old hotel. By far the most impressive
thing about the place was the large marble bathroom with the three
buttons on the wall next to the tub to summon the maid, the valet, or
a waiter. Ring for any one of them and, he or she appeared while you
were bathing to take your order. I was chicken to try, but Bob, who
had a similar setup, rang for all three. The waiter brought him a
scotch, the valet pressed his pants, and the maid turned down his bed
as Bob basked in the tub.

The crowning event of the evening was to be a dinner John had
arranged for us. He ordered for all of us, then asked the waiter to
bring on the wine, which John had evidently ordered in advance so
that it might be opened and allowed to breathe. A few minutes later
the sommelier arrived with the wine and poured a small amount in

John's glass. He swished it around in the glass, sniffed at it, sucked some in through his teeth, and finally declared it potable. When my glass was filled, I took a sip and immediately began eating. The others at the table did the same. Pretty soon we all were talking and joking. Every now and again one of us would grab the bottle for a refill. John, however, who had talked nonstop since we'd met, fell mysteriously silent. He was casting a pall on the entire dinner. "What is it, John?" I finally asked.

"Well?" he prompted.

"Well, what?" I had no idea what he was talking about. It turned out that the wine was a historic vintage that cost an astronomical amount of money, and I hadn't said one appreciative or astute thing about it. Playing to his belief that we all were hopeless rubes, I told him it tasted like grapes. It was the final straw, I'm sure.

With dessert came cigars. John produced his special cigar clipper for the occasion, then gave us a lesson on cigars and cigar paraphernalia. It was with a mixture of glee and scorn that he watched Tom and Bob clip their cigars with his clipper and fire them up. Marty and I demurred.

The London presentation was held at the Barber-Surgeon's Hall, famous for its meetings of heads of state. With three presentations under our belt, we all were now confident, and we did our best job. There was a lot of circling in London by investors who eventually bought our stock and held it for a long time. By day's end the European road show was over.

The road shows in the United States were run differently from those in Europe. In addition to presentations to the financial community at large, we were required to give a number of minipresentations at individual large fund management firms that had the potential for buying significant blocks of our stock. There were often a number of brokers, analysts, or fund managers present at what were known as one-on-ones. At one Boston pension fund, for example, we were escorted into what looked like a surgical theater ringed with tiers of seats and filled with dozens of eager fund managers, assistants, and analysts.

Unfortunately a few of the guys at these one-on-ones hadn't done their homework. At another Boston investment firm, for example, one question I remember being asked was: "How much does your software weigh?" When I suggested the weight of the software wasn't relevant to the product or the offering, the questioner insisted it was. By then, however, the entire offering had been virtually circled, and I was confident, even cocky. Walking out of the presentation, I turned to Rothschild's Boston guy and said, "Sheldon, I don't want you selling that man any shares."

Sheldon was flustered. "But he's an important customer."

"No shares," I insisted. "He can't have them."

We played the main Boston presentation to a standing-room crowd. The questions were good, and hundreds of thousands of shares of stock were circled. By the time we got to New York late that afternoon, there was not much left of the offering to sell.

That night Rothschild hosted a big dinner for ASK at the Four Seasons. The next morning we made our by now standard presentation at a large breakfast hosted by Rothschild, had a one-on-one with T. Rowe Price, followed by a one-on-one at Manufacturers Hanover and a large lunch group meeting and presentation at the Harmonie Club, then off to the airport for Chicago.

On the way to the airport Rothschild's limo driver, Murray, regaled me with stories, first about Tommy Unterberg and Bob Towbin, then about everyone else in the corporate and financial world. They were terrific, gossipy stories, "secrets," he claimed, about other public offerings, other CEOs, their quirks, and their special requests. Initially I felt like his confidante, as though I were the only one he'd ever told these stories to, but by and by I realized this wasn't the case. I felt suddenly vulnerable. What would he say about me to the next CEO? There weren't any secrets he could tell about me, were there? I retraced my steps in New York, recalling the one-on-one I'd sneaked out of early to shop for a dress for the Rothschild dinner. "Ahhh, Murray . . ." I began. But it was too late. I was already part of the mythology.

After putting on shows in Chicago, Minneapolis, Denver, and Los Angeles, we arrived in San Francisco for the final presentation on

September 18 to bad news. Actually the news had been following us around, but in the glitz and excitement of our coming out, it never quite registered. As ASK was becoming the darling of Wall Street, the stock market had gone south, plummeting 118 points since August, representing a 12 percent drop in 1981. A few days later Wall Street guru Joseph Granville in his widely distributed newsletter predicted a crash. The windows of opportunity were closing fast. Like it or not, ASK was about to put to the test Tommy's theory that a good company can always go public.

36

October 1, 1981

The day before the actual public offering there was a meeting at the printer's attended by ASK management, the lawyers, the accountants, the underwriters, and all associated gofers to proofread the prospectus a final time before it went to press. The meeting lasted until the wee hours, and the printer provided an ongoing supply of steaks, lobsters, and hundred-dollar bottles of wine. Early in the evening the registration statement that officially filed the offering with the SEC was printed. When it came off the press, it was hand carried to the airport to catch the last flight to Washington. When it arrived there, it was picked up by a courier and rushed directly to the SEC. It seemed a bit silly to me, but it was part of the game.

While we were at the printers, a conference call was set up between Tommy Unterberg in New York, representing Rothschild and the syndicate of underwriters, and Ken Oshman and myself, representing ASK. The reason for the call was to set the final offering price of the stock. In August the preliminary prospectus had proposed a range of eleven to thirteen dollars a share for the 1,350,000 share offering. At that time we were hoping to go out at near thirteen dollars. But with the downturn in the market, Granville's crash prediction, and dozens of less solid offerings being postponed, we were now looking at the eleven-dollar figure. Having guaranteed the offering, Rothschild wanted to go with a price that would assure a sellout. We all agreed, considering the economic climate, that if we went out at twelve dollars or more per share, some investors who had circled wouldn't actually buy. Going out a point lower would cost the company more than one million dollars. Still, as in any negotiation, it seemed best to leave something on the table. I was willing to have happy investors buy low and see their stock go up rather than do nothing or go down. We decided to go out at eleven dollars.

Fortunately we had another Silicon Valley company to look to for confirmation of our decision. Seagate, the company that had co-starred with ASK at the investment conference a few months earlier, had gone public a few days earlier at approximately the same price and had immediately climbed a couple of points. Their success proved that the market could still take a strong offering.

I was at the printers at 1:00 A.M., watching the prospectus being printed, when I learned that our registration statement had arrived at the SEC. Awakened at home a few hours later, at 6:00 A.M., October 1, 1981, I received confirmation that the offering was effective. Nine-year-old ASK was a public company.

The day of the ASK offering 1,350,000 shares of ASK stock were sold. That same day Rothschild exercised its 10 percent option for an additional 135,000 shares. The net to ASK was more than $9,000,-000. For the 546,550 personal shares I sold, I was to receive a check for $5,580,276. And I still owned more than 3,000,000 shares of ASK stock, 61 percent of the company.

I was not the only one who became a millionaire that day. As their stock options vested, most of the ASK officers became millionaires. Others in the company, while not millionaires, did very well, at least on paper.

I'd put an official stock option plan into effect in 1978, when I offered everyone in the company varying amounts of stock options with each option vesting at 20 percent per year. As the company began to take on value, these stock options bound some of the employees to the company and became known as golden handcuffs. The first person to exercise an option was Howard Klein. On January 2, 1979, he walked into my office with a check for two hundred dollars for four hundred shares of ASK stock, at fifty cents per share. The others were behind the door waiting to see what I'd do. They were expecting I'd say, "Well, we can't really do this. I can't really give you—" Instead I took his check and called Craig Johnson, our lawyer, to issue Howard his stock. In 1985 these initial four hundred shares, a small part of the total number of shares Howard eventually held, were worth thirty thousand dollars.

With virtually everyone in the company a shareholder, October 1, 1981, was an exciting day at ASK. But I couldn't quite get into the excitement. By the day of the offering I'd decided that whatever happened with the price of the stock was out of my hands. I'd built the company; I'd done the prospectus; I'd finished the road show. In my heart of hearts I never really believed the company was worth the one million dollars that Paul Ely had sort of offered, the twenty-one million that Tommy had estimated its value at in 1980, or the fifty-five million that October 1, 1981's eleven dollars per share seemed to indicate. I didn't truly realize what ASK had achieved. More important, I wasn't 100 percent certain I could keep it going, growing.

In the midst of all the hullabaloo I called an R&D review. Throughout the meeting my ex-hippie employees were taking calls from their brokers or interrupting to report what ASK was trading at. I was uncharacteristically quiet. At day's end Liz Seckler and Marty teased me about what I was going to do with all my money. I hadn't a clue.

That evening I went to Shreve's, a swanky jewelry store in the nearby Stanford shopping center and bought elegant watches for all the officers and a few of my oldest, most trusted co-workers—ten in all. I also bought diamond-rimmed watches for my mom and dad. "I'll have one of those and one of those and one of those," I said. The salesman was cool. In the heart of the Silicon Valley, with its superheated public offerings, I guess he was used to this kind of indulgence. "How fast can you engrave these and get them to me?" Very fast, it turned out. Also, he offered to come to ASK the next day to measure everyone's wrist. The tab came to more than forty thousand dollars, and I have no idea why he thought that I was good for it. A week later I saw him in a new Porsche, proof positive of the trickle-down theory.

Still, everyone teased me about not buying anything for myself. First, I couldn't think of anything I wanted. And second, I was concerned about how people would react. I didn't want there to be any jealousy. I wanted to downplay that I was suddenly worth so much money. So while the kid part of me wanted to take my $5,580,276 check, cash it in for a pile of $5,580,276 singles, and frolic naked through it, like Scrooge McDuck in the Disney comics of my childhood, the other part was saying, "If you got it, no need to flaunt it." But the continual teasing finally left me no choice but to buy a Ferrari.

That weekend I jogged in my sweats to the soccer field where Arie was coaching Andy's team, and the three of us drove to a high-ticket car dealer in nearby Los Gatos. A low-slung slinky red car was parked out front surrounded by a dozen tire kickers. "What kind of car is this?" I asked the salesman whose job seemed to be to protect the car, more than to sell it.

He looked pained. "A Ferrari," he said.

Good, I was on the right track. "Can I sit in it?"

The dealer eyed my jogging suit, then produced a key. I'm not certain what he saw that convinced him to do so, but I was soon the envy of the others milling around the car. I didn't have much trouble getting into the cockpit, but Ferraris sit really low, and getting out required more of an effort. "Can I take it for a ride?" I asked. This really piqued the interest of those in the crowd.

"Sure," said the salesman.

We got in the car. I drove it around the block a few times and then onto the nearby freeway to get it at least into third gear. Before I knew it, I was doing ninety. I slowed quickly and took the next exit. "Now *this* is a car," I thought as it took the curving off ramp as if on rails. Clearly some of the best things in life *weren't* free. Back at the dealership I said, "I'd like to buy this car. How much is it?"

The salesman gave me a wide smile. "Make me an offer."

I had no notion of what to offer. There was no price on the car, a new 308 GTSI. Was it worth a hundred thousand dollars? Fifty thousand? Less? I didn't want to come off as a total rube, so I told him I needed to use the phone. I found you can use the phone at a Ferrari dealer to call anywhere. First, I called Jimmy Treybig, the fellow who'd left HP to form Tandem and whom I was supposed to be on the lookout for when we were still spending nights at HP in sleeping bags. Jimmy's ship had come in at Tandem, and I knew he'd recently bought a Ferrari. When I couldn't reach him, I went to the library across the street and searched the phone books for Ferrari dealers in the western states. Using the library pay phone, I called the Ferrari dealer in San Francisco and told him I was in the market for a 308 GTSI and asked if he had a red one and how much would it cost. Since almost all Ferraris are red, that part was easy. He said that he didn't quote prices over the phone, that I'd have to come down. So I said, "Look, I don't want to waste my time," and picking a number out of the air, I went on, "I'm not going to pay a penny over sixty thousand."

"Well, come on down! We can put you into a three-oh-eight for that!"

Next, I called a Ferrari dealer in Monterey and told him I wanted a 308 GTSI. He also wouldn't quote prices on the phone, so I told him that I wasn't going to pay a penny over fifty-five thousand. "Well, come on down!"

I called a few more dealerships—Los Angeles, Las Vegas—lowering my price until I got the guy who said, "Lady, if you've found someone who'll sell you a three-oh-eight GTSI for forty thousand dollars, go for it!"

Having ascertained market value, I went back to my salesman and offered him thirty-eight thousand dollars. He looked aghast, as if I'd taken advantage of his good nature, then went through his repertoire of grimaces, contortions, and trips to the manager. In a few minutes, though, it was clear that I'd found someone who'd sell me a red Ferrari 308 GTSI for forty thousand dollars. Less, in fact.

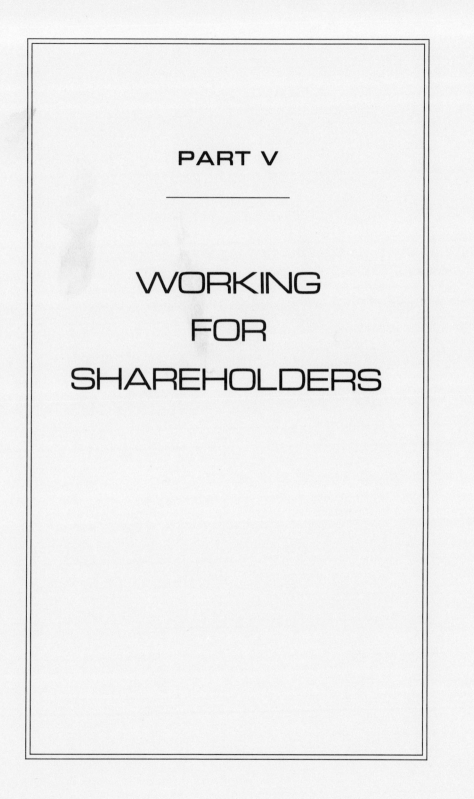

PART V

WORKING
FOR
SHAREHOLDERS

37

In the Public Eye

I had explained a bit about the stock market to Andy, my nine-year-old, and when ASK went public, he saved his allowance and did some odd jobs to buy a single eleven-dollar share. He had his eye on an eighteen-dollar model airplane. Every day he checked the paper to see how the stock was doing, and at the end of the first week, when it was only at thirteen, he was disappointed. I told him that things usually didn't happen so fast but that if I worked hard, pretty soon, maybe, he'd have his eighteen dollars. This seemed to satisfy him, but a few weeks later, when the stock was up two more points, he came back to me and said, "Mommy, the stock's only at fifteen dollars. You must not be working hard enough."

Andy was no different from anyone else who bought ASK stock, whether an institutional investor or a personal friend. They all were impatient, hoping for a quick return on their investments. When they got it—and over the years many made millions on ASK stock—everything was hunky-dory. But if they lost money, many were bitter and angry and, in some cases, let me know about it. Wanting to do a good job, wanting to please, I knew as long as they held the stock, they had power over me. They could check on ASK's value and tell whether I worked hard enough every day. Everyone could, including Andy, my parents, and my parents' friends. Paul Ely was right. As a public company you were in the public eye, constantly judged, like it or not.

As for ASK's past successes, they were just that—history. Stockholders weren't paying eleven dollars a share for what ASK had already accomplished. They were betting on what it would accomplish in the future.

So aside from the excitement of running a public business, of reading about myself and ASK in nearly every newspaper and magazine in the country, of being on talk shows, being asked to sit on boards, being invited to hotsy-totsy social events, and getting far, far more attention than I deserved, I spent my first year as CEO of a public company scared to death. Maybe we did just have a tiger by the tail with MANMAN? Maybe our success was just dumb luck? Maybe our competitors who'd never really made a convincing grab for the pie were getting smarter? Maybe, maybe. And everywhere there were analysts watching for that first misstep, that flat quarter, the new product that bombs. It was a fearful situation to be in, and though I had a very supportive board of directors and excellent vice-presidents, I felt as if I were facing it alone.

That's it for the complaining. The fact is, I wanted ASK to be a public company, and for the most part I thrived on our new, higher profile. I particularly liked working on the quarter system. I enjoyed having to prepare a report card to my stockholders every three months and the challenge of improving quarter by quarter. It suited my goal-oriented personality perfectly. I've always felt more comfortable when problems are broken down into manageable chunks, and that is precisely what making the quarter is all about. It's like cramming for a test. You turn all your attention to the obstacle ahead— your financial goal for that quarter. And when you surmount it, you tool up for the next. At the same time the trick is not to fall into the trap so many U.S. companies do of living quarter to quarter. You've got to balance quarterly performance with long-term goals.

After we went public, about 10 percent of my time went into

talking with and appearing before the financial community. This was a restless, fickle crowd, these analysts, brokers, and fund managers, and demanded a lot of attention, mostly at a never-ending stream of financial conferences. If you didn't show up, you were conspicuous by your absence. "What's going on at ASK? Are they being acquired? Are they having problems?" So I showed up.

Rather than just make an appearance to pitch my stock, I used the conferences to generate sales. Given a forum, I never failed to say, "Hey, I know you guys are looking real seriously at buying stock in such and such company, but do you realize it's thinking of buying an ASK system? If it does, it'll be a better company for you to invest in."

Traveling from conference to conference, I created a perception in the marketplace that if a company was using MANMAN, it was probably managing its manufacturing operation better than if it used a competitor's system. It even got to a point where almost every manufacturing company presenting at a conference was asked if it was using an ASK system. All this attention was not lost on the venture capitalists in attendance, who encouraged the start-up companies they were investing in to adopt MANMAN.

I also developed a scheme for getting analysts to provide us with sales leads. I passed out cards headlined GIVE ASK THE BUSINESS, with space for their names and the names of two manufacturing companies that could benefit from ASK's software. We also inserted the cards in our company newsletter, annual reports, press kits, and the promotional brochures we sent to brokers, analysts, customers, prospects, and shareholders. The response wasn't enormous, but with our product costing more than two hundred thousand dollars we didn't need thousands of leads—just a handful that panned out.

We also did some advertising, including a combined TV and *Wall Street Journal* print campaign that won our agency, Chiat-Day, a Clio—the Oscar of advertising—and recognition at the London International Advertising Awards for the best print trade campaign of the year. In the end, however, I'm convinced it was ASK's continued appearances at trade shows and seminars that really sold our systems.

Whatever we were doing, we must have been doing it right. By 1982 ASK was the eighth-fastest-growing public company in the United States and the nation's fastest-growing software company.

Venture capitalists were scouring the countryside looking for another ASK to invest in, whereas just a few years back VCs who heard I was "in software" often thought I was manufacturing women's lingerie.

In a poll of analysts conducted by the *Wall Street Transcript* I was selected one of the top three CEOs in the computer software industry. *Working Woman* hailed me as the "Queen of Silicon Valley." A local radio station asked me to be its guest weather reporter! I was getting invited to the social events and dinners of people I'd never met before, sometimes even reading the next day about my appearance at a dinner or party I hadn't attended. And everyone wanted my opinion. On September 30, 1981, most people didn't know my name. On October 1, whatever I thought about any topic was newsworthy.

In just a few years more than ten thousand articles about ASK appeared in magazines and newspapers around the world, usually focusing on me. A private person, I was uncomfortable with all the scrutiny. I also felt guilty that I was getting all the attention and that the others in the company weren't. One day I mentioned my concern in a meeting with Marty, Tom, Ken, and Bob. They'd just returned from a management development session put on by our accounting firm, Arthur Young, at which they'd been asked to write out their own job descriptions, and mine as well. For mine everyone had written, "To attract the press." Good publicity, they told me, regardless of whether it was centered on me or not, was good for the whole company. It boosted the value of the stock, helped sales, and improved morale. By then more than half the company was in sales offices scattered throughout the United States, and it was important for everyone to read about ASK and see ASK's name on television and in the papers. So I said okay, I'd go along with it.

One day, following a two-week climb of ASK stock for no apparent reason, I got a call from New York, from one of ASK's largest investors. He was planning a trip out west and was wondering if we could have dinner. Halfway through the meal I realized that our dinner was the *only* reason he'd flown from New York to California. I had no idea what was up, but I was my usual chatty self. When we were finished with coffee and about to leave, he suddenly leaned over and held my wrist gingerly.

"I have a very touchy question to ask you," he said. I liked him and wanted to put him at ease.

"Ask anything," I reassured.

"I just don't know how to go about asking you this but, but—"

At this point I was getting nervous. "But what?"

"Well, there's a rumor going around—"

"A rumor?" I couldn't imagine what it was.

Suddenly he blurted out, "A rumor that you have a terminal illness."

It's funny how you react to something like that. My first impulse was to laugh if only to release the tension. I tried, but the laugh wouldn't come. Oddly enough, my next thought was that maybe the rumor was true and I hadn't been told. I quickly realized it couldn't be; I hadn't been to a doctor in years. Again I tried to muster a laugh but couldn't. Instead, I flashed back to the dinner and replayed our entire conversation. Obviously uncomfortable, he repeated what he'd come three thousand miles to say. "There's a rumor on the Street that you have a terminal illness."

So I said, "Well, if it's true, I haven't been told yet."

"I'm glad to hear it," he said. "I'm truly glad to hear it."

As it turned out, with ASK's stock climbing and climbing, a large brokerage house had sold short thousands of shares of ASK stock, betting, in other words, that the stock price would go down. When it continued to climb and they had to cover their short, millions of dollars were at stake. So they started the rumor about my imminent demise, hoping it would send the stock on a nose dive. It didn't work.

38

D-i-v-o-r-c-e

Watching ASK investors take their money and kick back, I decided to do a little of the same. At thirty-five I wanted to cut back on my twelve- to fourteen-hour workdays and have a comfortable place to come home to. Arie and I and the kids were still living in Los Altos Hills in the starkly furnished house we'd moved to in late 1972. I'd never had the time or the inclination to make it homey or inviting, but now I wanted to. The consensus among the architects and decorators who traipsed through was that we should tear it down and start over. I thought we should move. Arie didn't want to. We argued about it every day for a week. Eventually, I went house hunting and found a new house in nearby Atherton I wanted to buy. Reluctantly Arie agreed to the move.

In and of itself the argument wasn't a big deal. Couples always argue, though Arie and I rarely did. To me, however, the nature of the argument pointed to a larger problem in the marriage: that Arie and I had grown apart and that we no longer wanted the same things. I wondered, Did I really want to spend the rest of my life with him? I began thinking about a divorce.

I was barely twenty-two when I married. Prior to that I'd led a very sheltered life. Most of that time I lived at home with my parents, who enforced a strict midnight curfew. Arie was the first man I'd ever slept with. But since my marriage a great deal had happened in my life. I'd been aged by business, motherhood, and travel. Arie, on the other hand, was much the same person I'd married. He was nervous about change and wanted a simple life with little risk and not too much excitement.

By many measures, Arie was a good husband. He had always been, and continued to be, an excellent friend. In the early going especially, he was a good soldier, coming down to OSI in the evenings to help out. More important, he never expected the things most men did of their wives in those years. He never complained about my hours, my traveling, my preoccupation with the business. As much as anyone can grant anyone else freedom, that's what Arie gave me. And that peace of mind gave me the opportunity to start ASK.

The one nagging complaint I had about Arie was that he rarely showed affection—not, at least, in the way it was shown in my family, where people were always hugging and kissing and where deep affection was always evident. The biggest argument Arie and I ever had, in fact, was over the fact that he didn't want my father kissing our young sons. While I understood the reasons for Arie's reserve—he'd lost his father when he was very young, and his mother wasn't particularly warm or demonstrative—I wanted more for my children and for myself. I missed the warmth of a loving family. I was getting stroked every day at work, but I didn't want to have to read the financial pages to see if I was loved.

The only other major argument I can recall from nearly fourteen years of marriage took place when we were living in New Jersey and I was fed up and wanted to move back to California. I didn't fit in; I hated the weather; I was lonely for my friends and family. Arie said it would be impossible for him to find a job in California. "What do you mean, 'impossible'? You haven't even tried."

"I don't have to try," he said. "I know."

His reluctance even to try was frustrating. True, in 1968 engineers in California were being laid off, and there were highly publicized cases of some engineers taking jobs as service station attendants. Still, as an engineer Arie was a catch. He'd gotten a Ph.D. from Stanford, a hotshot school. And Bell Labs wasn't exactly chopped liver. I couldn't believe I was married to a guy still in his twenties who already knew what was impossible. Angry, I stormed out of the room and locked myself in our bedroom. Next thing I knew, Arie put his fist through the door. It was the first time I'd ever seen evidence of his fury, his own frustration.

"Open up!" Arie demanded.

Suddenly my anger turned to fear. I unlocked the door and rushed past him. "Look, I'm going back to California. You can come with me or I'll go by myself."

I spent the night in a hotel. The next morning he came after me to apologize. He agreed to try to find a job in California, and together we went to New York and bought the San Francisco, San Jose, San Diego, and Los Angeles Sunday papers. It didn't matter to me if we ended up in Northern or Southern California. Back at the apartment we went through the want ads. Sitting on the couch in the living room, I kept looking up at the hole in the bedroom door.

The layoffs were for real, and Arie got a lot of rejections. I felt as bad about them as he did, worse maybe, because it was my wanting to move that accounted for them. But within the month he had an excellent offer to be a research manager at Itel's Information Storage Division in Northern California, which was subsequently sold to Univac.

It was not until after ASK had gone public that I mentioned the possibility of divorce to Tommy and ASK's lawyer, Larry Sonsini. Concerned by the effect a divorce might have on ASK's stock, they suggested I wait a year. We were in a nervous market, and Arie and I, living in a community property state, together held almost two-thirds of the outstanding shares. Wait and see what happens, they advised.

I waited, and not much happened. Arie and I continued to get along as we always had. Then, one night in fall 1982, Jerry Brown, who was then the governor of California and a good friend, invited me to accompany him to a party in San Francisco at the house of EST founder Werner Erhard. Erhard had made a bundle running seminars that helped people take charge of their lives, specifically to find the elusive "it" of existence—as those who had "it" proclaimed ad nauseam.

I'd told Arie I would stay only for cocktails and be home by nine. By the time I arrived at Werner's however, the cocktail hour was over, and I was escorted into Werner's living room. It was like walking into the American Museum of Natural History. The room was populated by huge stuffed animals, and enormous potted plants grew to its ballroom-height ceiling. Werner and Jerry greeted me. They said they'd been holding dinner until I arrived; that made it awkward for me to leave without staying through the meal. So I walked with them up two flights to the dining area, where tables were arranged in a large open square for about two dozen guests. My place card indicated the seat next to Werner's. At everyone's place setting was an exquisite hand-lettered menu complete with wines for each course. The meal that followed was one of the more elegant and elaborate I'd ever eaten, rivaling the birdcage lunch in Geneva.

Assuming Werner wasn't interested in manufacturing software, I quizzed him about the EST philosophy. Much of what I'd heard about it seemed like a crock. I quickly backed off when I sensed Werner go on the defensive. No need to spoil his dinner. Besides, the guy was the consummate salesman, and I wanted to let him do his number.

As it turned out, Werner didn't do his number; his disciples did. At the end of the meal Werner called on the guests who'd found "it" to give a little recitation on how EST had allowed them to get their lives together and how they'd found themselves in the process. I listened, but not very attentively. It was after ten and I was concerned that the night was dragging on and I should call Arie to tell him I'd be late. At first I didn't call because I didn't want to be rude to Werner and his guests, but when there was a break in the program, I stayed at my place at the table. I didn't want to call, I realized. I wanted Arie to worry. I wanted him to be angry because of my being late. I never did call.

When the evening was over, I drove home. I arrived a little

before midnight. Arie was in the kitchen, where I joined him. I don't recall what he said—probably nothing more than "I wish you'd called."

And I said, "Yes, I know. I want a divorce."

I don't know who was more surprised, Arie or I. I'd really not thought too much about divorce one way or another for months. It certainly wasn't any of the EST stuff either. I had simply realized I wanted to go on to the next phase of my life.

For a moment Arie and I just looked at each other in the unnaturally bright light of the kitchen. "A divorce . . ." It was a question, but now we'd both said the word. I'd set something in motion, and I realized there was nothing more I could say about it then. I had to let it sink in, to wait until the morning, at least, and make sure I still felt the same way.

When I awoke the next morning, Arie was gone. But we'd been gone from each other for years; I to work and Arie to retreat to his unemotional shell. So a divorce it would be. I felt neither good nor bad about the decision—only slightly sad. It was pointless to try to assess blame or indulge in "what if" fantasies. The only thing left for us both was to proceed to the next step.

That evening Arie asked what he had to do to convince me to stay. He suggested we see a counselor. But seeing a counselor meant trying to patch up the marriage, and I didn't want that. When I started the divorce process a few days later, Arie asked to remain at the house until the procedure was over. I wasn't angry at him, so I said okay, and for weeks we continued to share the same bed, even as we negotiated our divorce settlement.

Larry Sonsini wasn't a divorce lawyer, but any settlement would involve large amounts of ASK stock even though Arie had never been involved in the company, so I decided that as an interested party—and soon-to-be ASK board member, taking Craig Johnson's place—Larry would be my best advocate. Besides, he was the most effective deal maker and negotiator I'd ever met. Affable and easy to talk to, Larry always made everyone in a negotiation feel that he had his or her best interests in mind, even when he was representing the other side. Today he's one of the most respected lawyers in the Silicon

Valley, widely known for his fair play as well as for his classy, hand-tailored suits.

My initial offer to Arie was to pay him ten million dollars. I also asked for custody of Andy and Kenny. Arie turned down the offer. He wanted more money and joint custody of the children. We finally agreed on about twenty million dollars and joint custody. At the time ours was one of the largest if not *the* largest, cash and stock settlement in the United States ever given by a wife to a husband.

Since we continued living together while the settlement was being negotiated, Andy and Kenny weren't aware of what was happening until everything was just about settled, sometime in late November. The four of us sat down and talked it through. Andy was nine, and Kenny, six. We told them that we both would be spending time with them and that they could live with me part-time in the new house and part-time with Arie back in the Los Altos house, which we still owned since it hadn't been sold in the year since we'd moved to the new house. On the surface, at least, they didn't seem too upset. It seemed like the best of all possible arrangements. Knock wood, they are still happy, healthy kids.

39

ASK Goes Shopping

Having seen mainframes blindsided by time-sharing, and time-sharing blindsided by minicomputers, I knew that it was just a matter of time before something would come along and blindside minicomputers. In 1983 there was little doubt in my mind, and in the minds of many, that that something would be microcomputers, or PCs, as they are better known. The questions were, How long would it be before it happened and what could we do about it?

At first I thought we could develop our own micro-based system internally. But then I looked at all the mainframe companies that had tried to develop mini-based systems. None of them had succeeded. It takes a different mind-set to work with a mini from that needed for a mainframe. By extension I thought that ASK's mini mind-set would hamper our chances of developing a good micro product. So ASK went looking for an established microcomputer software company to buy.

I began my search by checking the trade papers and magazines for possible targets. I contacted each company that caught my eye and requested product literature and any other informational material they might have. Using this information and what I was able to glean from trade magazines, I developed a three-by-five card file on each company.

I didn't have to look far for what appeared to be an ideal candidate. A couple of hours northeast of Los Altos in the Sacramento suburb of Citrus Heights was a two-year-old company called Software Dimensions, Incorporated (SDI). SDI had landed in the fast lane of the emerging micro market. Two years after opening their doors they were generating a net profit of four hundred thousand dollars on three million dollars in annual revenues. Their accounting package, Accounting Plus, was a nationwide best seller, with a number of versions running on Apple and on other microcomputers running CP/M, the most popular operating system at that time. An IBM PC-DOS version was also in the works—vital, I was convinced, to the future success of the company. IBM had missed the boat in minicomputers, and they weren't about to make the same mistake with micros. It was only a matter of time before they became the major player.

Accounting Plus was being marketed to small businesses—smaller than the two-million-dollar-plus revenue companies we'd targeted for ASKNET or MANMAN turnkey systems—and I thought we could use the success of this package as a staging area for additional products, particularly a manufacturing product if and when microcomputers developed enough power to handle one or when we could develop a stripped-down version of MANMAN that wouldn't require as much power but that would still do the basic job. Tom, Ken, Bob, Marty, and I all agreed that acquiring SDI would be a smart move. The board, too, gave its blessing.

On April 4, 1983, ASK announced its intent to buy SDI from its owners, Ronnie and Linda Green, for approximately $12,000,000 in ASK stock. The Greens had been looking either to go public or to sell and agreed to stay on to ease the transition. The SDI name was to be changed to ASK Micro, which would become a separate ASK subsidiary.

Coinciding with our shopping for an acquisition was my search for a chief operating officer to run the everyday operations of the company while I focused more on long-range planning. I was tired of having to be at ASK every day for every decision and every crisis, which is precisely where my compulsive nature took me, often at the sacrifice of time with my family or friends. My sons were growing up without me, and since they were around only half the time, I wanted to spend some of that time with them. Also, now that I was single, I wanted to go out, and not only with clients. It was time to put my work life into perspective and create a more satisfying, fulfilling personal life. The divorce had been a first step. It was time to take the next.

My candidate for the chief operating officer job was Tom Lavey. My suggestion to promote him was not met favorably by the board members, however. They didn't think he'd be effective in that role. Tom was not the most organized person, and this shortcoming overshadowed his strengths in the eyes of the ASK board. I argued that he was an excellent leader and that ASK had strong, well-organized managers in Ken and Bob. Most important, I argued that for a company to remain dynamic and continue to thrive it needed both managers and leaders. It was finally agreed that I'd take a three-month vacation to give Tom a chance at running the company. But past commitments, my involvement in the acquisition, and my workaholic nature kept me around ASK for much of the three months. I never really gave Tom the opportunity to prove his ability to run the company in my absence.

Meanwhile, the SDI deal was about to close, and in my one concession to vacation, I'd left the legwork and the research to the rest of the team. At the eleventh hour, however, I got cold feet. I began poring over SDI's financials and looking in depth at their operation. I found a number of disturbing things. The management team wasn't very good. The company was about to move into a lavish new building, far too sumptuous for their projected near-term numbers. They were suing a number of competitors for copyright infringement, and the lawsuits were eating up time and money. The corporate culture at SDI wasn't very people-oriented. Their R&D people had little programming experience. The IBM PC conversion project was behind schedule. SDI's shipments weren't on track to meet their projected $3,500,000 sales number for fiscal 1983. And there was no way they'd meet their profit projection of $300,000—already lower than their previous year. In fact, the numbers looked more like $3,200,000 in sales and $200,000 in profits. Revenues weren't that far off, but earnings were a whopping 30 percent less than projected. Was it a trend? Was there a fundamental weakness we'd missed?

Ronnie and Linda explained that they'd lost several weeks of sales as the result of delays in receiving packaging materials from their suppliers. Fair enough. And the PC project was only slightly behind schedule. I could certainly sympathize with that. For every problem I brought up, they had a plausible explanation. But there were so *many* problems that my gut told me the acquisition was a bad idea. Impulsively, without checking with the ASK VPs or the board, I decided to withdraw ASK's offer for SDI.

I then told each VP individually what I'd done. Each said that he'd honor my decision but that he disagreed with it. The biggest advocate of going through with the acquisition was Tom. With all my VPs thinking we should go ahead with the acquisition, I was in doubt again. It was the first time I had been the odd woman out in a strategic decision at ASK, and I wondered if I was losing my touch. I called a board meeting. The board agreed that twelve million dollars might be too much to pay for ASK Micro, considering the potential problems I'd enumerated, but thought the acquisition still made sense. They also suggested that Tom become president of ASK Micro as a way of proving his ability to run a company. "And, Sandy," Ken Oshman said at the close of the meeting, "you just stay out of it, okay? Let it be Tom's baby."

When I told Tom that he'd been named president of ASK Micro—provided that Ronnie and Linda would accept a lower offer—he was delighted. By now he was chomping at the bit to run a company, and he had never really believed I'd turn over the reins at ASK. My nonvacation had supported his doubts.

The next day Tom, Bob, Ken, and I flew to SDI to meet with the Greens. Our initial offer was for 400,000 shares of ASK stock worth nearly $12,000,000. This time we offered 225,000 shares worth about $7,500,000. I wasn't surprised when they accepted. Tom moved to Sacramento, and shortly after, the Greens departed. On my vacation I'd bought a company.

I used to joke, "Don't waste my time with the good news. Bring me the problems." Though I was an optimist with an almost Pollyannaish view of the world, I saw my role of manager as that of a problem solver. But I would have liked, every now and again, to have seen something positive emerge from ASK Micro, particularly since the news with ASK on the home front was resoundingly good. Every month, however, Tom showed up at our month-end review meetings with ASK Micro's numbers, which were getting worse and worse. But he was such a terrific salesman he managed to convince the other officers that ASK Micro was on the verge of a turnaround. My gut said that things weren't about to turn around, but after making my skepticism known, I did as I had promised the board. I stayed out of ASK Micro. In the meantime, ASK was pouring more than three hundred thousand dollars of our hard-earned profits a month into our new subsidiary. This wouldn't have been a problem if I'd just seen the light that Tom saw at the end of the tunnel.

One of the more blatant indications that things were getting out of hand at ASK Micro was revealed at COMDEX, the semiannual microcomputer dealer trade show. The show was held in Las Vegas. ASK Micro had a large classy booth on the show floor, and upstairs they had rented a huge hospitality suite and were dispensing free booze and jumbo prawns for continuous happy hours with dealer prospects. As I watched platter after platter of jumbo prawns washed down with hard liquor compliments of ASK Micro, I thought, "This is *not* how to run a company losing three hundred thousand dollars a month."

I hadn't planned on going to COMDEX, but with ASK money disappearing into what seemed more and more like the black hole of ASK Micro, I had decided to participate in the development of the marketing message and in the COMDEX announcement of ASK Micro's new product, the IBM version of Accounting Plus. With Accounting Plus competing for shelf space and sales with hundreds of other IBM PC software packages in retail outlets like ComputerLand, it was vital that the product be correctly positioned, packaged, and promoted. The campaign that had been developed for the product was good, but because of poor planning, ASK Micro had incurred a substantial premium to have the packaging and promotional materials produced by the time of the show—costs it could ill afford.

Accounting Plus was positioned as easier to use than other IBM PC accounting software packages—as it was—and the KISS (Keep It Simple Software) campaign was created to convey our message. The plan was to create a "First KISS" product line of demonstration packages, accompanied by a computer-based tutorial called "KISS and Tell," and to offer a 20 percent off consumer promotion called "A First KISS for 1984" that bundled ASK Micro's three new IBM accounting modules with an interactive computer-driven tutorial and handbook.

To kick off the promotion at COMDEX, we gave away Hershey's Kisses in our booth and buttons with red lips and the legends "ASK for a KISS" and "KISS and Tell," People loved the campaign. They loved our booth, the prawns, the booze, the Kisses, the buttons, the hospitality suite. They were a lot less happy with the IBM PC version of Accounting Plus that ASK Micro had rushed to market. The program had a bug in it and often crashed.

By COMDEX it was clear that Tom wasn't the right choice as ASK's chief operating officer, even if he was able to turn ASK Micro around, as I now highly doubted. Intent on finding a good chief operating officer who could also become my successor as CEO someday, I looked for the next logical choice. I talked to a few people about the position but never went to a headhunter. I flirted briefly with a few names, including those of a well-respected former DEC executive and an IBM executive. But I was uncomfortable about taking someone from the outside. As it was, I thought that finding a new boss for a company run so much like my family would be like orphaning my kids.

Eventually I decided on ASK board member Ron Braniff, a Tymshare group vice-president. At least he wasn't a complete stranger. He had also been one of Tymshare's first employees and part of Tymshare as it grew from virtually nothing to a three-hundred-million-dollar company. He was a capable, stable, experienced manager who made a good professional appearance and was, I felt, very trustworthy.

I told the other board members that I saw Ron not only as ASK's COO but also as my potential successor as CEO. They approved of my choice of Ron as ASK's chief operating officer and agreed to my recommendation to make him president as well. No one believed or wanted me to relinquish my CEO role to him or to anyone else, for that matter. Instead of seeing Ron as a potential CEO, they saw Ron's appointment merely as a way of adding depth to the management team, which they favored.

Shortly before Ron's appointment was announced, I had dinner with Tom to tell him. He arrived in Los Altos looking terrible. He'd lost thirty pounds and had what seemed to be a miserable cold. I asked him if he was all right. He assured me he was. We made small talk through most of the meal, and when it was just about over, I told him that my long-term plans were to spend less time in the day-to-day operation of the company and that I needed someone to take ASK past the hundred-million-dollar mark. I didn't leave him any time to think I was referring to him. I told him I'd appointed Ron president and COO. It wasn't what he wanted to hear. I knew he wasn't very fond of Ron, but all he said was that he didn't think Ron was the right guy for the job. I had expected he'd try to sell himself as a candidate, but he didn't. He just repeated his concern about Ron's being the wrong guy. In retrospect, by then—January 1984—Tom probably knew he was in over his head at ASK Micro. And considering the way he looked, it was clear the pressures were getting to him. In any event, Tom was gracious and, at the end of dinner, drove back to Sacramento. And the lousy news from ASK Micro kept coming.

40

Out of
the Jaws of Defeat

Early that spring I decided I'd had enough hands-off at ASK Micro.
Knowing Tom was out of town, I flew up to Sacramento with Ken Fox
to have a look around the company. I wanted to see for myself what
was going on without Tom's salesmanship clouding the picture. Ken
and I talked with every department head as well as with other employees. I found a rattlesnake under every rock I overturned.

First, the distributors to whom ASK Micro was selling its products weren't paying. Second, they were returning for credit scads of
inventory that had been sold in the SDI era. Third, there wasn't a
standard price list, and distributors were buying at random prices.
Fourth, we were offering volume discounts of 40, 50, 60, 70 percent
off list to distributors who'd commit to buying large quantities of
ASK Micro software packages over a certain period of time. They'd
take the highest discount, sell a few packages, and return the rest for
credit, never selling anywhere near the quantities they had committed
to for the large volume discount they received. On the R&D side, our

IBM PC version was still crashing and had a random, unknown bug.

Worst of all, though, were the personnel problems. There were a lot of drugs around, a lot of alcohol. It had gotten so that some employees were embarrassed to attend the frequent ASK Micro parties because of what went on. And if that weren't enough, I was told that a male ASK Micro manager on a business trip with a female employee told her the company couldn't afford a separate hotel room, so she'd have to share a room with him.

Hearing this litany of obvious mismanagement made me furious, then sad, not because of the business or the money but because it was clear that the responsibility for much of what was happening lay with Tom. In Tom's defense, the entire micro market was highly disorganized. There were lots of Joe and Bill's garage-type retail software stores opening up, in some areas two or three to the block. In many cases the people running these stores knew little about computers and considerably less about how the software they were selling would be used.

Distribution and sales were also a can of worms. Distributors were undercutting one another, as they still do. But back then everyone wanted in on the action, and distributors were going into and out of business as fast as they could rent storefronts. One day they'd be selling products at list; the next day, at less than cost.

Finally, there were problems with the hardware. The machines of the day weren't quite powerful enough to run the software we were selling. More to the point, the software we were selling was too sophisticated for the times.

Ken and I flew back from Sacramento that night and met with Marty and Bob. We laid out the problems we'd unearthed, and there was little question what my first step would have to be. It was near midnight, Friday. Tom was due back at ASK Micro on Monday. Ken, Bob, Marty, and I arrived midmorning Monday to meet with him in his office. By then he knew of our visit the previous week. He started on the offensive. "It's terrible for you guys to come up here and snoop around when I'm gone."

"You're right," I said. "It probably wasn't the most appropriate thing to do, on the one hand." Tom nodded, as if by agreeing, he could soften the impact of what was coming next. "On the other hand, as CEO of ASK I'm responsible for what happens here. And unfortunately we've found that what's happening here is pretty serious."

The office overlooked a lake, and as the meeting went on, I found myself looking out over the lake to avert my eyes from Tom's face. We'd been through a lot together. More than anyone, Tom had built a viable ASK sales organization, a machine that worked and generated a constant flow of income. From the beginning he'd been a committed team player. When the money wasn't there, he never pushed to spend it. When we were low-budget and funky, Tom, who was used to better, never bitched and moaned. And now it was the end of the line.

Over the weekend I'd thought about bringing him back to ASK headquarters, but there was no longer any place for him, not where he could sustain his pride. His old job as VP sales had gone to Jim Manion. Plus we were a public company now, not a family circle. We couldn't sweep things under the rug. As a result of what was happening at ASK Micro, we were faced with potential liability and financial loss.

"Well," Tom said at one point, "I can't work in an environment where you come up here to snoop around."

"Does that mean you're resigning?"

Tom stood. "Yes, I'm resigning."

"We have to accept your resignation then."

Tom walked out of the office.

I had thought that after it was over, I'd feel better, but I felt miserable. I castigated myself for not seeing what was happening, not going up there earlier, not saving Tom. It seemed to me that the others, particularly Bob since all the invoices went through him, had had some idea of what was going on. When I questioned Bob why he'd let things get so out of hand, he said, right or wrong, Tom had been given authority to run ASK Micro, and although he questioned Tom about some of the expenses, he didn't think he should come running to me. Everyone had become protective of Tom. The team had played too well.

The question I now faced was how to turn ASK Micro around and who would do it. The way I saw it, I was the culprit who'd first approached SDI more than a year before. My fingerprints were all over the murder weapon. So it was my job to make ASK Micro go. Besides, my reputation as a CEO was at stake. Only a year earlier I was being hailed as one of the top CEOs in the software industry. With ASK Micro continuing to lose money, analysts were questioning my management skills. I started commuting to Sacramento a few days a week.

On the plus side, ASK Micro had a number of good, hardworking people. They were putting in fifty, sixty, seventy hours a week. They were dedicated and wanted to see the company succeed. For the most part, they were happy to see me. I was less happy to see them, face-to-face, because I knew I'd have to let a number of them go. In my first week I laid off about one-third of ASK Micro's sixty employees. Who left and who stayed were decided in a series of meetings with department heads. Everyone's name was put up on a board, and names and departments were shuffled around until we had the strongest, leanest possible team. A few were offered jobs in Los Altos. I felt awful about the entire process.

Next thing I did was reprice our software. We still gave volume discounts, but deeper discounts were given only after certain sales levels had been reached. I told distributors who'd bought at volume discounts and were now sending back inventory that we wouldn't accept returns if more than ninety days had passed since shipment. I didn't win any friends there either.

Just as HP had done with the early HP 3000, I withdrew the disk-crashing ASK Micro IBM PC product from the market until we worked out the bugs. There wasn't much time, however. As I'd expected, the IBM PC was sweeping through the consumer marketplace like wildfire, and I thought that a well-promoted, bug-free Accounting Plus package was our ticket to a turnaround—provided someone else didn't beat us to it. A second ticket, I decided, would be a manufacturing program that could run on a micro and was geared to the small business. I put Roger Bottarini in charge of the effort. The project was given the code name BOYBOY.

After poking around in the hornets' nest of distribution problems, I asked HP's Bill Richion, whose sales and distribution savvy I greatly respected, to come up for a look and offer some friendly advice. I wanted to know what a complete outsider would say about our chances for turning things around. We walked around the enormous, half-empty building. I could hear our footsteps echoing as we went from department to department. At the end of the day Bill said, "I think you're in deep, deep trouble here."

Still, I continued my two-to-three-times-a-week commute, passing Folsom Prison on the way to and from the airport, seeing prisoners on work details, feeling more and more like a captive myself. Often I was joined by Ken or Bob, and there were times when all three of us made the trip. By then, though I saw a turnaround possible, I wondered if perhaps we were squandering our resources. Was a microcomputer really a viable platform for accounting and manufacturing software at that time? Could we really make any sizable profit in that market? All it would take, after all, was three big system sales at ASK to generate as much revenue and a hell of a lot more profit than I could see coming from ASK Micro.

I was in the shower when I realized what we had to do. Years before, when I was doing next to zero, the few millions at stake at ASK Micro would have meant a great deal to me and I would have put in twenty-hour days to save it. But now, particularly as head of a public company with responsibilities to stockholders, I could no longer expend my energies and those of my staff for the small potential upside return ASK Micro might provide compared with the large downside possibility. After a year of pouring money into ASK Micro, it was time to cut our losses.

I got on the phone to Bob Riopel and asked, "If we were just to close ASK Micro down, write off everything we have to write off, pay severance pay for the employees left, and get out of our five-year lease on the building, what would be the hit on our earnings if we could do it all by the end of the fiscal year?" By now it was mid-May, and our fiscal year ended on June 30. Bob came back with something like three to five cents a share. "Do you mean to tell me we can put ourselves out of our misery for a three- to five-cent hit?"

"Now that you put it that way, yep."

In fact, the rest of ASK was doing so well that we could pull the plug on ASK Micro, write it all off, and still come up with a 50 percent growth in earnings per share over the prior year. Bob was always conservative in our accounting and had "reserves" for a rainy day. So the three to five cents were probably a worst-case scenario. Most likely we'd come in right on target.

Armed with this information, I called a meeting with Ron, Bob, Ken, and Marty. "Well, what are we going to do?" They all agreed it was time to move on. It was time to close down ASK Micro. "But let's not just close it down," I said. "Let's figure a way to sell it."

I have no idea why I said it or why I thought we could sell it or how to do it in the next few weeks, so we wouldn't have to carry the loss into the next fiscal year, a demoralizing prospect. Selling a business with the problems of an ASK Micro would mean shopping it around. And when you shop a company around, everyone knows it's on the block, and sales go to zero. You don't get a whole lot for a company that has zero revenues. Also, it was doubtful that even if we could find a buyer, we'd be able to close the deal before June 30. No, the smart thing to do was just to pull the plug on the whole operation. Say adios and take the few-cent hit. But it just rubbed me the wrong way.

The problem had nagged at me for a few days when I came up with the idea of selling ASK Micro—at least its assets—at auction. By late May it was looking more and more as if anything more than zero dollars for ASK Micro was gravy. And the good press something as offbeat as an auction would generate might soften the impact of closing down a company we'd paid nearly eight million dollars for less than a year earlier and had subsidized to the tune of another four million dollars. After all, the Accounting Plus program was still a top seller. And even if it wasn't running on IBM, it was running on a half dozen other machines. A hardware vendor like Apple or a chain like BusinessLand could pick up the license on the software at auction, then include the program as part of a hardware-software package. We decided to try the auction.

At the end of May I sent press releases to all the computer magazines and appropriate newspapers and trade journals announcing the auction and setting forth the ground rules. I also sent letters with the information to all the major hardware dealers and software outlets and any other company I thought could possibly be interested in owning a microcomputer-based accounting package.

The auction was to be conducted by sealed bid to be opened on June 23. There were ten products for sale. Licenses were available on an exclusive or nonexclusive basis, with the bidder to specify which he was bidding for. If the bid for an exclusive on a given package was higher than the sum of the bids for a nonexclusive, the exclusive bidder got it. All contracts would have to be signed and funds committed no later than June 30. I stipulated a minimum bid of fifty thousand dollars, which in retrospect was too high. It discouraged participation by smaller merchants, looking for nonexclusives.

The auction was a great success, not so much for the money it made—under one million dollars—but for the enormous amount of publicity it generated. Once again we were in the public eye as a gutsy, creative company. By far the best news of all came from the financial marketplace. Investors were becoming increasingly anxious about the overcrowded and disorganized microcomputer software marketplace. There was talk of a major shake-up in the air. And when ASK threw their hands up and yelled uncle—meaning no more future hits on earnings by ASK Micro—investors rewarded us by driving the ASK stock up three points, increasing our value by thirty-five million dollars. Not a bad reward for getting out of an investment we'd lost a total of about twelve million dollars on over the year.

On June 30, 1984, we were out of ASK Micro. And with ASK's overall earnings up 57 percent on total sales of sixty-five million dollars, we never missed a beat.

41

There Are
No Vacations

At about the time the trouble began at ASK Micro, my dad died of prostate cancer. He was only sixty-six and full of energy, and shouldn't have died. He loved life so. Besides, 99 percent of men with prostate malignancy don't die from it. How could Dad have been in the unlucky 1 percent? Still, after he'd been sick for more than a year and in the hospital a few weeks, the doctor suggested we stop giving him transfusions. The blood wasn't doing him any good. The time for heroic measures was past.

I flew down to L. A. to join my mother and brother at his bedside. When night fell, I begged them to go home and leave me alone with Dad. He was incoherent and barely knew I was there. I felt helpless. I didn't know what to do. To watch this strong man suffer so! He seemed lost and vulnerable. His mouth was dry, and as the night went on, I fed him ice chips, which seemed to soothe him. He died that morning while we all were at his bedside.

I'll always remember my dad for being able to fix anything, build anything. He built our house in Chicago almost single-handedly. No matter how busy he was—and there were times he worked on three jobs in a day—he always had time for me. When I was a kid, the two of us worked for hundreds of hours to construct an elaborate mock-up of the human nervous system, with soda straws for nerves and a multicolored fluorescent ball for a head. It created quite a stir at the science fair.

Dad was always there when I needed him. When ASK moved from the Los Altos house to larger quarters, Dad flew up to help me find a space. He was always helping out. If it weren't for his being there when things were at their most frantic, I'm sure my business would never have done as well as it did.

Like me, Dad was also extremely goal-oriented. Once he had decided he wanted something, he expended all his energies in making sure he'd get it. He met my mother on a Greyhound bus going to New York and the same day told her he intended to marry her. She was charmed by his earnestness but was too practical to believe in love at first sight. She didn't know Barney Brody. He wrote to her for months, and once he was earning a living as a salesman, he again proposed. Three years later he quit his job, moved to Chicago, and told her again he intended to marry her. He did, the following year.

Having bootstrapped himself out of the depression, Dad saw owning a Rolls-Royce as the pinnacle of success and vowed he would have one someday. But on his own terms; he refused to go to the bank and borrow for it. Owning a Rolls-Royce had to be a luxury he could afford, and affording it meant he could plop down the hundred thousand dollars in cash and not miss it. That is what he eventually did when he became a successful builder-developer in Los Angeles. Although I'm given credit for living the American dream, I had the support of my parents and a good education to help me along. Dad's was the real rags-to-riches story.

While he wasn't college-educated, my father respected the world of ideas and believed in the printed word. He loved reading and had an opinion on everything, usually with statistics to back it up. The only problem was, he believed too much of what he read. To make a point, he often quoted from the newspaper or *Time* or *Newsweek*, which he read religiously. If it concerned a topic about which I knew

the story behind the story, I'd suggest, "Dad, it's not really like that."
He wouldn't even bother to argue, just point to the article.

Dad's faith in what he read was one reason I agreed to give so
many interviews, knowing that he'd read the articles and believe
them. Even going public was partially motivated by my wanting Dad
to know how well ASK was doing. I could tell him the company was
worth such and such, but seeing it in the financial pages convinced
him.

Not long before he died, he came up to my house for a visit. I
took the day off. Dad was lying on the couch reading the afternoon
paper, and I was making dinner. "Will you look at this?" he called out.
I sat down next to him. On the front page of the business section was
the headline ASK STOCK SURGE A MYSTERY. The article began with the
fact that ASK's stock had climbed four points in early trading. It went
on to say that ASK's PR department couldn't explain the surge and
that CEO Sandra Kurtzig's whereabouts were a "mystery," the suggestion being I had disappeared with the deed to the ranch. It was the
first time I'd heard my dad laugh in months.

"Some mystery, huh, Dad?"

"Okay," he conceded, "maybe the press isn't always right."

My dad's death weighed heavily on me throughout the ASK Micro
mess. It was certainly one of the reasons I was looking for a chief
operating officer for ASK. I'd not spent enough time with my sons,
and I knew they'd both soon be too old to want to hang around with
their mother. Like my dad, I'd gone after things with a single-minded
interest. But when he finished a one- or two-year project, he'd take
time off and enjoy his life. Me, I'd find another project. I had the
formula only half right. It's not that ASK wasn't fun, but it had
become my only fun.

When ASK Micro was behind us, I decided to take a real vacation—total rest and relaxation, no business whatsoever. I was to leave
at the end of January 1985. Before I left, we held a two-day management meeting in Monterey with the entire board and all the company
officers. The purpose of the meeting was to review our current market
position and the business plan for the next five years. We were closing

in on a hundred million dollars in annual revenues and were ap-
proaching the end of the five-year business plan I had outlined before
our first public offering. At the meeting all indicators suggested that
ASK was in great shape.

After a few weeks of rest at home I went to the Caribbean with my
sons and Leo, the man I was seeing steadily at the time. We had been
there only three days when Tommy called. The market was heating
up, he said. Now was the right time to do another public offering.
"Right now?"

"Now," he insisted.

Before I left, Tommy had suggested that an offering might be in
order, but this latest phone call was clearly more than a suggestion.
High-tech stocks were going through the roof. Over the past month
ASK stock had climbed nearly 50 percent, from seventeen to twenty-
five. Our market value had gone from two hundred million to three
hundred million dollars. In spite of the fact that I had been selling
stock regularly to diversify, my remaining 2,500,000 shares—22 percent of the company—were worth more than sixty million dollars.

While ASK didn't need cash, Tommy reasoned that having
ready access to a larger war chest would give us the flexibility to buy
other companies in support of the new, aggressive five-year plan we'd
approved in Monterey. Generally not a believer in windows of opportunity, Tommy saw one gaping.

What followed was a series of phone calls, including a conference
call to the other board members. Everyone agreed the time was right.
Most important, we were on target to do twenty-five million dollars in
revenues in the quarter that closed March 31—our most successful
quarter ever—giving the company a revenue run rate of a hundred
million dollars.

I'd have to do another road show, of course. But it would be a
quick trip, a formality. Everyone in the investment community knew
who we were. We filed our registration statement with the SEC on
February 22 and did the offering on the twenty-eighth at twenty-one
dollars per share. A week later I was back on vacation in California,
planning a trip to Africa for mid-March.

A couple of days before Leo and I left on our high-ticket African safari—dubbed "Wings over Kenya" by its promoters because it partially involved traveling by air—I received a call from a friend and fellow entrepreneur, Sirtang Lal Tandon, or Jugi, as he was called. Jugi was from India and had made his considerable fortune at his company, Tandon, which developed and manufactured floppy disk drives for personal computers.

"Look," he said, "I've been invited to India to meet with Rajiv Gandhi. He wants to set up technology centers to develop computer software in India and wants to talk to people who know what they're doing."

"It just so happens I'm going to Africa in two days."

"Excellent. So you'll detour from Africa and join me in India then."

"But I'll need a visa, and it takes days—"

He told me not to worry. He'd call the embassy in San Francisco and have it arranged. I had the visa in a matter of hours.

There were four of us in the eight-passenger twin-engine Cessna flying over Kenya: Leo, I, our pilot, and our guide. Together we were to spend two weeks in the bush, flying from campsite to campsite, where we were joined by a driver in an open jeep. To beat the heat, we were up by 6:00 A.M., got into the jeep, and drove around until the animals took their morning snooze. Then we headed back to camp for breakfast. It was all very civilized.

After a nap we were usually back in the air, our pilot pointing out herds and flocks and prides and packs. When he saw something exciting, he'd swoop down low. It didn't seem to bother the animals, but Leo was a bit pale. I was expecting the terrain to be uniformly brown and scraggly, but much of it was green and luxuriant, with rivers and lakes.

One time, with me in the copilot's seat, the pilot leaned in my direction and asked, "Do you want to take the controls?" I'd taken flying lessons in the past and often had copiloted private airplane flights to ASK Micro. "Sure," I said. My mind hadn't been on the scenery but on what I would do when I returned to the States. "Sure."

I was a little uncomfortable with the controls at first and overcompensated, sending us up and down more dramatically than I intended. Leo gave me a queasy smile. The guide, whose only weakness I could detect was his penchant for sugar and whipped cream, was imperturbable. Ahead of me the terrain was flat, green, and gorgeous.

"Look!" the pilot called out. "Over there! Flamingos!" Off to my right, on an island in the middle of a winding river, I saw a mass of pink. "Take her down for a closer look," he urged.

"Won't I scare them?"

"Naw. We do it all the time."

I pushed the stick forward, swooping to my right and down until all I could see out of the windscreen was a sea of pink.

A few days later, April 3, we were back in Nairobi, our last night in Africa before heading for Bombay. I picked up a *Wall Street Journal* at the hotel. It was two days old but absolutely the most recent edition available in the city, the concierge assured me. I checked the over-the-counter listings to see how ASK was doing. We were at twenty-two, up one dollar from the offering price. I assumed we'd finished the quarter as planned.

Not ten hours later in Bombay I got a call from Larry Sonsini. It wasn't to catch up on the details of my vacation. "We didn't make the quarter," he said. "Instead of twenty-five million, we did eighteen million. The stock is down seven points, there's threat of a stockholders' lawsuit, and everyone wants to know what the hell happened. You've got to get back here. And quick!"

42

The Return

I cut short my trip to India and hightailed it back to ASK to find out what the hell had happened. There were three reasons we hadn't made our twenty-five-million-dollar number and why our stock had nose-dived to a low of thirteen and three-quarters, then settled to fifteen by the time I arrived home. First, almost six hundred thousand dollars' worth of software—nearly all of it profit and accounting for approximately four cents per share—had been left sitting on an order processing clerk's desk the Friday afternoon the quarter closed. The software was shipped the following week, but by then it was too late. The revenue and earnings were posted to the next quarter. Second, DEC had committed to shipping hardware that didn't make it off the loading dock. And third, as we rolled into the last weeks of the quarter, the entire computer industry was facing a slowdown that no one had predicted and that affected our ability to close the final sales we needed to make the quarter.

These problems were compounded by a general weakening of the manufacturing segment of the economy, on which ASK was exclusively dependent. Most unfortunately our flat quarter came on the heels of a stock offering one month earlier and seriously tarnished our previously shiny reputation.

Up until that quarter we had always been a predictable performer, consistently making or beating Wall Street's forecasts and growing at a phenomenal rate: 65 percent in 1984, 58 percent in 1983, and 86 percent in 1982. Our stock seemed almost always to be climbing, and had split two shares for one in 1983. Everyone was bullish on high tech. The economy seemed solid, as were our projections, which, as always, had been thoroughly developed and refined. We'd simply been caught unaware by forces we couldn't anticipate or control.

As it turned out, we weren't the only ones fooled that spring. A large number of high-tech companies in the country had at least one disappointing quarter in 1985. Among those announcing surprises was IBM, whose large staff of economists, you would think, could have predicted the slowdown. In a few cases the slowdown didn't affect some companies in the same quarter as us but then hit them even harder in a later quarter.

ASK, incidentally, rebounded in the fourth quarter, but one way or another, the slowdown in the business cycle would have caught up to us. Had the software gone out and the systems been shipped, we still would have missed the quarter. There was also no way to anticipate that our projections would be off as far as they were. Our forty-eight-quarter winning streak had simply been broken, a combination of good intentions, bad luck, and bad times. But it wasn't as bad as all that. Although third-quarter income was flat, revenues were still up 9.3 percent, and we finished fiscal 1985 with seventy-nine million dollars, a revenue growth of 22 percent over the previous year. It wasn't as good as I'd hoped, but it was none too shabby.

Larry had said that there'd be lawsuits, and there were. Five days after we announced our quarter, the first of three separate lawsuits was filed on behalf of ASK shareholders, claiming that ASK was guilty of some transgression. The three suits were quickly consolidated into a single blanket suit. In a nutshell—if I can summarize thousands of pages of legal documents—the grounds for the suit were that ASK had always been a predictable company that had made its quarters. And because we'd been growing at a consistent yet ridiculously high rate, the public's expectation was that we'd continue to grow at the same rate. The law firms hadn't the faintest idea what our transgression was, but suing gave them some right to discovery—meaning access to our files—with the hope they'd find a smoking gun.

The suits were a shot in the dark for these firms, which were well known in the industry for suing companies whose numbers fell below analysts' projections. Indeed, more than two dozen companies in the Silicon Valley were also being sued. What made ASK particularly vulnerable was that we'd done a public offering only five weeks before. ASK was an especially appealing target for these law firms because the company had a lot of money, as did the members of its board.

Generally, companies being sued by their shareholders for not making a quarter eventually lie down and die whether they're culpable or not. Shareholder suits are bad PR and take a lot of time and money to defend. Besides, most public companies—ASK included—are insured against shareholder suits, and usually, to avoid the cost of a trial, the insurance underwriters are more eager to settle than the companies themselves. As a result, very few, if any, of these lawsuits ever end up in the courts. Instead, there's a settlement in which each shareholder gets a few bucks and the law firms end up with millions, particularly if they can extend the litigation over a number of years. More than five years later, the shareholders' lawsuit (or what's left of it) is still pending.

By summer 1985 operating income had climbed to 15.4 percent and aftertax profits to 10 percent—good numbers by any measure. Confident the company was back on track, I decided it was finally time for me to put my personal life ahead of my business life. I submitted my resignation as CEO and recommended Ron Braniff as my replacement, retaining only my title as chairman of the board. I had tasted a few weeks of freedom from the pressures and responsibilities of running ASK and was eager for more. Most of all, I was determined to spend some totally uncompromised time with Andy and Kenny—and not just a few weeks. I figured I could always go back to business, but I could never relive my sons' childhood years. The board reluctantly accepted my resignation.

43

Madame Chairwoman

Every CEO has his or her own style. I'm an entrepreneur, and my style is aggressive, risk-taking, persistent, and demanding. I believe, as entrepreneurs must, in the survival of the fittest, and I was able to lead my team into the fray again and again—whether it was back to sleeping bags at HP or back to minicomputers when ASK Micro went bust. As a leader I tried to communicate my excitement and passion for the business and my vision of the future to those around me.

Ron Braniff, my successor at ASK, was more a manager than a leader. As the board of directors knew he would, he ran the company by the numbers and always looked more at the bottom line than at the big picture. It's the corporate manager's goal to make the quarter and to maintain equilibrium.

It was my impression at the time of my departure that Ron would continue to keep his eye on the bottom line, growing ASK at a moderate pace, and would maintain our position as the number one independent supplier of computerized manufacturing systems. With Ron at the helm and with the base I had left, I figured we'd reach a hundred million dollars soon enough, and a few years later probably hit two hundred million, and so on, keeping the board and the shareholders moderately happy. By contrast, had I given the company over to a more dynamic leader like Tom Lavey, we'd have either skyrocketed to one billion dollars or quickly been bankrupt. That was too high a risk for the board, the shareholders, and, ultimately, me. After all, ASK was my baby. And in 1985 I still owned 16 percent of the company. I'd left it in good hands, I thought.

I spent the summer of 1985 traveling with Andy and Kenny. We went to China, Hong Kong, Japan, Singapore, and Thailand. In the fall the kids were back in school, spending every other week with me. I went to soccer games and school meetings. I drove them to their friends' houses, and I picked them up again. I rarely went to ASK.

But I was only thirty-nine and it wasn't time for full retirement. I knew I had to do *something*. I'd been asked to sit on dozens of boards. But being on a board is frustrating for a hands-on person like me. I thought of starting a new company, but I'd been down that road before. I no longer had to prove to myself, my dad, or the world that I could do it. Nor did I need the power, the money, or the praise.

Another possibility was working in the media. I was asked to be the business correspondent for ABC's "Good Morning America," dabbled at this for a few months, then gave it up when I realized it meant spending too much time away from home. At one point a local congressional seat was up for grabs. With a constituency that included the Silicon Valley and Stanford, I might have had a good chance of being elected. But I'd seen the life of a politician close up through Jerry Brown and didn't think it would be one I'd enjoy.

The one project I did take on was writing this book. I'd been approached by a number of publishers who thought there was a good story to tell. I hoped my success would spur others to start a business and grab a piece of the American dream.

In 1987 I began dating Carl Brunsting, a surgeon in private practice in nearby Palo Alto. He was a long-divorced, unpretentious, soft-spoken guy, fourteen years older than I, with a grown-up family of his own. He loved telling and writing stories and limericks, was a wonderful pianist, had a great sense of humor, and was terrific with the kids.

On our first date he took me to see *Lady and the Tramp*. We've been together ever since.

As chairwoman of ASK's board I couldn't completely divorce myself from what was going on at ASK. Nor did I intend to. For the first two years after leaving, I stayed away primarily to give Ron a chance to build the company in his image, as he did. Soon after my departure Ken Oshman resigned from the board. Within a year Ken Fox and Bob Riopel had left the company. Ron brought in his former boss at Tymshare to take Ken Oshman's place on the board and promoted Marty Browne to replace Ken Fox as VP of R&D and Les Wright, our controller, to replace Bob Riopel as CFO.

While I managed to break myself of the habit of going to ASK as its chairwoman, I still kept up on things at the company, albeit on a slightly removed plane. I also continued to attend industry conferences and read dozens of trade and computer magazines a week. I might not have known what was going on at ASK day to day, but I did know what was going on in the world ASK served.

One thing was clear. Technology was changing and changing fast. There was much talk in the marketplace about portable applications that could run across different machines; superpowerful, freestanding individual workstations; and new, highly efficient data base software. The trouble was, ASK didn't seem to be listening. There was ongoing R&D, but from my vantage point it wasn't going in the right direction. Also, the R&D was almost entirely focused on product enhancements. There was virtually no new-product development. Good companies like HP get more than 50 percent of their annual revenue from products introduced within the previous three years. ASK had no new products. How, I wondered, could we continue to grow?

ASK, however, did continue to grow. While not as phenomenal as before, our numbers were good enough for Ron and the board. We hit almost $100,000,000 in revenues in fiscal 1987, climbed to $142,-000,000 in 1988, and hit $186,000,000 in fiscal 1989. However, operating income and aftertax profits were down from a high of 15.4 percent and 10 percent respectively in 1985, my last year as CEO, to

10 percent and 7.2 percent—a significant but not alarming drop. Outwardly ASK had made the transition from a glamorous highflier to a solid, stable, growing concern. Still, between 1985 and fall 1987, ASK stock had dropped from the mid-twenties to the mid-teens, where it hovered as the company coasted.

At board meetings I expressed my concern that ASK wasn't developing new products and wasn't positioned for the future, but the board didn't see any need for panic. The numbers simply didn't warrant too much concern. But I had a gut feeling that ASK was headed for trouble. Ron assured me we weren't. His sincerity and certainty had me questioning whether he even understood what I was talking about.

Then, in October 1987, the market crashed. ASK stock plummeted to six and three-quarters. Despite the doldrums the company was in, my first impulse was: Hey, here's a company that has a hundred and some millions in revenues and decent earnings; maybe I should buy some stock. By then I had sold off most of my ASK holdings, retaining less than 4 percent of the company. I put in an order to buy but chickened out. Owning much more of the company would mean having to take a more aggressive role, maybe even having to go back to protect my own interests. I didn't want to go back, though by now I was seriously questioning Ron's ability to run the company.

At the same time the board also considered tapping into ASK's cash reserves to buy back some of its own stock. We'd recently bought NCA, one of our competitors on the DEC machine, but still had a war chest of more than twenty-five million dollars. The decision was to forgo the stock purchase. The market and the economy were too shaky, and we might be better off with the cash, just in case.

By 1988, even with ASK's stock rebounding to slightly over fifteen, my frustration with what was happening was getting to me, and I was no longer able to keep my mouth shut at board meetings. I'd say, "Hey, this is what's happening in the market, and we'd better start developing new products to keep up. We haven't come out with a new product in three years," or, "We'd better start building up business in Europe. Selling direct won't work. We need to go through established local companies in each country. We're falling behind!" Ron disagreed.

At about this time I read a market survey done by the new advertising agency that ASK had hired. It said that ASK was no longer perceived as the leader in the manufacturing market, that there was no leader. No leader! I couldn't believe it. Here we were, outselling everyone in our portion of the market, and we were no longer considered the leader. Not only had ASK lost its glamour, but it had lost its reputation.

As all this gradually unfolded, I was becoming convinced that we either had to get a new CEO or sell the company. With revenues growing at more than 30 percent per year, however, my prognostication of a troubled future for ASK did not seem well grounded to the other directors.

Finally, in February 1989, attending board meetings had become too difficult for me. Seventeen years—the life of a U.S. patent—after founding the company, I resigned my chairmanship and cut my remaining ties with ASK. The stock was at eighteen. I figured the company had another year and a half before its problems came home to roost.

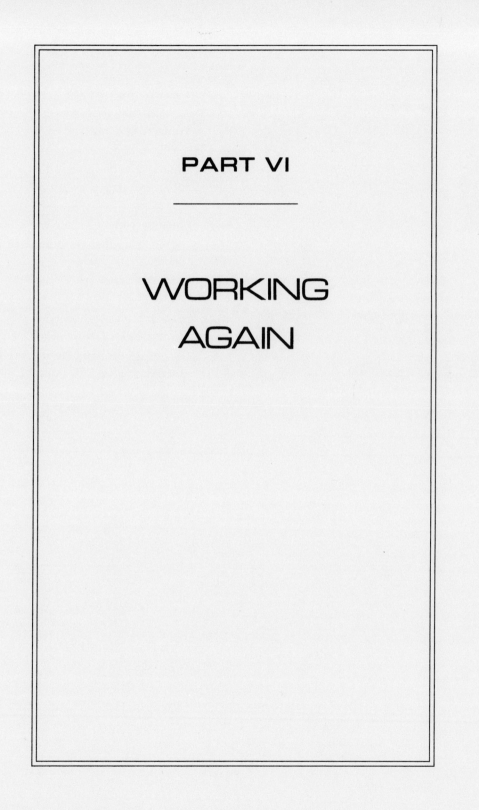

PART VI

WORKING AGAIN

44

ASK Redux

By September 1989 ASK stock had dropped to ten. Shareholders were obviously getting the message. Earlier that summer my older son, Andy, then sixteen, had taken an active interest in the stock market. This was the same son who seven years earlier had bought one share of ASK stock in our first public offering and complained when it climbed only four points in a few weeks. Back then he was saving for a model plane. Now he had his driver's license, and he wanted to buy a car. I made him a deal. I'd go halvsies with him on the car. Carl helped him get a summer job at Stanford University Hospital as a clerk in the emergency room. But when his hours were cut, he needed a new source of income.

During my years off I was spending a lot of time investing in the stock and bond markets and often discussed my investments with Andy. Andy's interest was piqued, and now, having earned a few thousand dollars of his own, he decided to try his hand in the stock market. After reasonably thorough research he picked two stocks he thought would earn him some money: Texas Instruments and Genentech. Impressed by his logic, seriousness, and single-mindedness, I coinvested with him. We sold in two months on Andy's urging and made a handsome profit. On a percentage basis I made more money on those two stocks than I made on any other in 1989.

In late August Andy came to me with another hot tip: ASK. "A one-hundred-thirty-million dollar market value with two hundred million dollars in revenues. Come on, Mom. You know someone's going to buy this company."

By then my break with ASK was complete. I had absolutely no inside information other than my own gut feeling that ASK's problems wouldn't catch up with the company until sometime in 1990. And Andy's hunches had proved themselves out in the past. So I bought some ASK stock at ten dollars per share.

Just how little did I know what was going on at ASK? At about the time Andy and I bought our ASK stock, Ron, as I later learned, informed the board that the company would not make its first quarter, ending September 30, and that the quarter would be significantly down from his projection. At best the revenue for the quarter would be no higher than the previous year's quarter. Worse, earnings would be nil; ASK might even post a loss. The day the company announced publicly it wouldn't make its quarter, the value of my shares dropped nearly 25 percent, as the stock plunged from ten and one-half to eight. I went back to Andy. "What now, chief?" I knew what his answer would be.

"Buy it, Mom." And I knew he didn't mean more stock. He meant I should buy the company.

Easy enough to say, but buying a company—any company—was a complicated process. Aside from my probably having to go back to manage it full-time, there were dozens of serious financial questions. But the financial person I trusted the most was Tommy, and I couldn't talk seriously to him about it because he was on ASK's board. Instead, if only to explore the possibility, I made an appointment with Warren Hellman, who ran a well-respected boutique brokerage that, among other things, did leveraged buy-outs (LBOs). I also talked to Marty Lipton, a longtime acquaintance and probably the country's most experienced and highly regarded mergers and acquisitions lawyer. He is known for his expert advice to Bendix, IBM, and others.

As I was walking out of the house to meet Warren for lunch in San Francisco, the phone rang. It was Tommy. He said he wanted to speak with me on behalf of the ASK board. Could we have lunch? I told him I already had a lunch appointment with Warren Hellman. Tommy knew Warren well and respected him. I'm sure that Tommy also knew what was on my mind. If he did, he knew more than I since I still had no clear plan.

"Come by my office before lunch then," he said. I told him I was already running late but agreed to come by afterward. In fact, I'd been in regular touch with Tommy since leaving the board, and at one point we'd talked about perhaps working together on some investment banking types of deals. But we never actually did a deal together. As ASK's stock was dropping from twenty-five dollars per share to ten dollars, I once joked that maybe I should buy the company back. Now it was no joke.

My lunch with Warren was very pleasant. It was a beautiful California day. We ate at an outside table in the courtyard of a stylish restaurant, part of a chain that Warren had invested in, so we were treated like royalty. Warren knew ASK by reputation, rather than in intimate detail. I myself didn't know exactly what was going on at ASK or how bad the numbers really were. But I thought that at eight dollars a share with no single, large controlling shareholder, ASK was vulnerable to a potential take-over bid at a low price. Warren agreed. We discussed the possibility of my doing an LBO with Warren's organization. I also told him that Tommy, on behalf of ASK's board, had asked for a meeting that afternoon but that I was uncertain what it would concern.

A board of directors has three key responsibilities: to review a company's financial statements, to ensure that the company is on track in setting and accomplishing its objectives, and to oversee the orderly succession of management. ASK's board, especially Tommy and Larry Sonsini, as I later learned, had responded surprisingly quickly for a corporate board to the problems at ASK. Immediately after Ron had told them ASK wouldn't make the quarter, they met with Les Wright, ASK's CFO, and other officers to determine the extent of the problems. By the time Tommy called me, only a few days after the unexpected quarter shortfall had been publicly announced, the board had already had an emergency meeting to discuss its options. Having ignored my earlier warnings, they acknowledged that they had burned a bit of a bridge between me and the board. It was a chasm, but it was not unbridgable, Tommy and Larry Sonsini assured the others. Was it? At that point they clearly knew something I didn't.

I also learned later that Ron was out of the country at the time the emergency meeting took place. In his absence the board voted unanimously to ask for his resignation and to request that I come back as CEO and chairman. I would also be given the opportunity to reconstitute the board with my choice of members.

Walking into Tommy's office after my lunch with Warren, however, I knew none of this and was surprised when virtually the first thing Tommy said was that the board needed me back at ASK to run the company. He laid out the situation and said that the board had empowered Larry and him to negotiate a good stock and compensation package for me if I'd return. Finally, knowing I'd just met with Hellman, he asked that I not come in the back door with a buy-out. I told him I'd think about it over the weekend.

By now, late September 1989, I'd been away from day-to-day operations at ASK for four years. I'd spent a lot of time with Andy and Kenny and made a warm, comfortable home for them. We'd had lots of great times together. I had also built a terrific relationship with Carl. I had nearly finished writing this book. And I had just finished building a house in Hawaii and enjoyed my unstructured time there immensely.

On the other hand, I missed the hurly-burly, the excitement, all the good parts of being in business. I'd gotten such great satisfaction from building the original ASK team, then working as part of that team to reach our goals. And with the distance I'd taken from the company in the last year, I thought I could be even more effective in grasping ASK's business situation and making the strategic and management changes that obviously had to be made to fuel ASK's resurgence. Maybe this time, with my life in balance, I could do it in moderation. Maybe it was worth a try.

For better or for worse, this wasn't the old ASK I would be returning to. Only a few people from the real old days were left. There were hundreds of new people I'd never even met. Nor was this the high-flying ASK of yore, but a troubled company that needed to be turned around. It was one business challenge I had yet to experience.

On Sunday afternoon I called Tommy with my answer.

45

The Four-Hundred-Million-Dollar Start-up

Much of the reason for ASK's early success was its ability to seize opportunities during times of technologic and economic change. We were an aggressive company willing to take risks. By 1989 ASK was no longer that company. Yet on the cusp of a new decade, computer technology and the needs of manufacturers were changing dramatically.

How dramatically? In the past many manufacturing companies were contained in a single building with a shop floor downstairs and executive offices and support services upstairs. Now even small companies were expanding nationally and internationally to compete better in a global market. Distribution and customer service were being ranked alongside production as keys to success.

On the technology side, high-performance PCs and workstations from vendors like Sun and Apollo were bringing computing power to the desktop—and to more and more desktops, as everyone from stock clerks to CEOs needed fast access to information. While machines and software to handle the demand were becoming increasingly complex, graphical user interfaces, as in the Apple Macintosh, that employed icons instead of text-based commands were actually making computers more accessible and easier to use, driving down training and support costs.

Sophisticated new relational data base software was also making it possible for the individual at the PC to retrieve information over huge, enterprise-wide networks without having to know where that information was stored. Networks themselves were becoming faster and providing more secure access to data. And new tools for creating software were speeding the development process and improving the final product. Most significant to ASK as we moved into the nineties was that proprietary operating system software—like that used to run MANMAN on HP and DEC computers—was gradually giving way to open, nonproprietary systems that would allow software to run on a number of different machines and provide users with the portability they were looking for.

Returning to ASK in fall 1989, I believed the opportunity for ASK in this new, still-evolving open systems marketplace was enormous. The movement toward industry-standard software was as significant as the one from mainframes to minis in the mid-seventies, when ASK had cut its teeth. The challenge of competing in this new marketplace was both exciting and daunting. I knew that to profit from this seminal change in the industry, we would eventually have to rewrite every piece of ASK software. We would have to reestablish our market position. We would have to rekindle the fire under our sales force. Most important, we would have to regain our entrepreneurial vision.

I made a list.

The first and certainly most challenging order of business was to put together a strong, creative, aggressive management team. When Ken Fox, Bob Riopel, and others left ASK in the mid-eighties, they were replaced by managers with narrower vision. As a result, the management team I inherited was weaker than the one we had had when ASK was a fifty-million-dollar company, nearly a decade earlier. Changes would have to be made, and at the highest levels. Fortunately there were a few excellent individuals still on the team from the old days—including Marty Browne—as well as a number of newer, highly capable players like Les Wright, the CFO. This gave me a core around which I could build.

The second order of business was to keep ASK's customer base growing with current product. To accomplish this, we'd have to expand our initial vision of selling only to discrete manufacturers, like audio component or tool companies, and begin selling to process manufacturers—producers of paper, pharmaceuticals, or food, for example. We'd also have to look beyond selling solely through our direct sales force and explore new ways of bringing our product to market—maybe even use distributors or agents in some areas to get broader geographical coverage.

Working for us on the product side was ASK's September 1989 acquisition of Data 3, whose SIM/400 manufacturing management software ran on IBM's AS/400 mid-range computers. This product supplemented our HP and DEC manufacturing product offerings.

The third order of business facing ASK upon my return was how to thrive in the new decade and how to take advantage, as ASK always had in the past, of a rapidly changing marketplace. The answer lay in new products.

No question, to continue to be a major player in our industry, we would have to develop new products to help current and prospective customers adapt to the demands of enterprise-wide computing. We'd have to help our customers with their transition to open systems. And we'd have to develop and/or acquire industry-standard, state-of-the-art open systems products.

Putting together a new management team, rebuilding a declining customer base, developing a whole new product line—these were tall orders, and ASK has a long way to go. But we'd already come such a long way. And I have no doubt we'll get there.

A great deal has happened at ASK since I returned. Joining Larry Sonsini, Tommy Unterberg, and me on the board are my former ally at HP, Paul Ely; Bob Waterman, coauthor with Tom Peters of *In Search of Excellence*; and Bob Sharpe, vice-president of business development for Electronic Data Systems, a multi-billion-dollar subsidiary of General Motors. I also assembled a topflight team of executive officers and managers. Together, we've stabilized the company and set a significant new product-development effort in motion.

Then, in the fall of 1990, ASK acquired Ingres Corporation, a worldwide leader in relational database and application development tools. Although Ingres had lost some money recently, it had excellent products, an extensive customer base, especially in Europe, and a large, growing revenue base. The acquisition brings ASK's annual revenues to nearly $400 million, making ASK the seventh largest software company in the world. To finance the deal we sold 20 percent of ASK to GM's EDS, and 10 percent to one of ASK's oldest friends, Hewlett-Packard.

But the saga—still underway—of the ASK turnaround and its repositioning as a key player in computing in the 1990s and beyond is another story for another time. For me, for now, it's back on the job—with a vision, a goal, a task, and a team to make it happen.

Acknowledgments

From the time I was a small child my mother always told me to just "hitch your wagon to a star." I hope that in reading my story many of you will be inspired to "hitch your wagon to a star" and "go for your goal."

I was blessed with health, a good education, and a warm, happy, challenging environment in which to grow up. For that I thank my always loving parents. Their love for each other and their love of life provided an enduring role model for me.

My loving brother, Greg Brody, is one-of-a-kind: entrepreneur, successful real-estate developer, sounding board, and natural comedian. Regardless of his responsibilities, he has always been there for me. His wit and humor invariably make me laugh. Many of the happiest, craziest, and funniest moments of my life have been shared with Greg.

My sons, Andy and Kenny, are the sweetest part of my life. Their patience with the long hours I spent away from home while building

ASK made this story possible. Beyond doubt, having them and watching them grow up to become young men is the most pleasurable and remarkable thing I've ever done.

I am very grateful to all the employees of ASK. They make ASK a fun place to work. Their hard work and dedication through the years have always made me "look good." I am especially appreciative of Marty Browne, Tom Lavey, Bob Riopel, Liz Seckler, Howard Klein, Ann Rehling, Ken Fox, Stewart Florsheim, Roger Bottarini, Bill Richion, Larry Sonsini, Tommy Unterberg, Paul Ely, Ken Oshman, and Les Wright who believed early on that ASK would be successful.

Without Tom Parker, my invaluable collaborator, this book probably would not have been written. His patience and fortitude go beyond the call of duty and we have become great friends.

Finally, my lasting love to Carl Brunsting, my best friend, whose love has given balance to my life.

Index